Praise for Nyogen Senzaki's *Like A Dream, Like A Fantasy*

"Nyogen Senzaki will always be remembered as one of the great patriarchs of American Zen. His impact on the transmission of Zen to the West is remarked upon in every study of the subject and yet his own writings and teachings have until now been difficult to find."
—*Buddhadharma: The Practitioner's Quarterly*

"Fearless and free-thinking, Nyogen Senzaki was the first great Buddhist teacher to immerse himself fully and without reservation in American life. The teachings and poems in this volume are as fresh, direct, and timeless as when they were first spoken."
—Melvin McLeod, editor-in-chief of *Shambhala Sun* and *The Best Buddhist Writing* series

"This collection will benefit all who read it."
—Sakyong Mipham Rinpoche, author of *Turning the Mind into an Ally*

"One of the first Zen masters to emigrate from Japan to the United States, Nyogen Senzaki's teachings and practice-centers influence a generation of Western Zen practitioners."
—*Eastern Horizon*

"A precious offering from a pioneer of Zen in America."
—Peter Matthiessen, author of *The Snow Leopard*

ELOQUENT SILENCE

ELOQUENT SILENCE

Nyogen Senzaki's Gateless Gate
and Other Previously Unpublished
Teachings and Letters

Edited and Introduced by
Roko Sherry Chayat
Foreword by Eido Shimano

 WISDOM PUBLICATIONS • BOSTON

Wisdom Publications
199 Elm Street
Somerville MA 02144 USA
www.wisdompubs.org

Library of Congress Cataloging-in-Publication Data
Senzaki, Nyogen.
 Eloquent silence : Nyogen Senzaki's Gateless gate and other previously unpublished teachings and letters / edited and introduced by Roko Sherry Chayat ; foreword by Eido Shimano.
    p. cm.
 Includes bibliographical references and index.
 ISBN 0-86171-559-4 (pbk. : alk. paper)
 1. Zen Buddhism. 2. Koan. 3. Rinzai (Sect). I. Chayat, Sherry. II. Title.
 BQ9265.4.S446 2008
 294.3'927—dc22
                          2008022859
 12 11 10 09 08
 5 4 3 2 1

Brief excerpts appear in this work from D.T. Suzuki's *Manual of Zen Buddhism,* originally published by Rider & Co. in 1950, and D.T. Suzuki's translation of Soyen Shaku's work, originally published in *Sermons of a Buddhist Abbot* by Open Court in 1906.

Designed and typeset in Adobe Garamond 11/16 by Gopa & Ted2, Inc.

Wisdom Publications' books are printed on acid-free paper and meet the guidelines for permanence and durability of the Production Guidelines for Book Longevity of the Council on Library Resources.

Printed in the United States of America.

    This book was produced with environmental mindfulness. We have elected to print this title on 30% PCW recycled paper. As a result, we have saved the following resources: 30 trees, 21 million BTUs of energy, 2,645 lbs. of greenhouse gases, 10,979 gallons of water, and 1,410 lbs. of solid waste. For more information, please visit our website, www.wisdompubs.org. This paper is also FSC certified. For more information, please visit www.fsuc.org.

師翁同臥澱風樓
覺夢橫身西半球
七十餘年唯一枕
賴耶海上放虛舟

For translation, please see beginning of Introduction, page 1

Having bid farewell to the far native country, wind and moon are in
  harmony
Not despising utter poverty, you continued to live in true Zen
The Hut of Morning Dew is like a dream, like a fantasy
Fifty years have passed since you departed. Aah!

nine bows,
Muishitsu Eido Shimano

Chinese poem composed and offered May 7, 2008,
at the Nyogen Senzaki Fiftieth Memorial Sesshin,
Dai Bosatsu Zendo

TABLE OF CONTENTS

Foreword by Eido Shimano   xiii

Introduction by Roko Sherry Chayat   1

Acknowledgments   23

PHOTOGRAPHS   27

PART I: COMMENTARIES ON THE *GATELESS GATE*   35

Introductory Comments   37

Mumon's Introduction   40

Case One: Joshu's Dog   43

Case Two: Hyakujo's Fox   47

Case Three: Gutei's Finger   51

Case Four: A Beardless Foreigner   54

Case Five: Kyogen's Man in a Tree   57

Case Six: Buddha Twirls a Flower   60

Case Seven: Joshu's "Wash Your Bowl"   63

Case Eight: Keichu's Wheel   67

Case Nine: A Buddha before History   70

Case Ten: Seizei Alone and Poor   74

Case Eleven: Joshu Examines a Hermit Monk in Meditation   77

Case Twelve: Zuigan Calls His Own Master   80

Case Thirteen: Tokusan Holds His Bowls   83

Case Fourteen: Nansen Cuts the Cat in Two   87

Case Fifteen: Tozan's Three Blows   91

Case Sixteen: The Bell and the Ceremonial Robe   94

Case Seventeen: The Three Calls of the Emperor's Teacher   97

Case Eighteen: Tozan's Three Pounds   100

Case Nineteen: Everyday Life Is the Path   104

Case Twenty: The Man of Great Strength   107

Case Twenty-one: Dried Dung   110

Case Twenty-two: Kashyapa's Preaching Sign   113

Case Twenty-three: Think Neither Good, Nor Not-Good   116

Case Twenty-four: Without Speech, Without Silence   121

Case Twenty-five: Preaching from the Third Seat   124

Case Twenty-six: Two Monks Roll Up the Screen   127

Case Twenty-seven: It Is Not Mind,
It Is Not Buddha, It Is Not Things   130

Case Twenty-eight: Ryutan Blows Out the Candle   133

Case Twenty-nine: Not the Wind, Not the Flag   137

Case Thirty: This Mind Is Buddha   141

Case Thirty-one: Joshu Investigates   144

Case Thirty-two: A Philosopher Asks Buddha   147

Case Thirty-three: This Mind Is Not Buddha   151

Case Thirty-four: Wisdom Is Not the Path   154

Case Thirty-five: Two Souls   158

Case Thirty-six: Meeting a Master on the Road   163

Case Thirty-seven: The Cypress Tree in the Garden   166

Case Thirty-eight: A Buffalo Passes through an Enclosure   169

Case Thirty-nine: Ummon's Off the Track   172

Case Forty: Tipping Over a Water Vessel   175

Case Forty-one: Bodhidharma Pacifies the Mind   178

Case Forty-two: The Woman Comes Out from Meditation   182

Case Forty-three: Shuzan's Short Staff   185

Case Forty-four: Basho's Staff   188

Case Forty-five: Who Is It?   191

Case Forty-six: Proceed from the Top of the Pole   194

Case Forty-seven: The Three Barriers of Tosotsu   197

Case Forty-eight: One Path of Kempo   200

Amban's Addition   203

PART II: COMMENTARIES ON THE
BLUE ROCK COLLECTION   207

Case One: I Know Not   209

Case Two: The Ultimate Path   211

Case Eight: Suigan's Eyebrows   213

Case Twelve: Tozan's Three Pounds of Flax   216

Case Twenty-two: Seppo's Cobra   218

PART III: COMMENTARIES ON THE
BOOK OF EQUANIMITY   221

Introduction   223

Chapter One: Buddha Takes His Preaching Seat   226

Chapter Two: Bodhidharma Walks Out from Samskrita   229

PART IV: DHARMA TALKS AND ESSAYS   235

An Ideal Buddhist   237

A Meeting with Sufi Master Hazrat Inayat Khan   242

Seven Treasures, Part One   244

Seven Treasures, Part Two   249

Seven Treasures, Part Three   253

The Ten Stages of Consciousness   257

Emancipation   260

How to Study Buddhism   265

Zen Buddhism in the Light of Modern Thought   268

Buddhism and Women   272

Obaku's Transmission of Mind, Part One   276

Obaku's Transmission of Mind, Part Two   279

Obaku's Transmission of Mind, Part Three   282

Obaku's Transmission of Mind, Part Four   286

Esoteric Buddhism in Japan   289

Shingon Teachings   296

What Is Zen? An Evening Chat   299

What Does a Buddhist Monk Want?   305

On Zen Meditation   309

On *The Lotus of the Wonderful Law*:
Introducing Soen Nakagawa   315

Bankei's Zen   322

PART V: CALLIGRAPHIES AND SELECTED POEMS   325

"Basho"   327

"Opening words of Wyoming Zendo"   328

"Evacuees make poinsettia"   329

"Autumn came naturally"   330

"In this part of plateau"   331

"This desert on the plateau"   332

"My uta (Japanese ode)"   333

"Those who live without unreasonable desires"   334

"The mother was named an enemy-alien"   335

"Naked mountains afar!"   336

"No spring in this plateau"   337

"Closing the meditation hall"   338

"Bodhidharma"   339

"This world is the palace of enlightenment"   340

"Until now the radiant moon"   341

Bodhidharma Commemoration   343

Celebration of Buddha's Birth   343

Translations of Three Poems by Jakushitsu   344

Commemoration of Soyen Shaku   346

Thirty-third Commemoration of Soyen Shaku   346

PART VI: THE AUTOBIOGRAPHY OF SOYEN SHAKU
*(Translated and with Comments
by Nyogen Senzaki)*   347

PART VII: CORRESPONDENCE   363

To Soyen Shaku, December 25, 189?   365

To Soyen Shaku, March 21, 1905   378

The Purpose of Establishing Tozen Zenkutsu,
April 8, 1931   382

Article and Related Letters to the Editor,
Second General Conference of Pan-Pacific
Young Buddhist Associations, 1934   384

Exchange with Myra A. Stall, July 11 and 16, 1956   402

Newly Translated Correspondence   404

Notes   407
Bibliography   411
Index   413
About the Editor   435

Foreword

In 1952, the United States government extended a special invitation to Sogen Asahina Roshi, the former Abbot of Engaku-ji in Kamakura, Japan, in order to promote cultural exchange between the two countries. The purpose was also to heal the wounds of the war in people's hearts and to allow Japanese representatives to experience American culture first-hand. After visiting Washington, D.C., Sogen Roshi visited Los Angeles to meet Nyogen Senzaki, since they had both trained at Engaku-ji. On that occasion, Sogen Roshi composed a Chinese poem, the last line of which reads, "Daisetsu preaches Zen; Nyogen practices it."

Daisetsu refers to D.T. Suzuki. He was a lay practitioner under Soyen Shaku Roshi at Engaku-ji, simultaneously with Nyogen Senzaki, who was then an ordained monk in training. In 1893, their teacher, Soyen Shaku, was invited to attend the World Parliament of Religions in Chicago. It was the first time in history that Buddhism was introduced to the North American continent. Soyen Shaku made a second trip in 1905, but in both cases, his stays were very short. D.T. Suzuki lived in the United States on and off for nearly twenty years. His contribution through an intellectual approach cannot be measured, and indeed he was instrumental in sowing the seeds of Zen in the West.

On the other hand, Nyogen Senzaki lived in "this strange land" for fifty years, remaining mostly inconspicuous, with a sincere willingness to blend into American culture. In fact, he had no choice but to give up the hope of returning to Japan. I can easily imagine his struggle and loneliness, especially longing to continue his practice under Soyen Shaku. But somehow, the Dharma said "No."

Soyen Shaku was a pioneer in spirit, but the two vessels he used to transmit his Zen were D.T. Suzuki and Nyogen Senzaki. Both were equally indispensable. Given the Western tendency to approach everything intellectually, without D.T. Suzuki, Zen would have never been accepted here. D.T. Suzuki presented a mixture of both the logical and enigmatic aspects of Zen Buddhism, which was the perfect combination to attract and fascinate Westerners. Nyogen Senzaki's way, on the other hand, was to come down to the streets and teach whomever he met. He had a small zendo, literally *small,* first in San Francisco and later in Los Angeles. He conducted zazen meetings twice a week at his apartment zendo. The rest of the time, he was either working to support himself in the early days, or studying the Dharma. According to his letter addressed to Soyen Shaku, as a young boy he was sent to his grandfather's temple, which belonged to the Pure Land School, where he read the entire Pali Buddhist canon, the *Tripitaka,* before reaching the age of twenty. After becoming a Zen Buddhist monk, he received strict training from Soyen Shaku. Upon coming to this country, against his first plans to stay for only three years, he cultivated a Buddhist field, obeying the silent voice of the Dharma. This book is a testimony of his life-long struggle and devotion to transplant this great legacy to the West.

To commemorate the fiftieth anniversary of his departure, the time has come for us to truly appreciate what he has done. Although I met him only once, this meeting drastically changed my life. I sincerely hope that reading his life's work will give the readers a similar impact.

Eido Shimano

Eido Tai Shimano is the abbot of the New York Zendo in Manhattan and Dai Bostatsu Zendo in the Catskills.

Introduction

In a dream I'm lying in a pagoda with my old teacher.
When I awaken, I am on my single pillow in the
Western Hemisphere.
For more than seventy years I have floated
On the Alaya Sea in this illusory boat.

NYOGEN SENZAKI, JULY 7, 1955

Like the great Zen ancestors Bodhidharma and Huineng, Nyogen Senzaki
has, in the fifty years since his death, become something of a Zen legend—
despite the fact that he lived in obscurity and spoke of himself as "a mushroom, without a very deep root, no branches, no flowers, and probably no
seeds," and as "a lone cloud floating freely in the blue sky."[1] These five
decades since Nyogen Senzaki's passing, in commemoration of which this
book is offered, have seen the emergence of Zen in the West not merely
as an intellectual pursuit, but as a rigorous and life-changing daily practice. This emergence is in no small way Nyogen Senzaki's legacy. As Eido
Shimano Roshi notes in his Foreword, while D.T. Suzuki brought the
philosophy and culture of Zen Buddhism to America, it was Nyogen Senzaki who taught Zen as a steady, disciplined, unromantic yet transforma-
tive path of everyday life.

The biographical details of Nyogen Senzaki's life contribute to the legend. In the essay in this volume titled "What Does a Buddhist Monk

Want?" written while interned at Heart Mountain, Wyoming, in 1942, he said he was abandoned as a baby, and never knew his biological parents. "My foster father, a Japanese scholar-monk, picked me up at the death bed of my mother, who was, I was told later, Japanese. (I look more Chinese than Japanese.) In those days the Japanese census was not very strict, so I was booked as the first-born baby of the Senzaki family. The Senzakis lived near the temple of my foster father."

The boy was entered in the records of the town hall of Fukaura, Aomori Prefecture, as having been born on October 5 (which happens to be Bodhidharma's Commemoration Day), 1876, and was given the name Aizo Senzaki. In an early letter to Zen Master Soyen Shaku (presented in the Correspondence section of this book), Nyogen Senzaki wrote about losing his adoptive mother when he was five years old, and being sent to live with his grandfather, who was the priest at Soko-ji, a Buddhist Pure Land temple. The elderly priest taught the boy the Chinese classics, and had a profound influence on him, which was, as Nyogen Senzaki later wrote, "to live up to the Buddhist ideals outside of name and fame and to avoid as far as possible the world of loss and gain."[2] When Nyogen Senzaki was sixteen, his grandfather passed away. In his last words to his grandson, he warned him not to join the ranks of Buddhist priests, whom he regarded as "a pack of tigers and wolves."

Aizo Senzaki went back to his village, and decided to enter medical school. While studying for the entrance examination, he kept thinking of how his grandfather's congregants' offerings to the temple had made it possible for him to live. Increasingly he felt that the only way to requite their kindness would be to relinquish secular life and become a monk. Discovering Zen through a friend who introduced him to the haiku poet Basho, he began zazen practice. After reading about Zen Master Tokusan, the *Diamond Sutra* scholar who burned all his commentaries upon realizing his true nature, Nyogen Senzaki dropped his medical studies and entered a local Soto Zen monastery.

He was ordained on April 8 (the date on which Buddha's birthday is observed), 1895, and given the name Nyogen ("Like a Phantasm"). Later he studied under a Shingon Buddhist teacher, but it was only upon meeting Soyen Shaku Roshi that he knew he had met his true master. He became a training monk at Soyen Shaku's monastery in Kamakura, Engaku-ji, one of the headquarters of the Rinzai School (where D.T. Suzuki was also studying, as a lay Buddhist scholar). However, due to ill health, Nyogen Senzaki had to leave before finishing his training, and he returned to his village in Aomori prefecture, Fukaura. There he was horrified at the moral failings of the villagers, the indolence and hypocrisy of the temple priests, and the sorry state of primary school education. His monk's vow, which had never faltered, became even stronger as he returned to secular surroundings: his resolve was quite simply to bring Buddha's loving-kindness to everyone he met, particularly children. To this end, he decided to establish what he called the Mentorgarten, a school based on the German kindergarten model in which, he wrote, "boys and girls could polish their wisdom and virtue" and he could "teach Buddha's Dharma as well as the necessary subjects." He coined the name *Mentorgarten* to express his feeling "that the whole world is a beautiful garden, where everyone can associate peacefully and be mentors to each other. I used the German word *garten* instead of the English 'garden' because of my fondness for Froebel's theory of the kindergarten.[3] We are all children of the Buddha, who is our ideal of supreme knowledge and moral perfection."[4] In a letter written some decades later to one of his students, Nyogen Senzaki described the way he taught:

> Every morning, before I opened the play-house, I burned incense and meditated for half an hour. I did not, however, recount colorful religious stories for the children; I only guided and watched over them, helping them to learn about nature while they were playing. Sometimes I called to their attention a sunrise or sunset, or the different shapes of the beautiful moon, or the stars scattered in the heavens. As for their manners, I just tried to train them to be in a harmonious relationship with their parents.

Even today I do not believe in molding children in accordance with any dogmatic religious creed. Some churches utilize children for their own propagandistic purposes, but the natural power of children is so strong that they are able to outgrow such exploitation, and the churches are eventually made to realize that they have labored in vain after all.[5]

Polishing wisdom and virtue and teaching Buddha's Dharma were the leitmotifs of Nyogen Senzaki's life. He had a rare purity of intent and an unswerving dedication to the ideals his grandfather had imparted to him. Indeed, his impatience with those who put on a show of piety while indulging their basest instincts kept him from ever joining that "pack of tigers and wolves," motivating him instead to seek the life of a homeless monk. He lived among ordinary people as a mentor, not as a temple priest, and endeavored to extend his Mentorgarten ideals not only to the children of his village, but to women and older boys as well. However, he was going against the grain of secular society as well as that of the Buddhist establishment, which regarded him with scorn and, with few exceptions, ignored his pleas for financial support. Soyen Shaku tried to help, writing a strong letter of support in the fall of 1901 for Nyogen Senzaki to use as needed:

If there were a man whose behavior was so pure that even the Puritans would admire him, if he did not have the vow to save all sentient beings, I would not respect him. However, what if I met a bodhisattva such as Jofukyo in the Lotus Sutra with no ego whatsoever? When he raises his hand, it becomes the hand of compassion; when he stretches his feet, they become a Moses basket of generosity. If he sees young boys and girls, it is as if they are his own children; if he sees handicapped people, it is as though they are himself; although he has no wife and children, he makes a family wherever he goes, and teaches the true Dharma to all who come to him. If he were to devote himself to the realization of buddha-nature only, I would shed tears and not hesitate to respect him. In this day and age, among ten thousand Buddhist priests, how many are like this? Here is a monk named Nyogen. He is poor. He has no position, no fame, but he has a vow stronger than fame. His Dharma treasure is worth more than any material wealth. He has compassion, which is higher than any position. After leaving Engaku-ji, he went into the secular world, and now he wants to establish the Mentorgarten and devote his body and mind to the young people's spiritual growth.... I, Soyen, give one hundred percent moral support to his project. May this good student, with great vows for all, manifest both flower and fruit simultaneously.[6]

Despite this letter and his own strenuous efforts to promote and maintain the Mentorgarten, Nyogen Senzaki's struggles became more acute with the economic crisis caused by Japan's war with Russia in 1904. At the turn of the century, in many countries around the world, America figured large in potential immigrants' minds—the expression "streets paved with gold" was viewed more as a descriptive than an apocryphal one. Nyogen Senzaki wrote a second letter to his teacher in which he outlined his plans to try raising funds for the Mentorgarten in that land of opportunity.

In 1893, Soyen Shaku was invited to the United States to represent Japan at the World Parliament of Religions in Chicago, becoming the first Rinzai Zen master to speak on American soil. As Louis Nordstrom notes in *Namu Dai Bosa: A Transmission of Zen Buddhism to America*, "In Japan, Soyen Shaku was considered somewhat unconventional. After having become a roshi, he not only went on a pilgrimage to Ceylon where he studied Theravada Buddhism, but he also undertook the study of Western philosophy and culture, encouraging others to do so as well."[7] Among those who were deeply affected by his teaching in 1893 was a woman, Ida Russell, who became the first Zen student in America, later traveling to Japan to study with Soyen Shaku. In 1905 she and her husband, Alexander, invited the Zen master and his student, D.T. Suzuki, to come for a protracted visit to their home in San Francisco, where she had begun leading a small Zen group.

Soyen Shaku's admiration for her dedication and his vision of Zen's revitalization on American soil were conveyed in a poem he wrote for her:

> The Fifth Patriarch told a new monk,
> "Southern monkeys have no buddha-nature."
> That monk proved he had buddha-nature
> By becoming the Sixth Patriarch!
> In any part of the globe
> Where there is air, a fire can burn.
> Some day my teaching will surely go to the West,
> Led by you!

Knowing that Nyogen Senzaki hoped to garner support in America for his efforts to maintain the Mentorgarten, Soyen Shaku invited the young monk to accompany him on his second trip to the United States. However, just before they were to leave, Nyogen Senzaki again became ill, this time from an eye infection, trachoma. These illnesses—first at Engaku-ji, now when he was about to depart to America—seem in retrospect to have been the Dharma's way of emphasizing that his path would always be that of a solitary wandering monk. He recovered, and was able to get passage on a freighter to Seattle, and then make his way south to San Francisco by train. He spent a short time in the Russell home with Soyen Shaku and D.T. Suzuki, but then was on his own again—one account in the legend has Soyen Shaku walking away from him in a park.

Eido Roshi, in *Like a Dream, Like a Fantasy*, says, "In my opinion, this is when Nyogen Zen—the starkly simple, deeply idealistic, pure Zen that was Nyogen Senzaki's gift to America—took root. At least twice during the ensuing year, according to Soyen Shaku's diary, Nyogen Senzaki visited his master in San Francisco. I assume it was during these visits that the teacher told his student to remain in this 'strange land' and adopt its new language and culture. He also told him to remain anonymous and not to teach Zen for at least seventeen years."[8]

Nyogen Senzaki was brilliant. He had read the Chinese classics and the entire *Tripitaka*[9] by the age of eighteen; he had trained in Zen with one of the most important masters of the century, as well as in esoteric Buddhism through his studies with a Shingon master; he had plumbed the teachings of Christianity, and had read widely in Western philosophy. But he knew hardly any English and had little comprehension of American culture when he found himself alone in San Francisco. Those first seventeen years in this "strange land" were unimaginably difficult. He took whatever jobs he could get, struggling to learn English during the few hours he wasn't working. He did zazen alone in Golden Gate Park, and studied at the Public Library of San Francisco. In 1917 he wrote to a brother monk, Kishu, "Nowadays I work from 7 P.M. throughout the night as a telephone operator and bookkeeper for this hotel. Then from 7 A.M. to 11 A.M. I work as a housekeeper, with three American women and one Italian man as assistants. The only time I can sleep is from 2 P.M. to 6 P.M., and when it is too busy, sometimes I don't sleep for two or three days. Between 2 A.M. and 5 A.M., the telephone rings less often, and during that time, I study.... Nevertheless, I am still having financial problems.... I work so hard; why can't I save any money? My debts increase every month, so I cannot conduct my own independent business."[10]

Not long after that letter, Nyogen Senzaki was befriended by a young American woman who was soon smitten with him. Evidently the feelings were mutual, because in 1919 he wrote to his teacher and asked for permission to marry the woman he called his "Yankee Girl." Soyen Shaku was gravely ill at the time, but he wrote back giving his consent. However, on November first of that year, the great Zen master passed away. Losing his beloved teacher must have been too overwhelming for Nyogen Senzaki to consider his own personal happiness; perhaps he viewed his teacher's departure at that time as a message from the Dharma to eschew such fleeting joys and embrace his solitary monk's path with renewed vigor. In any case, the marriage did not take place, and in ensuing years, Nyogen Senzaki often railed against Buddhist priests who married and lived according to their own selfish desires.

Every November first from that year on until his own death, Nyogen Senzaki conducted a memorial service and wrote poems commemorating his teacher (see those from 1950 and 1951 on pages 345–46) and one reproduced in his beautiful calligraphic hand ("In this part of plateau," on page 331); many others appear in the 1976 volume *Namu Dai Bosa: A Transmission of Zen Buddhism to America*, and in the 1978 and 2005 editions of *Like a Dream, Like a Fantasy: The Zen Teachings and Translations of Nyogen Senzaki*. He was an excellent poet, writing on many subjects, most often in classical Chinese forms; he usually translated each poem himself into English and typed it or wrote it in script on the same page as his brushed kanji.

Starting in 1922, three years after Soyen Shaku's death and exactly seventeen years (as mandated by his teacher) after his arrival in the United States, whenever he could save enough money, Nyogen Senzaki would hire a hall to present lectures on Buddhism. He called these meetings his "floating zendo." Gradually, people began asking to sit with him. "I at last established a zendo in 1928, which I have carried with me as a silkworm hides itself in its cocoon," he told a student.[11] Now the adult Mentorgarten Sangha was born—a Sangha that had no divide between East and West, no connection with any religious organization or establishment, and very little of the hierarchy typical of Japanese Zen. In his talks, he addressed his students as "Bodhisattvas" or "Fellow Students," and noted, "The same spirit of Sangha found in my Mentorgarten movement may be found in early Buddhism—nay, not only in early Buddhism, but in both ancient and modern Buddhism as well. If there is true Buddhism, there is this Sangha spirit."[12]

In 1931, Nyogen Senzaki moved to Los Angeles, and it was there that he met two women who would be of major importance to his life's work: Shubin Tanahashi and Ruth Strout McCandless. Mrs. Tanahashi and her husband ran a laundry not far from Nyogen Senzaki's quarters. One day he left some articles of clothing to be washed, but was unable to reclaim them because he had run out of money. The next time she saw Nyogen

Senzaki passing by, Mrs. Tanahashi asked him why he had not picked up his clothing, and he quietly explained. Mrs. Tanahashi then came up with a mutually helpful proposition: her son, Jimmy, was a Down Syndrome child who was wheelchair-bound and unable to speak; she was very busy with the shop. Could Nyogen Senzaki care for Jimmy from time to time, in exchange for having the Tanahashis do his laundry? Thus a very special friendship was born. Of course the arrangement pleased both Nyogen Senzaki and his young charge, who, with the monk's gentle tutoring, was eventually able to repeat the first line of the "Great Vows for All," *Shu jo mu hen sei gan do*—"However innumerable all beings are, I vow to save them all." Shubin herself became Nyogen Senzaki's first Zen disciple in Los Angeles.

One day in the fall of 1934, she excitedly showed him a women's journal, *Fujin Koron*, which had a selection of poems and diary entries by a young monk living in seclusion on Dai Bosatsu Mountain, near Mount Fuji. The monk's name was Soen Nakagawa. Nyogen Senzaki was so deeply moved by what he read that he wrote to Monk Soen, and a life-long friendship between the two began. Monk Soen would send letters about koan practice with his new teacher, Yamamoto Gempo Roshi, at Ryutaku-ji in Mishima, as well as haiku, often written during solitary retreats in his hermit hut on Dai Bosatsu Mountain. Nyogen Senzaki would send letters about the Mentorgarten Sangha that met in his little zendo called *Tozen Zenkutsu*, "The Meditation Hall of the Eastbound Teaching." He would also mail selections from his ongoing project, translating the *Gateless Gate* (with the editing help of Paul Reps, who would later publish that and a selection of Zen stories Nyogen Senzaki had translated in a book that became very popular, *Zen Flesh, Zen Bones*). Nyogen Senzaki continued his own work on the *Gateless Gate*, writing the commentaries that appear in this present volume from 1937 through 1939.

Nyogen Senzaki and Soen Nakagawa discovered in each other the values of moral integrity, resolve, and purity they both found gravely lacking in the Buddhist establishment in Japan. In his commentary on Case Twenty-two of the *Gateless Gate*, Nyogen Senzaki quoted a New Year's Day poem he had written:

> One hundred thousand *bonzes*[13] of Japan are intoxicated with sake on this New Year's Day.
> Alone, Brother Soen is sober—nothing is able to tempt him.
> I light a lamp on my windowsill, and pine for him from this side of the ocean.
> He must be very happy when the plum blossoms herald the coming of spring!

Then he added, "This monk is my discovery, being of the same name, by pronunciation, as my teacher Soyen Shaku, but written differently in Chinese characters. He is in Mishima, Japan, these days. His full name is Soen Nakagawa. He will come to America in the future, gather the old assembly around him, and tear Kashyapa's preaching sign into rags."

Eido Roshi writes in his section of *Namu Dai Bosa*, "The Way to Dai Bosatsu":

> One of the reasons Nyogen Senzaki had come to the United States in 1905 was because he was disenchanted with modern Buddhism in Japan. He wanted to revive it in fresh soil. Now he had found someone in Japan who understood the true Way. Soen Nakagawa himself was frustrated with the overly structured modern Japanese temple life. In his own country his idealism was not well understood by those around him, but across the Pacific there was someone who, it seemed, was actualizing his own ideals.[14]

They eagerly wanted to meet, and it was arranged that Soen Nakagawa would come to California, but hostilities leading to the war between Japan and the United States intervened (the latter had cut off all credit to Japan, which meant all oil supplies, in response to Japan's invasion of

Manchuria). On October 12, 1941, two months before the bombing of Pearl Harbor, Nyogen Senzaki wrote:

> No ships cross the Pacific Ocean from Japan.
> We commemorate Bodhidharma in the loneliness of autumn.
> My brother monk does not come to America, and I do not
>   go to Japan.
> Listen to the incantation of the Dharani of the Great
>   Compassionate One!
> My voice is my Brother's voice!
> Yes, all these voices come from just one throat.

They agreed that since they could not meet in person, they would continue doing so every month in spirit. In the spring of 1938, while helping his teacher, Gempo Roshi, establish a Buddhist temple in Manchuria, Soen Nakagawa had written the following letter to Nyogen Senzaki:

> In Japan, on Mount Dai Bosatsu, the local deity festival is held on the twenty-first day of every month. Therefore, let us set this day as Spiritual Interrelationship Day. Those who are interested in seeking the Dharma, wherever they reside on this planet: start zazen at eight p.m. local time, entering into samadhi, and from 8:30, listen to the spiritual broadcasting of *kenteki*, the offering of the *shakuhachi* flute. Then chant the twenty-fifth chapter of the *Lotus Sutra*, 'The Great Compassionate Dharani,' 'Namu Dai Bosa,' and then the dedication to the Dai Bosatsu Deity. After that, at each place have a joyous gathering. Is this not a Universal Bodhisattva occasion? What a joyous event! This Spiritual Interrelationship Garden has no specific place; rather, the entire cosmos is the garden. The members of the Dai Bosatsu group are all animate and inanimate beings.... On the evening of the twenty-first of every month, we will go into the depths of form and nonform. For now, we call it Dai Bosatsu Deity, but fundamentally it is the sunyata-of-sunyata, or the profundity-of-profundity. What a liberated spirit!

In 1942, Nyogen Senzaki was imprisoned by the American government in an internment camp for Japanese nationals. First he was sent to Santa Anita, and then put on a train headed for barracks surrounded by barbed wire on the barren plateau of Heart Mountain, Wyoming. Some of Nyogen Senzaki's most poignant and, at times, most acerbic poetry was written during his three years there, and many, with his original calligraphy, are reproduced in this volume (see the Calligraphies and Selected Poems section, pages 324–46). One such poem not mentioned elsewhere in this work, "Leaving Santa Anita," of September 5, 1942, reads:

> A government must practice its policy without sentiment.
> All Japanese faces will leave California to support their government.
> This morning, the winding train, like a big black snake,
> Takes us away as far as Wyoming.
> The current of Buddhist thought always runs eastward.
> This policy may support the tendency of the teaching.
> Who knows?

Sharing a twenty-by-twenty-foot room with a family, Nyogen Senzaki's first efforts were to set up a zendo, and on December 20, 1942, he held an opening dedication, writing a poem for the occasion:

Opening Words of Wyoming Zendo

> The evacuation crammed Japs by heads into the units of barracks.
> Fortunately, the monk could stay with a Buddhist family.
> He called his share of space "E-kyo-an," Room of Wisdom Mirror.
> He suffered heat with the family in Santa Anita.
> He suffered cold with the family in Heart Mountain.
> He and the family and a number of Buddhists in the two places
> Meditated together, recited sutras, and studied Buddhism every morning.
> America gave the monk alms, a single room, today.

He now reopens Tozen Zenkutsu, the Meditation Hall of the Eastbound
  Teaching.
He had it twenty years in California
Inviting many Caucasian Buddhists from all parts of the world.
He has to wait exclusively for Japanese Zen students to come,
In this snow-covered desert of internment, a Wyoming plateau.
He has nothing to do with the trivialities of the dusty world.
He rather prefers to sit alone, burning the lamp of Dharma,
Than to receive any insincere visitors and waste time.

In addition to holding zazen and Buddhist study sessions at the
camp, Nyogen Senzaki translated and wrote commentaries on several
cases of the Soto koan collection called the *Shoyoroku*, or *Book of Equanimity*, Chapters One and Two of which are included in the present
volume.

Before the war, an unassuming yet remarkably insightful woman
named Ruth Strout McCandless met Nyogen Senzaki as a result of her
serious inquiry into Zen Buddhism. She became one of Nyogen Senzaki's most treasured disciples, studying with him individually and then
joining his Sangha. On December 5, 1941, he gave her the Buddhist precepts and a rakusu inscribed with the Dharma name Kangetsu, which
means "Cold Moon"; he took the name from a poem by the fourteenth-
century Japanese Zen master and poet Jakushitsu Genko, whose work he
greatly admired:

To make every day a pleasant day is not an easy task.
The doors please and the lights smile in this house.
If you want to know why,
Sit on the veranda and face the cold moon.

Some years later, he presented her with his Buddhist robe and kesa.
Kangetsu helped Nyogen Senzaki immeasurably with his writing and his

life. They collaborated on two important books, *Buddhism and Zen*, published in 1953, and *The Iron Flute*, which came out in 1961. On January 16, 1946, he wrote a poem dedicated to her:

> My English writings
> Have too many rips and rents.
> Who else can stitch and mend
> Except the old friend, Kangetsu?

She and her husband, John, and their two sons, Keith and Duncan, lived in a big house in Pasadena, California. When Nyogen Senzaki was informed that he would be sent away to the Heart Mountain camp, he asked Mrs. McCandless to keep his precious library of Buddhist books. After the war ended, it was to their home that Nyogen Senzaki went for a restorative two months. Duncan McCandless, who kindly made available many of Nyogen Senzaki's poems and several photographs from his mother's archives for this volume, remembers the Buddhist teacher's presence in their home and on visits with great fondness: "He had a kind and magnanimous dignity," he told me. "There was never any imposition from him in the way of personality, but always a sense of benign interest. The Japanese aesthetic was the highest of the high to me even when I was nine or ten years old; I built a little Japanese garden with a one-*tatami* hut, and he gave me little treasures to put in them." Kangetsu and Nyogen Senzaki remained in close contact until the latter's death. "My mother never spoke to others about Zen," Mr. McCandless said. "Her dedication was deep and personal. I sensed a strong communication between my mother and Senzaki Sensei that went way beyond words, and she enjoyed a similar kind of relationship later with Soen Roshi, with whom she shared a marvelous sense of humor."

After leaving the McCandless home, Nyogen Senzaki returned to Los Angeles. For a time, he could not find a space for his zendo, and wrote on October 29, 1945:

> For forty years I have not seen
> My teacher, Soyen Shaku, in person.
> I have carried his Zen in my empty fist,
> Wandering ever since in this strange land.
> Being a mere returnee from the evacuation
> I could establish no zendo
> Where his followers could commemorate
> The twenty-sixth anniversary of his death.
> The cold rain purifies everything on the earth
> In the great city of Los Angeles today.
> I open my fist and spread the fingers
> At the street corner in the evening rush hour.[15]

Not long after that, one of his followers, the owner of the Miyako Hotel, offered him a room and a small space for a zendo. On April 8, 1949, after fifteen years of correspondence broken only by the war years, Nyogen Senzaki and Soen Nakagawa were at last able to meet face to face, on Pier 42 in San Francisco. In June, Soen Nakagawa gave his first talk in America as part of a presentation at the Theosophical Society Library, San Francisco (see page 315). Then they spent several months together in Los Angeles, in Nyogen Senzaki's new space at the Miyako Hotel. Nyogen Senzaki had written a poem on October 10, 1948, in commemoration of Bodhidharma Day that anticipated Soen Nakagawa's arrival:

> Zen students practice perseverance age after age.
> They climb the mountains of meditation.
> They sail the seas of wisdom and knowledge.
> Where is their goal?
> Bodhidharma says, "I know not."
> A blue-eyed youth enters the monkhood.
> A brown-eyed monk crosses the Pacific.

Who knows their purpose?
What are they going to do?
Bodhidharma says, "I know not."[16]

Soen Nakagawa stayed with Nyogen Senzaki for nearly half a year, returning in the fall of 1949; he had been named the Dharma successor of Yamamoto Gempo Roshi, and his installation ceremony as the abbot of Ryutaku-ji took place in 1950. Nyogen Senzaki wrote this parting poem on September 23, 1949:

A monk's life is like a floating cloud
Or moving water—
No one can stop him.
Six months have passed like a dream;
Spring became summer
And summer became autumn.
Nansen left abruptly
Baso's moonlight party.
So Brother Soen goes back to Japan,
Crossing the Pacific Ocean
Lightheartedly as a seagull.
The moon follows him ten thousand miles with varying faces.[17]

In the early 1950s, at the suggestion of Shubin Tanahashi, the aging Nyogen Senzaki moved his zendo and residence into a house across the street from her apartment, on Second Street, in Little Tokyo. There was a bit more space and comfort in the new place, but most importantly, his loving disciple also wanted to be able to take care of him.

In 1955, Soen Roshi returned to the United States, and the two friends again were able to enjoy their deeply intimate Dharma relationship. Nyogen Senzaki continued to teach and write, helped greatly by Kangetsu Ruth McCandless's editorial assistance and keen understanding. Later that year he, Kangetsu, and her close friend Kokin Louise Padelford went to Japan, flying in a Stratocruiser—a propeller plane with sleeping sections. It was his first and only trip back; fifty-one years had passed since he had walked on Japanese soil. How inconceivably different his country must have seemed in the wake of Hiroshima and Nagasaki, the U.S. Occupation, the political and educational reforms, the headlong rush into industrialization and economic revitalization—and at the same time, how unchanged, particularly at Soen Roshi's rural temple on the outskirts of Mishima.

Eido Tai Shimano had his first and only opportunity to meet Nyogen Senzaki on that visit. He had been training under Soen Roshi at Ryutaku-ji since October 1954. He wrote in "The Way to Dai Bosatsu":

> Before [Nyogen Senzaki's] arrival, Soen Roshi had requested that a Western-style toilet be made for him. He knew it had been fifty years since Nyogen Senzaki had used Japanese toilets.... He made a drawing of an American toilet, and gave it to a carpenter, who was amazed, as were all of us monks. We had never seen anything like that before. The finished product couldn't be flushed, as it was impossible to change the whole plumbing system at Ryutaku-ji, but at least there was a place to sit!
>
> As I was a new monk, I did not know why Nyogen Senzaki had come to Japan. I did not even know who he was. However, when he gave a talk to all the monks, I was moved by this elderly man, with his exotic-looking silver hair, his vital voice, his strangely accented Japanese, and most importantly, by the content of his talk.[18]

As it turned out, it was Eido Roshi—then the young monk known as Tai-san—whom Soen Roshi asked to go to the United States to be an attendant to Nyogen Senzaki. Tai-san had studied English, and was responsible for helping foreign students at Ryutaku-ji with their questions and requests, so Soen Roshi thought he would be the most appropriate monk to send. At Soen Roshi's request, Tai-san wrote to Nyogen

Senzaki about the plans, and in one of his return letters, Nyogen Senzaki wrote that his disciple Shubin Tanahashi would be coming to Japan for a visit. When she arrived, Soen Roshi made ceremonial tea for her and asked Tai-san to join them. After her visit, Tai-san began preparing to leave for America. But on May 7, 1958, a telephone call came from Los Angeles during morning zazen. At the age of eighty-two, Choro-an Nyogen Senzaki—Morning Dew, Like a Phantasm—had returned to no-form.

The next day, Soen Roshi wrote a letter in which he addressed his beloved friend, saying that when his attendant monk informed him of the telephone call, "At that very moment, as though struck by a bolt of lightning, my mind was joined by yours." He returned to the zendo after taking the call, conducted dokusan, and then went to tell Gempo Roshi of Nyogen Senzaki's passing. Gempo Roshi said, "He was a reincarnate, and will work even harder for the Dharma now that he is without hindrances." Soen Roshi wrote, "I completely agree with him. Nyogen, Nyoho [Like a Phantasm, Like Dharma], please guide us on our path and in our practice with all your might. Please give us your encouragement in our pursuit of Buddha's incomparable Way." At the end of his letter he composed a haiku:

> *Dokoku no*
> *Hatete arikeri*
> *Satsuki Fuji*

> Cries of grief have ebbed
> Here it stands
> Mt. Fuji in May

Half of Nyogen Senzaki's ashes were placed in Evergreen Cemetery, Los Angeles, where the headstone is carved with an inscription he had written some time before he died:

Friends in Dhamma, be satisfied with your own heads. Do not put on any false heads above your own. Then minute after minute, watch your steps closely. These are my last words to you.

The other half were reserved and later mixed together with Soen Nakagawa Roshi's ashes beneath a stupa at Dai Bosatsu Zendo's Sangha Meadow Cemetery, in the Catskill Mountains of New York State.

In his will, Nyogen Senzaki had left all his manuscripts, both in Japanese and in English, to Soen Roshi. That summer, Soen Roshi went to California, led two sesshins, and moved his beloved friend's personal belongings to Shubin Tanahashi's house; he took three large boxes of manuscripts back to Japan. In August 1960, two years after Nyogen Senzaki's passing, Tai-san did in fact leave for the United States; Soen Roshi went to see him off and gave him the three boxes containing Nyogen Senzaki's manuscripts, and asked him to publish them as the opportunity arose. In 1984, after many teaching trips in America leading sesshins on both coasts, Soen Roshi passed away. He left his Dharma successor Eido Tai Shimano Roshi as literary executor of all his work and holdings, including Nyogen Senzaki's writings. Eido Roshi published some of these in *Namu Dai Bosa: A Transmission of Zen Buddhism to America*, to mark the formal opening in 1976 of Dai Bosatsu Zendo; more appeared in the 1978 and 2005 editions of *Like a Dream, Like a Fantasy: The Zen Teachings and Translations of Nyogen Senzaki*.

It is with deep gratitude to all these pioneers of Zen Buddhism in America that I have worked to bring together a further volume of hitherto unpublished material from these holdings, to commemorate the fiftieth anniversary of Nyogen Senzaki's passing. The book begins with the complete *Gateless Gate*, including Nyogen Senzaki's commentaries on each case. This section is drawn from talks he gave over a period of two years, from September 21, 1937, to July 6, 1939; they were recorded and transcribed by his students. His initial translation of the koans from the

Chinese, done in 1934 with the editing help of Paul Reps, appeared many years later in the 1957 book *Zen Flesh, Zen Bones* without commentaries, but in Nyogen Senzaki's talks on the *Gateless Gate* he often revised and corrected that translation to be in closer accordance with the original Chinese. The manuscript edited for this volume is based on those talks, using Nyogen Senzaki's revisions and my own editorial changes made for purposes of clarity and English usage.

The book continues with undated translations and commentaries on Cases One, Two, Eight, Twelve, and Twenty-two from the other principal koan text of the Rinzai Zen School, the *Hekiganroku*, or *Blue Rock Collection*, and with an Introduction, translations, and commentaries on Chapters One and Two from the *Shoyoroku*, or *Book of Equanimity*, which he worked on while interned at Heart Mountain.

The next part consists of a selection of Dharma talks and essays in chronological order from 1931 through 1954. Nyogen Senzaki's poems in his beautiful calligraphy, with his own English translations typed or written on each page, and selected poems without his calligraphy, follow. These include his translations of the fourteenth-century Japanese Zen master and poet Jakushitsu Genko, and his commemorative poems to Soyen Shaku. Next is his translation of and explanatory notes on Soyen Shaku's unfinished *Autobiography*. The final grouping consists of Correspondence, including a lengthy letter Nyogen Senzaki wrote to his teacher not long after leaving Engaku-ji about his struggles to establish the first Mentorgarten; a subsequent letter in which he broaches the subject of going to the United States; an article published in a Tokyo newspaper that generated a flurry of letters to and from Nyogen Senzaki; and one of his last epistolary exchanges. These letters are particularly significant in that they illustrate Nyogen Senzaki's uncompromising adherence to Buddhist teachings, his humility, his unswerving dedication to the precepts, and his impatience with those who were more interested in their own comfort than in striving for realization.

In my editorial decisions, I have made every effort to retain Nyogen Senzaki's style, which is enlivened by his knowledge of American slang, his peppery exhortations, and his vivid allusions and metaphors, while eliminating awkward phrasing and polishing his word usage. I changed the pejorative term "Hinayana" ("Lesser Vehicle"), used by writers of Nyogen Senzaki's time, to the more accepted term "Theravada" ("Teaching of the Elders"). He often used the Pali word *Dhamma* rather than the Sanskrit *Dharma*, because, he said, European Buddhist scholars were more familiar with the Pali. Since he also spoke of "Buddha's Dharma" and "Dharmakaya," and used other Sanskrit terms, and since readers today are quite familiar with the Sanskrit word *Dharma*, for the sake of consistency I have used the latter.

Certain themes recur throughout Nyogen Senzaki's koan commentaries, talks, essays, poems, and letters: "Block the road of your thinking," he tells us again and again. That's all we need to do. "Give the uppercut to your own dualistic ideas." The simpler the better, he emphasizes; no word is best of all. We must continually strive to actualize the truth of Zen for ourselves, since realization "will not come to us by luck, as in a lottery" (Case Twenty-two of the *Gateless Gate*). If we are filled with "emotional pining" for something outside, for someone else's understanding, we are cut off from our own inner wisdom. He notes that real Zen teachers never give anything; rather, they take away whatever their students are attached to.

Stressing that silence is the most eloquent vehicle for expressing Zen, in his commentary to Case Twenty of the *Gateless Gate* he says, "I appreciate your enthusiasm in copying my lectures and keeping them, but remember that I speak them with shame and tears. I do such a dirty job (this talking on Zen) because nobody else has done it here before me. Please do not show my lectures to any outsiders and say that they are a part of my Zen. I have no such funny business as preaching Zen. Whatever I say passes away before you record it. You only catch my yawns and coughs."

Nyogen Senzaki had no use for Buddhists who sought renown or used propaganda to attract students. "The teachings lose their richness when they have many followers" (Case Twenty-six of the *Gateless Gate*). Indeed, he held most of his contemporaries in the Zen Buddhist establishment in disregard, particularly in Japan, but in America as well, as is evident in this paragraph from Case Two of the *Blue Rock Collection*: "Here in America, many so-called spiritual teachers gather students who bring many questions; they then patiently try to entertain them with favorable answers."

In the United States, Nyogen Senzaki lived as an ordinary citizen, not calling attention to himself in any way. He wore a suit and tie, placing his robe over them when engaged in zazen or giving a lecture; he did not shave his head, but, as the young monk Tai-san observed when Nyogen Senzaki visited Ryutaku-ji, had a beautiful silver crown of hair. "Those who digest Zen well should do their work in the world without displaying any trace of Zen," he says in "Amban's Addition" to the *Gateless Gate*, and in the same commentary he tells us, "Monks have no monopoly on Zen. Zen belongs to the world. Laymen and laywomen adherents should study Zen—even children in kindergarten should be trained in the Zen way. The shrubs and grasses around this humble house also study Zen. They show the color of Zen through their own natural green.... Zen monks are like street cleaners. They do their work so that others can go their different ways.... True monks who guard the lamp of Dharma are becoming fewer and fewer."

The world—not just the Zen world, not just the Buddhist world— needs the cool-headed, compassionate, and incisive teachings of this true monk more today than ever. With palms together, in commemoration of his life of integrity, simplicity, wisdom, and unstinting loving-kindness, this book is offered to men, women, children, shrubs, grasses, and street cleaners!

Acknowledgments

My first debt of gratitude goes to Nyogen Senzaki himself, who has been such an inspiration to my own practice these past fifty years. I can still remember the excitement with which I picked up the beautifully presented *Zen Flesh, Zen Bones*, slid it out of its slipcase, and knew that despite the meager state of my finances, I had to buy that book filled with stories and koan selections compiled and translated by Nyogen Senzaki with Paul Reps's editing. It's still with me, slightly the worse for wear after decades of good use; the little paper band that went around the book is now a tattered bookmark. Along with D.T. Suzuki and Alan Watts, it was Nyogen Senzaki who guided me in my first untutored years of Zen.

The saying goes, "Rare it is to be born in human form; rarer still to encounter the Buddha-Dharma; and even rarer to meet a true teacher." My gratitude to my teacher, Eido T. Shimano Roshi, is beyond words. I am particularly indebted to him for entrusting me with Nyogen Senzaki's manuscripts, letters, poems, and photographs from the collection that his teacher, Soen Nakagawa Roshi, had given to him, and for encouraging me to bring together this fiftieth commemoration volume.

I am grateful to Josh Bartok of Wisdom Publications for suggesting the project, for making available to me a Xeroxed selection of Nyogen Senzaki's manuscripts, and for his willingness to work on a short timetable in order to present this as a fiftieth anniversary publication.

Thanks, too, to Pat Stacy and Gerry Shishin Wick, who called those ancient Xeroxes to Josh's attention and provided him with his first look at that material.

My deep appreciation goes to my first husband, Louis Nordstrom, editor of *Namu Dai Bosa: A Transmission of Zen Buddhism to America*, in which he presented a selection of Nyogen Senzaki's writings from Eido Roshi's collection, and for his excellent Introduction, to which I have referred several times in the present text. One unexpected but very enjoyable aspect of bringing this book into being was meeting Duncan McCandless, a son of Nyogen Senzaki's disciple and colleague, the late Ruth Strout McCandless. Mr. McCandless was generous in lending the calligraphy poems that have been reproduced in this volume, as well as several rare photographs. I am deeply indebted to him.

My profound thanks go to Professor Tsutomu Nakatsugawa, as well as to his friend, Mitsuo Ishida, Ph.D., both of whom worked diligently at the very difficult task of translating Nyogen Senzaki's letters to his teacher, Soyen Shaku; they were written in old-style characters, and it required long hours and a good deal of research in various dictionaries to bring these into print.

Many Zen students helped me with this project. I am grateful to my Dharma brother Zenshin Richard Rudin in California, who drove me here and there and helped with many details, and to Sunyana Graef Sensei of Vermont Zen Center for her proficiency at computer scanning. For their prodigious work typing the texts from Xeroxed manuscripts into the computer, I wish to express my appreciation particularly to Kanro Christine Dowling at the Zen Center of Syracuse Hoen-ji, and to Andrea Rook at Dai Bosatsu Zendo, with additional help from Kigetsu Jennifer Sampson of Hoen-ji and Tetsunin Pat Yingst of Austin Zen Center, who spent time at Hoen-ji as well. My thanks, too, to Fujin Zenni, head monastic at Dai Bosatsu Zendo, for her warm encouragement, and to Jokei Megumi Kairis, also at Dai Bosatsu Zendo, for scanning and mailing photographs from Eido Roshi's collection.

I also owe a debt of gratitude to all my students, whose patience during my busy time with this project is greatly appreciated.

To my husband, Andy Hassinger, whose enthusiasm for Nyogen Senzaki's teachings began in 1978, the year we met and the year the first edition of *Like a Dream, Like a Fantasy* came out, and who has been an ever-encouraging, inconspicuous yet constant bodhisattva, I offer my most loving thanks.

And finally, with a reverential heart, I dedicate this book to the Zen Studies Society, which, under the direction of Eido Roshi since he came to New York on the first day of 1965, has brought the teachings of Nyogen Senzaki to generations of American students. In addition to being the fiftieth anniversary of Nyogen Senzaki's passing, 2008 is the fortieth anniversary of the Zen Studies Society's New York Zendo Shobo-ji. Happy Birthday, New York Zendo; congratulations, Eido Roshi and Aiho-San Yasuko Shimano and all Sangha everywhere!

Roko Sherry Chayat
Zen Center of Syracuse Hoen-ji
Syracuse, New York
September 2007

Photographs

Except where otherwise noted, photographs are
courtesy of Eido Shimano Roshi

Mentorgarten Sangha, Fukaura, Aomori Prefecture, Japan, early 1900s

28

Left: Nyogen Senzaki, 441 Turner Street, Los Angeles, 1934

Right: Nyogen Senzaki, May 1, 1935, with inscription to Shubin Tanahashi

Below: Jimmy and Shubin Tanahashi at the laundry shop in Little Tokyo, 1935

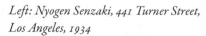

Above: Nyogen Senzaki in Soto-style kesa, January 14, 1942
Archival materials courtesy of estate of Ruth Strout McCandless

Below: Heart Mountain Barracks, 1944
Archival materials courtesy of estate of Ruth Strout McCandless

Above: Nyogen Senzaki in his study, late 1940s
Archival materials courtesy of estate
of Ruth Strout McCandless

*Right: Nyogen Senzaki and D.T. Suzuki,
California, late 1940s*
Archival materials courtesy of estate of
Ruth Strout McCandless

*Below: Nyogen Senzaki and Soen Nakagawa
(standing, front row) on the latter's first trip
to the United States, in Los Angeles, 1949,
with Sangha members including Shubin
Tanahashi (kneeling, front row, left)*

*Below: Soen Nakagawa at Miyako Hotel,
Los Angeles, 1949*

Above left: Shubin Tanahashi, Jimmy Tanahashi, Nyogen Senzaki, Los Angeles, 1949

Above right: Nyogen Senzaki at his Second Street Zendo, with photograph of Soyen Shaku, Los Angeles, 1952

Nyogen Senzaki in kesa at his altar, with photograph of Soyen Shaku, Second Street Zendo (his last dwelling), Los Angeles, 1954

Above: Nyogen Senzaki's altar at his Second Street Zendo

Right: Nyogen Senzaki with Soen Nakagawa Roshi, 1955

Above: Nyogen Senzaki at Ryutaku-ji, Japan, 1955, seated front row center; at his left are Yamamoto Gempo Roshi and Soen Nakagawa Roshi; back row, third from left, Soen Nakagawa Roshi's mother; back row, fifth from left, Ruth Strout McCandless; seventh from left, Eido Tai Shimano

Right: Soen Nakagawa Roshi, Nyogen Senzaki, and Ruth Strout McCandless, Ryutaku-ji, 1955

Above left: Rev. Inoue and Nyogen Senzaki in Kamakura, Japan, 1955

Above right: Nyogen Senzaki, Los Angeles, ca. 1957

Shubin Tanahashi at Ryutaku-ji, 1957, seated with Soen Nakagawa Roshi and Yamamoto Gempo Roshi, front row; second row, third from right, Eido Tai Shimano; second from right, Soen Roshi's mother.

Nyogen Senzaki's funeral, Evergreen Cemetery, May 1958

Nyogen Senzaki's grave at Evergreen Cemetery, Los Angeles, 1958; Soen Nakagawa Roshi and Shubin Tanahashi, seated, with other Sangha members

Soen Nakagawa Roshi, Shubin Tanahashi, and Los Angeles Sangha at Nyogen Senzaki's Second Street Zendo, September 1960

Soen Nakagawa Roshi and Jimmy Tanahashi, Los Angeles, September 1960

Shubin Tanahashi and Eido Tai Shimano inside Mrs. Tanahashi's house, Los Angeles, 1961

Introductory Comments

BODHISATTVAS: Let us begin to study the *Gateless Gate*. These commentaries, telling about the experiences of teachers of old, are first of all to encourage your meditation. Second of all, they aim to assist you in learning systematically about Buddhism. The two ways should advance together. Otherwise our meditation may turn into mere formality. Saladin Paul Reps and I made an attempt at a translation of the *Gateless Gate*. Using this translation as our text and revising it to be in accordance with the original Chinese, I will add my comments to each case. Buddhist scriptures were translated into Chinese by both Indian and Chinese scholars, dynasty after dynasty, from the first century C.E. on. The essence of Buddhism, however, was carried from India to China in 520 by Bodhidharma, known as the first Zen patriarch. The wisdom of enlightenment, that is, the essence of Buddhism, was transmitted from the Buddha to the silent-sitting Bodhidharma in natural succession through twenty-seven generations, and was then transmitted from Bodhidharma to his Chinese successor, and similarly handed down through the centuries.

Bodhidharma was called the silent-sitting monk because he did not preach or translate the sutras as did the other monks who came to China before him. Meditation was his work, and he did nothing else during the nine years he spent in China until he passed away there. It was thus that Zen Buddhism entered and was nurtured in and spread through China and Japan. Before and after Bodhidharma, many thousands of scriptures were translated and ten times that number of commentaries were written and published, creating many sects and schools of Buddhism.

Zen, the most radical (as in essential, not extreme) interpretation of Buddhism, maintains that it transmits the essential teaching. The Japanese word *Zen*, from *Chan* in Chinese, and *dhyana* in Sanskrit, means meditation, and is a method to attain enlightenment. Zen is the attainment itself. While the word Zen was originally Japanized Sanskrit, it is now more than an abbreviation of the original word. It represents an accomplishment that the original word did not contain.

The Sanskrit word *dhyana* was transcribed into two Chinese characters and later abbreviated into one character, which was pronounced "Chan" or "Shan" in Chinese, and "Zen" by the Japanese. If China had, in the modern age, a Zen scholar like our Professor D.T. Suzuki, who began writing Zen books in English forty years ago, the teaching of Bodhidharma would be called Chan or Shan by Europeans and Americans, instead of Zen.

The essence of Bodhidharma's teaching was:

> A special transmission outside the scriptures,
> Rising through and beyond words and letters;
> Direct pointing to one's mind-essence,
> Seeing into one's nature and attaining enlightenment.

These words were, according to Chinese tradition, spoken by Bodhidharma. Let me make a plain, literal translation from the original Chinese:

> Outside the scriptures, there is a special transmission.
> It has no form, neither written nor spoken.
> It opens your essence of mind.
> You can realize your true nature and become buddha.

Zen has many classic texts, of which the *Gateless Gate* is one. The *Gateless Gate*, our translation of *Mu-Mon-Kan*, literally "No-Gate-Barrier," was recorded by Zen Master Mumon Ekai, who lived in China from 1183 to 1260. The work consists of narrated interactions between ancient Chinese teachers and their pupils, illustrating means employed to break through dualistic, externalizing, generalizing, and intellectualizing tendencies so that students might realize the essence of Zen. The problems or inner challenges with which these masters confronted their pupils came to be called *koans*. They used slang freely to actualize the highest teaching, that of seeing into the nature of one's own being. They made no pretense of being logical. Koans deal with states of mind rather than words. Unless this is understood, the point of this classic text will be missed. The whole intent is to help the pupil break through the shell of limited mind and attain a new, eternal birth—enlightenment.

Life itself offers many problems. These teachers offered problems to their pupils to lead them to an understanding of life. Zen is liberation. Each problem is a barrier. Those who have the spirit of Zen pass through it. Those who live in Zen understand one koan after another as if they are seeing the unseen and living in the illimitable.

Mumon's Introduction

BODHISATTVAS: We now begin to study our text.

Mumon says in his Introduction:

Zen has no gates. The purpose of Buddha's words is to enlighten others; therefore, Zen is gateless. Now, how does one pass through this gateless gate? There is a saying that whatever enters through the gate is not the family treasure. Whatever is produced by the help of another will dissolve and perish.

In the Bible we often see such an expression as, "That which the Lord has declared unto his prophets should come to pass...." This is a distorted view of the teachings of Revelation. The young stage of a religious mind always lingers around such an idea. One thus has to have a Supreme Being, and the agency of prophets. The compilers of old scriptures had to work hard to satisfy those childish minds, and thus stitched together the ragged pieces of old traditions and legends.

Zen has nothing to do with such antiquities. You are here to meditate only because you want to know your true self. No agent of a Supreme Being provoked you to come. No scriptures enticed you to study meditation. As Mumon says, "Zen has no gates." All of you have gathered here by your own will. The purpose of Buddha's preaching is to dispel the clouds of delusion and to allow the sun of enlightenment to blaze forth from your own mind. Just as medicines are prescribed by a doctor according to the nature of the sickness, the teachings are provided by Buddha according to the condition of the disciple's mind. Therefore, the essence of the teaching has no particular form or mold. This is what Mumon means in saying, "Therefore, Zen is gateless."

In his time, all students of Buddhism understood that Zen is the essence of Buddhism, not a school or a sect of it. Mumon quotes a Chinese saying, "Whatever enters through the gate is not the family treasure," and to make the meaning clear, he adds another saying of Buddhism, "Whatever is produced by the help of another is likely to dissolve and perish." In the West you say, "Heaven helps those who help themselves." Buddhism says, "One creates heaven and earth by oneself." You must discover your own family treasure within yourself. I am a senior student to you all, but I have nothing to impart to you. Whatever I have is mine, and never will be yours. You may consider me stingy and unkind, but I do not wish you to produce something that will dissolve and perish. I want each of you to discover your own inner treasure.

Mumon continues: *Even such words are like raising waves in a windless sea or performing surgery upon a healthy body. If you cling to what others have said, and try to understand Zen through explanations, it is as though you are trying to hit the moon with a pole, or scratch your itchy foot from the outside of your shoe. It is not at all possible.*

Those who understand Zen need not listen to Mumon or anyone else. But most students have something lurking in their minds, something that is bound to become a harmful parasite: a feeling of dependence upon others for their own growth. These students need sharp and emphatic encouragement, not soft and kind words.

The following part of Mumon's Introduction will be understood without comment. I will offer it here and stop raising waves in a calm sea, or performing surgery upon a sound body.

In the year 1228, I was giving Dharma discourses to the monks in the temple of Ryusho, City of Toka, in the Province of Onshu, and at their request I retold old koans, endeavoring to inspire their Zen spirit. I meant to use the koans as one uses a piece of brick to knock at a gate: after the gate is opened, the brick is useless and is thrown away. Unexpectedly, however, my notes were collected as a group of forty-eight koans, together with my comments in prose and verse on each, although their arrangement was not in the order in which I spoke about them. I have titled the book the Mumonkan *(Gateless Gate), and offer it to students to read as a guide.*

If you are brave enough and go straight ahead in meditation, you will not be disturbed by delusions. You will attain Zen just as did the ancient masters of India and China; perhaps even more so. But if there is a moment's hesitation, it is as though you are watching from a small window for a horse and rider to pass by: in a blink of your eye, they are missed.

Mumon ends the Introduction with his verse:

The great Way has no gate;
Thousands of roads enter it.
When one passes through this gateless gate,
One walks freely throughout heaven and earth.

Soon we will begin a week of seclusion in commemoration of Bodhidharma, from the third of October to the ninth. This is a fine opportunity for all of you to practice Zen with self-determination. Let us see what we can do for attainment.

Case One
Joshu's Dog

A monk asked Joshu, "Does a dog have buddha-nature or not?" Joshu answered, "Mu." [19]

BODHISATTVAS: The first koan in the *Gateless Gate* is "Joshu's Dog." This koan is usually the first one given to the Zen student. Many masters in China and Japan entered Zen through this gate. Do not think that it is easy just because it is the first. A koan is the thesis of the postgraduate course in Buddhism. Those who have studied the teachings for twenty years may consider themselves scholars of Buddhism, but until they pass this gate of Joshu's Dog, they will remain strangers outside the door of Buddhadharma. Each koan is the key of emancipation. Once you are freed from your fetters, you do not need the key any more.

A stanza from the *Shodoka* ("Song of Realization") goes:

> The wonderful power of emancipation!
> It is applied in countless ways—in limitless ways.
> One should make four kinds of offerings for this power.
> If you want to pay for it,
> A million gold pieces are not enough.
> If you sacrifice everything you have, it cannot cover your debts.
> Only a few words from your realization are payment in full,
> Even for the debts of the remote past. [20]

You can get this power of emancipation when you pass "Joshu's Dog." Your answer to this koan will be your payment in full, even for the debts of the remote past.

The great Chinese Zen master Joshu always spoke his Zen, using a few choice words, instead of hitting or shaking his students as other teachers did. I know that students who cling to worldly sentiments do not like the rough manner of Zen. They should meet our Joshu first, and study his simplest word, "Mu."

Each sentient being has buddha-nature. This dog must have one. But before you conceptualize about such nonsense, influenced by the idea of the soul in Christianity, Joshu will say "Mu." Get out! Then you may think of the idea of "manifestation." Fine word! So you think of the manifestation of buddha-nature as a dog. Before you can express such nonsense, Joshu will say "Mu." You are clinging to a ghost of Brahman. Get out! Whatever you say is just the shadow of your conceptual thinking. Whatever you conceive of is a figment of your imagination. Now, tell me, has a dog buddha-nature or not? Why did Joshu say "Mu"?

MUMON'S COMMENT

To realize Zen, one has to pass through the barrier set up by the patriarchs.

Do not think that the barrier is in the book. It is right here in front of your nose.

Enlightenment is certain when the road of thinking is blocked.

Meditation blocks the road of thinking.

If you do not pass the patriarchs' barrier, if your road of thinking is not blocked, whatever you think, whatever you do, will be like an entangling ghost. You are not an independent person if you do not pass this barrier. You cannot walk freely throughout heaven and earth. *You may ask, what is the barrier set up by the patriarchs? This one word, Mu, is it. This is the barrier of Zen. If you pass through it, you will see Joshu face to face. Then you can walk hand in hand with the whole line of patriarchs. Is this not a won-*

COMMENTARIES ON THE *GATELESS GATE* 45

drous thing? If you want to pass this barrier, you must work so that every bone in your body, every pore of your skin, is filled through and through with this question, What is Mu? You must carry it day and night.

Didn't I tell you it is not an easy job? Don't be afraid, however. Just carry the koan, and ignore all contending thoughts. They will disappear soon, leaving you alone in samadhi. Do not believe Mu is the common negative. It is not nothingness as the opposite of existence. Joshu did not say the dog has buddha-nature. He did not say the dog has no buddha-nature. He only pointed directly to your own buddha-nature! Listen to what he said: "Mu."

If you really want to pass this barrier, you should feel as though you have a hot iron ball in your throat that you can neither swallow nor spit up.

Don't be afraid; he means you should shut up, and cut off even the slightest movement of your intellectual faculty.

Then your previous conceptualizing disappears. Like a fruit ripening in season, subjectivity and objectivity are experienced as one.

There you are, in samadhi.

You are like a dumb person who has had a dream. You know it, but you cannot speak about it. When you enter this condition, your ego-shell is crushed, and you can shake the heavens and move the earth. You are like a great warrior with a sharp sword.

Neither Japan nor China has such a warrior; therefore they have to fight each other.[21]

Cut down the buddha who stands in your way.

What Mumon means here is complete unification.

Kill the patriarch who sets up obstacles.

This is an expression in Chinese rhetoric, meaning once you become a buddha, you have no more use for buddha. Some Japanese blockhead could not understand such a peculiar expression, and many other quaint Chinese terms as well, and took them all as invitations to stir hatred. This is one of the causes of the conflict between China and Japan. Ignorance is not bliss, it is a terrible thing.

You will walk freely through birth and death. You can enter any place as if it were your own playground. I will tell you how to do this. Just concentrate all your energy into Mu, and do not allow any discontinuity. When you enter Mu and there is no discontinuity, your attainment will be like a candle that illuminates the whole universe.

Discontinuity may be allowed at first while you are engaged in your everyday work, but when you are meditating in the zendo or in your home, you must carry on with this koan, minute after minute, bravely. Our seclusion week is an opportunity for you to engage in this sort of adventure. After you train yourselves well, then even in the midst of your everyday work you will find your leisure moments filled with the koan.

Mumon's verse

> *Does a dog have buddha-nature or not?*
> *This is the most profound question.*
> *If you say yes or no,*
> *Your own buddha-nature is lost.*

Case Two
Hyakujo's Fox

Hyakujo was delivering a series of Zen lectures. An old man attended them, unnoticed by the monks. At the end of each talk, when the monks left the hall, he would follow them out. But one day he remained, and after the monks had gone, Hyakujo asked him, "Who are you?" The man replied, "Many eons ago, I was a human being. This was in the time of Kashyapa Buddha (the prehistoric Buddha), and I was a Zen master living on this mountain. One day a student of mine asked me whether or not an enlightened person is subject to the law of causation, and I foolishly replied, 'An enlightened person is not subject to the law of causation.'

"For this answer, evidencing a clinging to the absolute, I became a fox for five hundred rebirths, including this present one. Will you free me with a Zen word from this prison of a fox's body? Please tell me your answer. Is an enlightened person subject to the law of causation?"

Hyakujo replied instantly, "An enlightened person is one with the law of causation!"

At these words, the old man was enlightened, and cried out, "Now I am free!" Paying homage with a deep bow he said, "I am no longer a fox, but I must leave this body in my dwelling place behind this mountain. Please give me a monk's funeral." Then he disappeared.

The next day Hyakujo told the head monk to make preparations for a monk's funeral. "But no one has been sick in the infirmary," wondered the monks. "What can this mean?"

After dinner, Hyakujo led the monks out of the dining hall and around the mountain. There they found a cave. Taking his staff, Hyakujo poked around in the leaves at the cave's mouth until he uncovered the body of a fox. He then performed the ceremony of cremation.

Later that evening, Hyakujo related the story to the monks. Obaku, after listening carefully, asked Hyakujo, "I understand that a certain person, many ages ago, gave a wrong answer. For this he was turned into a fox for five hundred rebirths. Now please tell me—if some modern master, being asked many questions, always gives the right answer, what then?" "If you will come up here to me," Hyakujo replied, "I will tell you."

Without hesitating, Obaku got up and hurried to his teacher, giving him a resounding slap on the cheek, for he knew that this was the answer his teacher intended for him.

Hyakujo clapped his hands and laughed aloud at this discernment. "I thought the foreigner had a red beard," he cried, "and now I know it!"

BODHISATTVAS: It is probable that Hyakujo made up this tale himself, in order to impress on his monks the authority of the law of causation. He chose his material carefully, so as to best appeal to their level of understanding.

At the Flower Festival this year, I said, "Every action brings its own results in the material world, in the realm of the mind and in society. Cabbages and kings, rich men and paupers, wise birds and stupid asses—none can break the law of causation." This is my answer to this koan. Enlightened person or unenlightened person, it makes not the slightest difference.

The person who understands the law is wise enough; the person who knows to beware of the law can live righteously. One who does as one pleases, yet stays within the bounds of the law, is a great sage; that one is an enlightened person.

Those who believe in the power of the church or priestcraft to erase their sins are all foxes. When they believe the church or priest is not subject to the law of causation; they expose their inability to live congenially within the law. Their children will do as they do, and society will imitate them. This is the power of their evil karma.

Obaku was the best disciple of Hyakujo, and knew what his teacher meant. What he was asking was, "Where is the person who is always one with the law of causation?" Hyakujo did not dare say, "I am that person." Instead, he would have said, "You are the one, my dear Alfonse," and would have slapped his disciple's face. But Obaku prevented this by slapping his teacher's face: "You are the one, my dear Gaston."[22]

Hyakujo then clapped his hands and laughed. "I thought the foreigner had a red beard, and now I know it."

MUMON'S COMMENT

"An enlightened person is not subject to"—How can this answer make the monk a fox?

Because he postulates an enlightened person, and separates himself from the law of causation.

"An enlightened person is one with the law of causation"—How can this answer emancipate the fox?

When you are enlightened, you can do as you please, yet you will always live within the law.

To understand this clearly, you must have only One eye.

That's what Mumon says, but it's too late in this zendo. All who have attended this class know very well, "The eye with which I see God is the very eye with which God sees me!"[23] Mumon, Mumon, are you trying to sell the "Extra, extra!" of the day before yesterday?[24]

MUMON'S VERSE

Subject to or not subject to?
The same die shows two faces.
Not subject to or subject to?
Both are mistaken!

In Zen, thinking and acting must be without an instant's hesitation, otherwise your action or word will be an uncertain gamble.

Case Three
Gutei's Finger

Whenever he was asked a question about Zen, Gutei raised his finger.
A young attendant began to imitate him. When anyone asked the boy
about his master's teaching, the boy would raise his finger.

Gutei heard about the boy's mischief. He seized him and cut off his
finger. The boy cried and began to run away. Gutei called out to him.
When the boy turned his head, Gutei raised his finger. At that, the boy
was enlightened.

When Gutei was about to pass from this world, he gathered his
monks around him and said, "I attained my one-finger Zen from my
teacher, Tenryu, and throughout my whole life, I have not exhausted
it." Then he passed away.

BODHISATTVAS: In the time of Gutei, the Chinese government perse-
cuted Buddhism, destroying 40,000 Buddhist temples and cancelling the
ordination status of 260,000 monks and nuns. This took place in 845
C.E.; the tyrannical rule lasted for twenty months. As a monk, Gutei lost his
temple home. He hid himself in a remote mountain, begging for his food
secretly among the villagers. One evening a nun came to his shelter and
walked around him three times with her traveling staff without taking her
hat off. It was very impolite to act that way at a monk's shelter. She made
it clear that she considered him a stone image, not a living monk. Gutei
commanded her to take off her hat. The nun said, "If you are not a stone

image, say a word of Zen, and then I will properly pay you my respects." Gutei had never attained Zen; therefore, he could not say a word. The nun called him a stupid monk, and went away. Gutei was ashamed of himself to no small degree. He made up his mind that he would undertake a journey through which he might attain understanding. Before he could start out, however, he was visited by an old monk. Gutei expressed his shame and resolve, frankly, in a man-to-man talk. The old monk then raised his finger. Seeing this, Gutei was enlightened. The old monk was Tenryu, a great teacher of that time.

Although the Chinese government's persecution resulted in the worst circumstances for the Buddhist establishment in its history in China, it created the opportunity for good monks and nuns to set out on pilgrimages. Gutei, too, caught his chance at this time of oppression. He sensed keenly that the opportunity for realization is rare and noble. This was the reason why, in our present story, he cut off the boy's finger.

An imitation of the teaching seems at first rather innocent, but if it is not nipped in the bud, it will grow into the ugly weed of religious complacency, or into the troublesome weed of hypocrisy. To open the gate of realization, one must block off one's road of conceptualization. Gutei seized the boy and cut off his finger. The boy cried and began to run away. It was too sudden for the boy to think of anything; there was only the pain. At that moment, Gutei called for the boy to stop. The boy turned his head toward Gutei, and the master raised his finger. There! With his road of thinking blocked, the boy could be enlightened.

This koan not only teaches you to realize Zen for yourself, but also shows you how to open the minds of others and let them see the truth as clearly as daylight. The power of Zen that Gutei received from Tenryu was not merely the act of raising a finger; it was the means to enlighten others. Therefore he said on his deathbed, "I attained my one-finger Zen from my teacher, Tenryu, and throughout my whole life, I have not exhausted it."

MUMON'S COMMENT

The enlightenment that Gutei and the boy attained has nothing to do with the finger. If you cling to the finger, Tenryu will be so disappointed that he will annihilate—another Chinese expression; we should probably use the word "disown," or "expel"—*Gutei, the boy, and you.*

MUMON'S VERSE

> *Gutei cheapens Tenryu's teaching*
> *Emancipating the boy with a knife.*
> *Compared to the Chinese god who divided a mountain with one*
>   *hand,*
> *Old Gutei is a poor imitator.*

A Chinese myth tells us that the Yellow River at first could not run toward the east, as there was a great mountain in the way. A god came to help, and divided the mountain into two parts, so that the water could run through. If you look carefully at those two mountains, you will find the fingerprints of this god. Such a story! Zen never asks us to believe in miracles, but we Zen students perform miracles without knowing it ourselves. Didn't I give you a koan in this seclusion: "After you have entered into the house, then let the house enter into you." Now, show me how you accomplish this trick! Those who are still working on this koan: have a cup of tea and go home. You will sleep soundly tonight.

Case Four
A Beardless Foreigner

Seeing a picture of Bodhidharma, Wakuan asked, "Why does that son of a western barbarian have no beard?"

BODHISATTVAS: Zen master Wakuan was born in 1108 and died in 1179, in the Sung dynasty. In his time many foreigners entered China from India, Persia, and other countries of Central Asia. The Chinese called them all foreigners. The majority of Chinese people even called them barbarians, as they thought they themselves were the only civilized people, living at the very center of the world. Zen teachers used the slang of the day freely to express direct meaning. They called Bodhidharma "a son of a barbarian," or "that old blue-eyed barbarian."

Today, too, Zen monks are so intimate with Bodhidharma that they do not call him master, lord, or teacher. Instead they call him "that fellow," and many a time, "this fellow." Thus Bodhidharma is the monk, and the monk is Bodhidharma. To pay homage to Bodhidharma is to respect oneself, and one's cup of tea is actually sipped by the lips of Bodhidharma. Probably Wakuan had shaved that morning, and, rubbing his chin with his hand, he might have said, "Well, well, the beard of Bodhidharma is all gone."

In a picture, even in a photograph, we can see only the shadow, but not the real substance. If you add to the picture of Bodhidharma the missing beard, then you will miss his ears, or else his wrinkles. When you gather together all sorts of attributes, you can never encounter the real substance. No poem or prose can describe the fullness of Bodhidharma's image. No music of worldly instruments can reproduce the voice of Bodhidharma's preaching. Only in the palace of your inner self do you meet Bodhidharma face to face—nay, you open his eyes, and he smiles with your mouth and all your features.

Do not call it realization or enlightenment; such names will spoil your fun. You are a son of a barbarian. You ought to be satisfied with the name.

Mumon's comment

If you want to practice Zen, it must be true practice. When you attain realization, it must be true realization. You yourself must have the face of the great Bodhidharma to see him. Just one glimpse will be enough. But if you say you have met him, you have never seen him at all.

The last sentence is the most important for you. Did you ever experience meeting a person for the first time whom you did not feel was a stranger at all, or walking through a place that was somehow very familiar? Your friends may explain it to you using the theory of reincarnation, or else they may pull you into the concoctions of astrology. As long as you hold your individuality tightly and cling to an ego-entity, you can please your friends by listening to their nonsense, but once you smell even a whiff of Zen, you cannot help but laugh at your friends' ignorance.

Suppose you and I were business partners in a past incarnation, and I owed you some amount of money; you cannot collect even a cent from me, from this penniless monk. Suppose your stars indicate that you have a tendency to argue; if you make any noise and disturb others in the zendo, astrology or no astrology, I have to put you out. The stars are not forming your character now. Your own thoughts and actions are forming it. Even if you were a queen of Africa in your past incarnation, you cannot go back to being one now. So what is the use of worrying about meeting somebody from a former time or visiting some former place in person? In fact, no such animal to be called a person exists here. You feel familiar because you are one with that other person. You remember the place because you are in the place connected with all other places. You are on the verge of awakening to oneness; only your dualistic ideas prevent you. You and I have met each other many millions of years ago. Now, tell me where we have met!

If you pass this koan, you will also pass the fourth koan in the *Gateless Gate*, "A Beardless Foreigner." Mumon said, "If you say you have met him, you have never seen him at all." He really said a mouthful.

MUMON'S VERSE

> *One should not discuss a dream*
> *In front of a fool.*
> *Why does Bodhidharma have no beard?*
> *What an absurd question!*

We are barbarians, and ought to be satisfied just to smile at each other.

Case Five
Kyogen's Man in a Tree

Kyogen said, "It is like a man who is hanging by his teeth from a tree over a precipice. His hands cannot grasp a branch, and his feet cannot reach a limb. Beneath the tree is someone who asks him, 'Why did Bodhidharma come to China from India?' If the man in the tree does not answer, he fails the questioner, and if he does answer, he falls and loses his life. Now, what shall he do?"

BODHISATTVAS: Most koans are put in the form of one or more questions. When the koan is in the form of a statement, you must ask yourself why the master made such a statement. You cannot squeeze out the answer by thinking about the koan. Simply concentrate your whole being upon it. This is the proper way to work on a koan.

This koan is expressed here only partially; the entire dialogue is as follows: A monk asked Kyogen, "Without using either relative or absolute terms, please tell me why Bodhidharma came to China from India." Kyogen answered, "You are hanging from a tree by your teeth over a precipice, and your hands grasp no branch and your feet rest on no limb, and you must answer the question. If you do not answer, you are a dismal student of Zen, but if you answer, you fall from the tree and lose your life."

Mumon tries to make a long story short, and makes the matter confusing. Kyogen here is not giving his opinion about Zen. If he were, he would have to use a relative term. He is not pointing at Zen through postulation, because if he were, he would have to use an absolute term. He addresses through his question the very being of the monk, the questioner himself. Why does the monk have to worry about Bodhidharma? The blue-eyed Indian passed from the world a long time ago. It does not matter whether Bodhidharma came from the West to the East, or from the East to the West. The concern of the moment for this monk is to realize Zen, nay, even to forget the term *Zen*, but to see his own true self the moment he acts.

If I serve you a cup of tea and say, "This is a symbol of Zen," none of you Zen students of the Mentorgarten[25] will enjoy such a lukewarm beverage. A stranger may come among us, and after sipping my tea, may express his appreciation. Because he is a stranger, I will not say anything about it. But if it were the case of an old-timer here, I would not allow such an unworthy comment. Why? Because the sipping is the appreciation, and the appreciation is the sipping. The thriftiest Zen student does not waste one-tenth of one word, or the slightest movement of a thought. Kyogen wanted to teach the monk the thrift of Zen, and thus he stopped the use of his hands and feet; he required the monk to be enlightened before he opened his mouth and fell from the tree into the precipice. It is the same trick as cutting off the finger of the imitator in the third koan. The kindness of such an unkind action is to block off the road of thinking. Zen never says, "Try this method, and then you will be enlightened." It only demands that action which is enlightenment itself.

MUMON'S COMMENT

In such a predicament—which the man in the tree faces squarely—your eloquence is of no use. You may have memorized all of the sutras, but they are of no use to you. When you can give the right answer, even if your past path was one of death, a new path of life opens to you. But if you cannot answer, you will have to wait and ask the future Buddha, Maitreya.

Maitreya is the Buddha who comes to the world five billion six hundred and seventy million years after the death of Shakyamuni Buddha. Mumon was being ironic. Those who are looking for help to be enlightened, whether from a Buddha or from a master, are hopeless customers of Zen.

MUMON'S VERSE

> *Kyogen is truly a fool*
> *Spreading ego-killing poison*
> *That shuts his pupils' mouths*
> *And causes tears to stream from their dead eyes.*

Here again, Mumon uses an ironical expression. He means, "A fool always keeps his own company." The monk who asked Kyogen to express Zen without using either relative or absolute terms was a fool from the beginning. He wanted to know the value of zero, and he was ready to keep the accounts of nothingness in his book of foolishness.

A good Zen student always looks like a fool, and never shows others his smartness. Thus others' feelings are soothed, and less harm is done. Kyogen showed his foolishness and told the monk such a foolish story. I admire his kindness.

Fools are born every minute. Even in our time here in America, we need this foolish koan. Those who use this ego-killing poison as a medicine try to shut their mouths and cause tears to stream from their dead eyes. What a pity!

Why don't they open their true eyes and laugh at the foolishness of both Kyogen and Mumon?

Case Six
Buddha Twirls a Flower

When Buddha was on Grdhvakuta Mountain, he twirled a flower in his fingers and held it before the assembly. Everyone was silent. Only Mahakashyapa smiled at this revelation, although he tried to control the expression on his face. Buddha said, "I have the eye of the true teaching, the heart of Nirvana, the true aspect of non-form, and the ineffable gate of Dharma. It is not expressed in words, but is transmitted beyond the teachings. This teaching I give to Mahakashyapa.

BODHISATTVAS: Buddha preached many important doctrines on Mount Grdhvakuta, which means Mount Eagle.[26] The minds of the disciples were quite developed intellectually at that time. They had never dreamed that a moment might come when their attainment would be examined. Buddha suddenly showed his Zen, twirling a flower that someone had offered him. He usually mentioned flowers in simile, in metaphor, in synecdoche, in metonymy, in allegory, and in allusion—if we were to use the terms of modern rhetoric to describe his sermons. On this occasion, however, it was entirely different. Buddha expressed his own enlightenment in such a simple manner—twirling a flower before his listeners. Everyone was silent; yes, apparently silent, but each mind was filled with commotion; each was bewildered by thoughts about what the teacher meant.

Mahakashyapa, the chief disciple, was the only one who was in real silence. He entered into the inner realm, the Buddha's realm. He smiled innocently, like a happy child. "Only Mahakashyapa smiled at this revelation, although he tried to control the expression on his face." The original Chinese says, "His serious features crinkled into a smile."

Buddha said, "I have the eye of the true teaching (the nucleus of wisdom), the heart of Nirvana (buddha-nature), the true aspect of non-form (*suchness* or *thusness*), and the ineffable gate of Dharma (the passage of realization). It is not expressed by words, but is transmitted beyond the teachings. This (esoteric) teaching I give to Mahakashyapa." Buddha was like a traveler who carries a suitcase with the labels of all the ports he has passed. No matter how many labels are pasted on it, they do not indicate the contents of the suitcase. No matter how many good names he mentions, they do not describe exactly what he gave Mahakashyapa at that moment. Seeing is believing. Each of us has to open the suitcase and witness what the content is.

MUMON'S COMMENT

Golden-faced Gautama thought he could cheat anyone. Buddha's face was always luminous; therefore the people of the time called him Golden-faced Gautama. He thought he could cheat his listeners with his ironical expression.

Buddha made good listeners appear bad, and sold dog meat under the sign of mutton. Mumon, Mumon, are you not his agent? Tell the truth, nothing but the truth to your judges.

Buddha thought it was wonderful. What if everyone in the audience had smiled? Nonsense, Mumon, then they would not have been the audience; they would all have been buddhas.

If everyone had smiled, how could Buddha have transmitted the teaching? If Mahakashyapa had not smiled, how could Buddha have transmitted the teaching? What are you talking about, Mumon; Mahakashyapa never smiled. We all witnessed it. What you call a smile is not a smile at all. Who called you a Zen master? Your wisdom is turning sour; I pity you.

If Buddha says that realization can be transmitted, he is like a city slicker who cheats a country bumpkin, and if he says that it cannot be transmitted, why does he approve of Mahakashyapa? Mumon is like a clown in a circus. He is seemingly disturbing the performers, but just the same, he is making the show go on.

MUMON'S VERSE

At the twirling of a flower
His disguise was exposed.
No one in heaven or on earth can surpass
Mahakashyapa's crinkled face.

To make this koan's account of transmission clear, I will read D.T. Suzuki's translation of my teacher's words. The Dharma was transmitted genealogically through seventy-seven ancestors, from Mahakashyapa to my teacher, Soyen Shaku. So whatever he said is the actual voice of the Dharma, which I have heard directly, and the translator, Dr. Suzuki, has heard and transcribed vividly. I wish all of you to make these words your own koan: "Buddha once brought a flower before an assemblage of his disciples and showed it to them without any comment whatever, and the entire congregation was bewildered as to what to make of this strange behavior on the part of their Master, except Kashyapa, who, thoroughly understanding the import of this incident, softly smiled and nodded. Thereupon the Buddha solemnly proclaimed, 'I am in possession of the Eye which penetrates into the depths of the Dharma and the mysteries of Nirvana. I now give it to thee, O Kashyapa, that thou mayest guard it well.' What sort of eye could it have been which was transmitted from the Buddha to Kashyapa and which made the latter comprehend something incomprehensible in the flower in Buddha's hand?"

Case Seven
Joshu's "Wash Your Bowl"

A monk said to Joshu, "I have just entered the monastery; please teach me." Joshu asked, "Have you eaten your rice porridge?" The monk replied, "Yes, I have." Joshu said, "Then you had better wash your bowl." At that moment the monk was enlightened.

BODHISATTVAS: Mumon puts only the last part of the dialogue between Joshu and the monk in the text. I shall relate it to you from the beginning, otherwise you may overlook something important:

A monk came to Joshu. "Where did you come from?" the teacher asked. "From the South," the monk replied. "All Buddhism is in the South; there is nothing here for you," said Joshu.

He did not mean this geographically; rather, he meant that one who cannot attain wisdom in the South has no hope in the North, West, or East.

The monk tried to start a debate with Joshu, saying, "But Buddhism does not belong to any particular place." If the monk had been a student in this class, I would have said, "Show me the Buddhism that does not belong to any particular place! Show me, now!"

Joshu told the monk, "Even if you were to meet the best teacher in China, you would attain nothing, for you have tightly shut the door of your inner shrine. You will not let yourself see the Buddha." The monk then asked, "What is Buddha?" Joshu replied, "You can find him in the shrine."

The stupid monk looked up at the shrine in the room and said, "But that is only an image of Buddha. Where is the real Buddha?" Joshu repeated, "In the shrine." Slowly the monk began to comprehend. "Do you mean the Buddha in me?"

Now, if Joshu said "yes" at that moment, the monk would get a conception of Buddha that would be nothing but an inchoate shadow. If the monk were to outlive Joshu and survive to this day, he might study the up-to-date sciences of physiology and psychology. He might thus search for the Buddha within himself, but all in vain, after all. Christians think that the word "no" is the hardest one to say when facing temptations. Buddhists consider "yes" the most dangerous word, for it prevents realization.

Joshu said neither "yes" nor "no." He asked the monk, "Have you eaten your rice porridge?" The monk replied, "Yes, I have." Joshu said, "Then you had better wash your bowl."

Here the teacher has shown the pupil how one may act gracefully without hesitation, without entanglement in the slightest delusion. It is the direct action of the essence of mind. It is the actual work of buddha-nature itself. When one eats too much, one's stomach suffers. When one thinks too much, one's mind becomes stuck. Zen's economy is like that used in arithmetic. It always expresses its fraction in the lowest possible terms. Joshu showed the monk the fraction of Zen reduced to its lowest common denominator!

Mumon reduced the dialogue to the heart of the matter, expressed by this sentence: "I have just entered the monastery; please teach me."

MUMON'S COMMENT

Joshu opened his mouth and showed his heart, but I doubt if this monk really saw Joshu's heart. I hope he did not mistake the bell for a pitcher.

After having eaten one's rice porridge, one must wash one's bowl. This is the first lesson in the monastery, and even old-timers cannot neglect this duty. I know this monk did not mistake the bell for a pitcher when he received the reduction of Joshu's arithmetic. He realized a bell is to be rung, and a pitcher is to be filled with water.

Mumon is like a poor gardener; one cannot trust his art of grafting. He doubts whether the readers of the *Gateless Gate* understand his shortcut. That is why I have reproduced the complete dialogue between Joshu and the monk.

MUMON'S VERSE

> *It is too clear, and so is hard to see.*
> *A fool once searched for fire with a lighted lantern;*
> *Had he known what fire was,*
> *His rice would have been cooked much sooner.*

This poem is from an old Chinese story. A fool in China wanted to cook rice for his supper. He could not see the fire under the stove, so he searched the whole house for fire with a lighted lantern.

In our class, we always recite the *Pancha Sila* in Pali. It is the recitation of the Five Precepts:

> The first: Kill not any living thing for your own pleasure.
> The second: Take not anything that does not belong to you.
> The third: Respect your beloved as a fellow traveler on the road to enlightenment.
> The fourth: Do not speak a word that is not true.
> The fifth: Avoid intoxication; always have a sober mind.

These five precepts may seem too simple for you to observe, and too easy and common for deep thinkers like yourselves. You would rather investigate a higher theory or more complicated koans; yet this is the fire you have been looking for from the very beginning!

Those actions that are purified through keeping the five precepts are the echo of buddha-nature. Why study the profound teachings of the sutras? Because you want to develop a mind that will always work harmoniously with these five precepts. Why learn to meditate? Because you want to train yourselves to master mind and body, as if you had just eaten your rice porridge and then washed the bowl, easily and freely.

Buddhism begins with your everyday action, and soon inundates the whole world in its ever-widening rings of karmic ripples.

Case Eight
Keichu's Wheel

Getsuan said to his students, "Keichu, the first wheel-maker in China, made two wheels of fifty spokes each. Now, suppose you remove the nave uniting the spokes. What would become of the wheel? If Keichu had done this, could he be called a master wheel-maker?"

BODHISATTVAS: The teacher who presented this koan belongs to the same lineage as Mumon, the author of the *Gateless Gate*. The relationship between these two teachers is that of great-grandfather and great-grandson. Therefore, the koan must have been kept among the ancestors like a family code, for no other Zen books have recorded Keichu's Wheel.

Keichu was the man who invented the two-wheeled wagon. He lived in China twenty-two centuries before the Common Era. His vehicle's wheel consisted of a tire, a wooden rim, fifty spokes, a hub (or nave), and an axle nut, almost the same as what we see in modern times. Now, the question is, "If you remove the nave that is uniting the spokes, what would become of the wheel?" If you pile up all the separated parts of an automobile, how can you recognize your own car? The translation continues as follows: "And if Keichu had done this, could he be called a master wheel-maker?" I suggest we read this as follows: "And had Keichu done this operation, where would he find his invented wheel? Is he a master or is he not a master?"

If you read Chapter Eleven of the *Tao Te Ching* you will see this koan, together with the answer to it. The original was written by Lao-tsu, six hundred years before the Common Era. It was then that Buddhism met Taoism, the teaching of Lao-tsu, in China. They joined forces and produced Zen. Let me read this chapter of the *Tao Te Ching* to you: "The many spokes unite in one hub; but it is on the empty center that the use of the wheel depends. The usefulness of a vessel is in its hollowness. The usefulness of a room depends upon the space within it. Therefore that which has material existence serves for profitable adaptation, and that which has no material existence is the truly useful."[27]

What do you think of these words of Lao-tsu? Monks should answer the question and say, "Nothingness is the very source of everything." I do not know whether Keichu, the master wheel-maker, would use the same words, but I can see him vividly, making wheels from nothingness, and letting every wheel revolve freely. Modern inventors aim at material profits; therefore the results they get are mostly destructive and inhuman. They envision an ego-entity within themselves, and imagine something that rules and controls a wheel. If there is something that gathers together a tire, a wooden rim, a certain number of spokes, a hub, and an axle nut that controls the resulting wheel, the result might not be the same as the wheel at all.

A wheel is merely a product of karma relations of spokes, hub, and other parts, and there is nothing to be called a center or a controlling entity. Keichu never thought of mastership; therefore he was a master. Listen to what Lao-tsu says in Chapter Ten: "When the body and mind are held together in one embrace, they can be kept from separating. When one gives undivided attention to the breath and brings it under the utmost degree of control, one can become pliant as a child. When one has cleansed away the most tempting sights and thoughts, one can become perfect." Is this not the very same way in which we count our breaths in meditation? Again in that chapter Lao-tsu says, "He can produce and nourish without claiming anything as his own. He can do anything without anyone being aware of it. He can preside over all, and yet without controlling. This is the Mysterious Quality."

Is this not the very same attitude as that of a bodhisattva?

MUMON'S COMMENT

If you can answer this question immediately, your eyes will be like a comet and your mind like a flash of lightning.

That was all Mumon said. He meant to praise a brilliant Zen thought and a graceful Zen action. If you do not watch your step, you will be caught by the trap that Mumon set out for you. Do you remember what the Buddha said in the *Diamond Sutra?* "If a bodhisattva retains the thought of an ego, a person, a being, or a soul, he is no more a bodhisattva." Zen has nothing to do with wheels or wheel-makers. The reason why Master Getsuan asked the monks this question, and why Mumon recorded these words in the *Gateless Gate*, is to let all of you see clearly the creative source of nothingness, which is the original person in full.

MUMON'S VERSE

> *When the hubless wheel turns,*
> *Neither master nor no-master can stop it.*
> *It turns above the heavens and below the earth—*
> *South, North, East, and West.*

I will add a line to the poem and say, "This is the life of Zen students."

Case Nine
A Buddha before History

A monk said to Seijo, "I understand a buddha who lived before recorded history sat in meditation for ten cycles of existence and could not realize the highest truth, and so could not become fully emancipated. How could this be?" Seijo replied, "Your question is self-explanatory." The monk asked, "Since a buddha was meditating, why couldn't he realize buddhahood?" Seijo replied, "He was not yet a buddha."

BODHISATTVAS: The original story of a prehistoric buddha was derived from the *Saddharma-pundarika Sutra, The Lotus of the Wonderful Law.* Like most other Mahayana sutras, this sutra is a dramatic work, depicting the highest principles of Buddhism. The questioning monk could not enjoy the beauty of the drama, but tried to argue using everyday logic. Seijo did not take the trouble to explain the original story, but simply snapped the questioner's weapon and cornered him.

All sentient beings have buddha-nature, but none can enter buddha-hood without effort. There are many ways of striving, but until one is actually enlightened, one is still on one's way, and has not as yet become a buddha. The original story emphasizes this point and describes the duration of meditation as ten cycles of existence. It suggests that buddhahood does not come in gradual stages, so the monk who questioned had become discouraged. "Meditating for ten cycles of existence," he must have thought, "and yet he could not attain buddhahood! Then how can I accomplish it in this short life?" If one aims to become a buddha, no matter how many cycles of existence he strives in meditation, he will always be a scandal-monger of dualism, never an enlightened buddha.

The other day, I read an article in a Japanese magazine regarding a lotus seed one thousand years old. It was discovered in the depository of a carved wooden buddha, with the record of the date when it was inserted. The seed was planted in a pond, and no one believed that a bud would emerge from it. To the surprise of the botanist who made the experiment, a now fully grown lotus has blossomed after one thousand years. If anyone had discovered it five hundred years ago and planted it, the seed would surely have blossomed just the same, for whenever a seed meets water and sunshine, it strives of itself to grow. Until that time it is only a seed and not a lotus flower. Similarly, all sentient beings have buddha-nature. You can call it the seed of enlightenment, but unless one actualizes it within one-self, one cannot call it a *pundarika*, the lotus flower of realization.

Seijo at first answered the monk, "Your question is self-explanatory." But the monk said, "Since a buddha was meditating, why couldn't he real-ize buddhahood?" Seijo replied, "He was not yet a buddha." Some of you have studied philosophy, science, religion, and other such subjects for many years, and may wonder why you do not reach the ultimate stage of wisdom. Please do not blame old man Time. He has nothing to do with your tardiness or dualistic ideas. Just blame yourself, and jump into the ocean of oneness. Then you can swim by your own efforts and reach the other shore with your own power.

MUMON'S COMMENT

I will allow the realization, but I will not admit the understanding. When one who is ignorant attains realization, that one is a sage. A sage who begins to understand is ignorant.

In realization one enters into the source, the mind essence. In understanding, one comes out of the oneness, and the mind can work within dualism. Those who have attained realization always know how to return to the source. Therefore, even though their minds can function in dualism, their manner is playful. Sometimes they venture into dualism on purpose, to lead others into the wisdom of the universe. There must be a distinction made between a sage and an ignorant person concerning this wisdom. Do not think that Mumon is clinging to the absolute.

MUMON'S VERSE

> *It is better to realize mind than body.*
> *When you realize mind, you need not worry about body.*
> *When body and mind become one, you are free*
> *And desire no praise.*

Certain students of Theravada Buddhism realize easily the emptiness of the body, but they stick to the mind as if it were an entity that exists and carries the seeds of karma. In Mahayana teaching, we see clearly the fact that mind and body are not two separate things. It is only by comparison that they appear to be different. There is no mind without body, and there is no body without mind. After all, there is nothing but emptiness. But that emptiness produces everything. This is the source of the universe; this is the essence of mind. You may call it buddha-nature, or Dharmakaya, but be careful. When you call it, it is not there. When you name it, you have already missed it. A really free person desires no praise, nor holds any dislike for those who slander him or her.

The original Chinese poem says in the last line: "A sage never wishes to become the governor of a state." I suppose, in the time of Mumon, a governor was highly honored by the people. When I translated this line, I simply wrote it as "You are free, and desire no praise." I have heard that even here in America, a man sacrifices his wealth to be elected governor. Such a man is far from being a sage. He should study the *Gateless Gate*, realizing mind and body thoroughly until they become one.

Case Ten
Seizei Alone and Poor

A monk named Seizei asked Sozan, "Seizei is alone and poor. Will you give him support?"

Sozan called out, "Seizei!"

Seizei responded, "Yes, sir."

Sozan said, "You have already finished three cups of the best wine in China. Why, then, do you say you have not even wet your lips?"

BODHISATTVAS: A monk is always alone and poor. A monk who has a family and a savings account is not a monk. Japanese Buddhist teachers these days all have families, and naturally they cannot afford to be poor. The term "monk" means "novice" in the Buddhist circles of modern Japan. One who remains a mere monk for more than sixty years, as I have, will be stamped a failure. It proves how Japanese Buddhism has degenerated and has become commercialized.

In this koan, Sozan the teacher and Seizei the student are both monks, so naturally each is alone and poor. What the student asked of the teacher was an immaterial treasure, the wisdom of Buddhadharma. Therefore he said, "Seizei is alone and poor. Will you give him support?" He meant, "I have never met a good teacher, and have worked alone for my emancipation. Please impart your wisdom to me." He was not looking for comfort or pleasure. He was not seeking fame or glory. He had even given up the desire to accumulate knowledge through book-learning. He was on the verge of accepting Zen, beyond intellectualism. He was really alone and poor, both materially and spiritually.

Sozan, the teacher, called out to him, "Seizei!" Sozan just called his name, and Seizei responded, "Yes, sir." The switch was turned on, and in no time there was the light of Zen. Sozan had nothing to impart to Seizei. There was just a tiny catch that had kept the switch from turning on. That was an idea of "alone and poor"—an idea of "I am on the verge of accepting Zen." As I always say, when you recognize that you are going to enter into samadhi, you are just leaving it. Sozan said, "You have already finished three cups of the best wine in China—Zen—and still you are saying that you have not even wet your lips." These words allowed the attainment of Seizei.

A priest of the Soto sect arrived in Los Angeles about ten days ago. All Buddhist priests in the city, except me, welcomed him and gave a party with sake, Japanese wine. There was another party given by his church members to welcome him, and still another by his co-workers and their church members. They all drank sake and had a good time, but no preaching has been heard as yet. That priest probably only remembers the part of the koan that refers to the wine! Sozan was a Zen master who lived in China in the ninth century. His teacher was Tozan, and the "To" in the name Soto was derived from Tozan. I suppose the priest who just arrived here simply wanted to commemorate his ancient masters by drinking wine!

MUMON'S COMMENT

Seizei overplayed his hand. Why was that so? Because Sozan had eyes to see, and knew with whom he had to deal. Even so, I want to ask: At what point had Seizei drunk the wine?

Mumon is blaming Seizei for his self-recognition. I do not doubt the sincerity of this monk, but only see his fault in clinging to nothingness.

Mumon thinks Seizei challenged Sozan to a game of Zen and overplayed his hand. I do not agree with this. A monk asked Joshu, "I have nothing in my mind. What shall I do now?" Joshu said, "Throw it away." The monk said, "Since I have nothing, what can I throw away?" Joshu said, "Then you had better carry it away." Here Joshu showed the monk his mistake of holding on to the idea of nothingness. Sozan used the same method to wake up this student.

Mumon says, "Even so, I want to ask, at what point had Seizei drunk the wine?" Mumon himself is quite intoxicated with the wine of Zen. Come on, Mumon, we belong to the temperance group. Join us this evening, and sip a cup of tea with us!

MUMON'S VERSE

The poorest man in China,
The bravest man in China,
Although he barely sustains himself,
He wishes to rival the richest.

Seizei was certainly the poorest man in China, and also the bravest man in China. He barely sustains himself, since he has nothing worldly in his view. Mumon says, "He wishes to rival the richest." I would rather say, "He became the wealthiest when he responded, 'Yes, sir.'" It reminds me of a stanza of the *Shodoka:*

Sons of the Shakya are known to be poor,
But their poverty is of the body; their spiritual life knows
    no poverty.
The poverty-stricken body is wrapped in rags,
But their spirit holds within itself a rare, invaluable gem.

Case Eleven
Joshu Examines a Hermit Monk in Meditation

One day, Joshu visited a place where a monk had retired to meditate in solitude, and asked him, "What have you now?" The monk raised his fist. Joshu left, remarking, "Ships cannot anchor where the water is too shallow." A few days later, Joshu went again to visit the monk, making the same abrupt query. The monk repeated his surly gesture in response. Joshu said, "He can give, he can take. He can kill, he can save." And he bowed to the monk.

BODHISATTVAS: Zen monks, as a rule, decline to make compromises with worldly life, preferring to remain in seclusion. The monk in this koan had no wish to become a teacher and waste precious moments of meditation. He lived alone in a little hut, known to nobody. To him, every hour in the day and every minute in the night were for nothing but meditation. He sat and walked in meditation. He ate and slept in meditation. He thus preached without words, and taught all sentient beings without exception.

Joshu came upon the monk and asked him, "What have you now?" Joshu saw vividly what the monk had, before he asked, but wanted to make sure. The monk raised his fist in the manner commonly adopted by the Zen teachers of the time. Joshu replied, "Ships cannot anchor where the water is too shallow," and then left. He knew that the monk raised his fist impersonally, but he was disgusted with the conventional manner of Zen teachers, and could not help but complain at the sight of the fist.

A monastery may be formed any time a group of Zen students gather around a teacher. It is like a bay that connects with the great ocean. If anyone foolishly makes a demarcation, thinking that he alone has a view of the water, who would not pity him for his ignorance? Yet there are many monasteries, schools, religions, and sects, each considering its own teaching to be a private lake rather than a bay, forgetting the inlet to the ocean of Dharma, the universal truth.

Joshu therefore said, "Ships cannot anchor where the water is too shallow." But the mind of this monk was no puddle, no matter what Joshu said. Its waters may have appeared to be merely rippling, yet every wavelet echoed the surges of the great ocean.

A few days later, Joshu went again to visit the monk, and asked the same question, "What have you now?" The monk answered the same way: he raised his fist. Even if the Buddha confronted him, this monk would have raised his fist. If Bodhidharma visited him one hundred times, the monk would do the same each time. He would not be copying the conventional manner of Zen teachers, but would simply be creating his own Zen from the essence of mind; to each question he would be giving a fresh and original answer, without hesitating. He is the creator. He is the master. To this, Joshu gave recognition, bowing and saying, "He can give, he can take. He can kill, he can save."

MUMON'S COMMENT

The raised fist was the same both times. Why, then, did Joshu scorn the first, and approve the second? Where is the fault? Whoever answers this knows that Joshu's tongue has no bone, so he can use it freely. Yet perhaps Joshu is wrong; through that monk, he may have discovered his own mistake. One who thinks that the insight of the one exceeds that of the other has no eyes to see.

Some Japanese teachers claim that there were two different monks to be examined in this koan, but since the fist is one, considered impersonally, we may regard it as involving only one monk.

Joshu's first impression differs from his second, but the monk doesn't care either way. His fist is like a big tree; it is rooted in the good earth, and boldly aspires to heaven. It is not a part of the monk's body. All monks and all Zen teachers, including Joshu himself, are present in this fist. They lecture from within it, and no matter how they praise or slander it, it is the source of all their strength.

MUMON'S VERSE

> *The light of his eye is like a comet,*
> *His Zen activity is like lightning.*
> *The sword that kills*
> *May also save!*

The first line is praising Joshu's keen observation, and the second is admiring the monk's Zen. If anyone thinks that Buddhist activities are embodied only in the building of temples, or in the noise of propaganda, such a person has no right to read this poem.

A Japanese Zen master of the fourteenth century wrote a poem in honor of this monk:

> Like Vimalakirti, he follows the ancient way
> With a closed mouth.
> He tells no one of his inner treasure.
> When he sees the blue mountain from his veranda,
> He feels he has said too much.

Only such a man can attack Joshu with his fist!

Case Twelve
Zuigan Calls His Own Master

Zuigan would call out to himself every day, "Master!" Then he would answer himself, "Yes, sir." After that, he would say, "Be alert!" Again he would answer, "Yes, sir!" And then he would say, "Do not be deceived by others," and would answer, "No, sir! No, sir!"

BODHISATTVAS: Every koan calls out to your own master. When you meditate on the koan "The Sound of One Hand," the voice of silence is the master. You walk with it, you sleep with it. You can neither work nor study without it. Gradually your whole being becomes the voice of silence, and you realize that there exists nothing but your true self. You may call it "master," as Zuigan did, but you can also name it the essence of mind. If you were seeking buddha, it would be Dharmakaya, the origin of all processes. Zuigan realized it clearly and enjoyed living in it. It was in a somewhat playful manner that he called out to it every day, "Master," and then answered himself, "Yes, sir." Some of you have passed the koan "The Sound of One Hand," and enjoy the voice of silence, glancing at it every now and then. You are playing at banking with your own money, being both debtor and creditor, just for fun. Zuigan was playing in the same way. He said, "Be alert!" and answered himself, "Yes, sir!" and then, "Do not allow others to cheat you!" and responded, "No, sir! No, sir!" He was counting his money, as did Shylock in Shakespeare's play.

To meditate on this koan, you must meet the master face to face.

Through constant effort, you will be able to enter the samadhi where there is no "master" to meet, and no "you" to meet the master. Unless you pass this gate of samadhi, which is the gateless gate, you will only see the shallow part of this koan, thinking of "master" as your own conscience. That would be just gratuitous speculation, which has no place in Zen.

MUMON'S COMMENT

Old Zuigan buys and sells himself. He is putting on a puppet show. He uses one mask to call "Master," and another to answer the master. A third mask says, "Be alert," and another, "Do not be cheated by others." If you cling to any of his masks, you are mistaken; yet if you imitate Zuigan, you will turn yourself into a fox.

In Japan, the fox is believed to have a strange power, enabling it to imitate and deceive human beings. The fox will present itself as your friend, and invite you to the forest, if you carry a gift of food good enough to tempt it. You may think you have spent the night in the forest with a friend, but in cold fact, you have only met a fox, and have lost your gift.

Once a man on his way home from a masquerade met a fox. The man wore the mask of a young wife. The fox turned himself into a husband, and tried to take the box lunch from the man. The fellow happened to have another mask, representing an old woman. Suddenly he exchanged the first mask for that one. The fox saw the mother-in-law and ran away.

There are some Zen teachers who simply imitate the ways of old masters. In their haste to seize upon fame and glory, they cheat their students. If you do not cling to your mask, you can easily outwit any foxy Zen teacher. Know that under your mask, you each have a real and true face of your own.

A monk came to Gensha, a contemporary of Zuigan, and was met with the question, "Where did you come from?"

The monk answered, "From Zuigan."

"Why didn't you stay there?"

"Because Master Zuigan passed away."

"I am very sorry to hear that. How did Zuigan teach you?"

"He always called to himself and answered himself with his own voice."

"Hold on!" Gensha, the new teacher, exclaimed. "Now that Zuigan has passed, who is going to ask the question, and who will reply?"

The monk hesitated. Gensha beat him with a big stick, and kicked him out of the monastery.

MUMON'S VERSE

Some students cannot pierce the guise;
Their glance is turned by an opaque exterior.
On finding the seed of birth and death,
Foolish people call it the true person!

The monk who went to Gensha was a dull-witted fellow! He slandered his poor teacher, and deserves a good many more blows from that big stick!

Case Thirteen
Tokusan Holds His Bowls

Tokusan went to the dining room from the meditation hall, holding his bowls. Seppo was on duty as the cook-monk. When he saw Tokusan he said, "The dinner drum has not yet been struck. Where are you going with your bowls?" Tokusan turned and went back to his room.

Later, Seppo told Ganto about this. Ganto said, "Old Tokusan does not understand ultimate truth."

Tokusan heard about this, and asked Ganto to come to him. "I have heard," he said, "that you do not approve of my Zen." Ganto whispered something to his teacher. Tokusan said nothing.

The next day Tokusan gave an entirely different kind of talk to his monks. Ganto laughed and clapped his hands, saying, "I see our old man understands ultimate truth indeed. None in China can surpass him."

BODHISATTVAS: Tokusan was the master of the monastery. He was eighty years old at the time, and his Zen was also aged, like the best wine. Seppo was a young monk whose duty was to cook for the master and other monks. His Zen was still green, and he had to fret or get excited every once in a while. Ganto was his brother monk, who was trying to help him attain Zen.

One day, the cooking was delayed and Seppo was somewhat upset, hurrying to catch up with his work. Tokusan, the master, knew the time instinctively, and came down to the dining room holding his bowls. In a monastery there is no "set table"; each monk brings his own bowls and takes them away with him after he finishes eating. Seppo said, "The dinner drum has not yet been struck. Where are you going?" It is monastic custom to beat a drum [or strike a gong] when dinner is ready to be served.

Master or no master, Tokusan should have waited for the signal before entering the dining room. Thus, the old master "got the goat" of the cook. The cook should have considered his own rule-breaking—delaying the dinner—before criticizing his teacher. Because his Zen was green, he was not master of his mind; he could not see both sides of the wrong. Tokusan came out quietly, and also quietly went back to his room.

Seppo, the cook, told Ganto, his brother monk, about this. Seppo still thought he was right and the master was wrong. Ganto wanted to teach Zen to Seppo, so he said, "Old Tokusan does not understand ultimate truth." If he had blamed the cook he would have had to have heard a noisy argument, so he switched the blame to the master. The aim of Zen is to attain peacefulness, not to settle a matter of right or wrong.

There was another monk whose name is not recorded in the text, as he is not worthy of being recorded. I can call him "Buttinsky." He told the master what Ganto had said about his teacher. The teacher asked Ganto to come to him. "I have heard," he said, "that you do not approve of my Zen." Ganto whispered to his teacher that what he had said was in hopes of enlightening his brother monk. Tokusan said nothing.

Do you remember the Zen poem about the bamboo shadows and the moonlight?

> Bamboo shadows sweep the stairs
> Yet not a speck of dust is stirred.
> The moonlight penetrates to the bottom of the pool,
> But in the water not a trace remains.

You see how gently the master listened to the tale-teller, and how naturally he asked Ganto, the monk, about it, and how easily and freely he listened to the whisperer, just nodding to him.

The next day, Tokusan gave an entirely different kind of talk to the monks. Ganto laughed and clapped his hands, saying, "I see our old man understands ultimate truth indeed. None in China can surpass him." Now what kind of lecture do you think the master gave? I asked my teacher about this, and he kept silence for a long while. I thanked him for the instruction. Now, I will hand it over to you. To work on this koan you must watch your step minute after minute. This is not a monastery affair. In your home, in your community, and in your world, you must polish and practice your own Zen. Do not blame the law-breakers until you examine yourself as to whether you are a law-breaker or not. A Zen master said, "I have a very strong power: when the wind blows I bend gracefully." Yes, such a flexible power is the strongest one of all. When you meet a strong person, if you do not give in, you have to fight. All the troubles of this life are caused in this way. If you know that there is no ego to be supported, you can easily and gracefully give in. Most of the time you gain by giving in, and you lose by persisting.

MUMON'S COMMENT

As for ultimate truth, neither Ganto nor Tokusan even dreamed of it. After all, they are like puppets on a shelf.

There is no such thing called "ultimate truth" outside your everyday life. You may attend meditation classes to seek enlightenment; but if you neglect to look for it in front of your nose, you will never find it, no matter how many weeks of seclusion you faithfully attend.

MUMON'S VERSE

Whoever understands the first truth
Should understand the ultimate truth.
The last and the first,
Are they not the same?

Case Fourteen
Nansen Cuts the Cat in Two

Nansen saw the monks of the eastern and western halls fighting over a cat. He seized the cat and told the monks, "If any of you can say a word, you will save the cat." No one answered, so Nansen boldly cut the cat in two. That evening, Joshu returned, and Nansen told him about the affair. Joshu removed his sandals and, placing them on his head, walked out. Nansen said, "If you had been there, you could have saved the cat."

BODHISATTVAS: Nansen's monastery was overcrowded with monks. They were divided into two dormitories, eastern and western, where they stayed during their leisure time or sleeping hours. They would assemble in the zendo for meditation, and in the lecture hall to attend the master's discourses. It happened, one sunny afternoon, that some of the monks were sitting on the lawn between the two dormitories, quarreling over the ownership of a cat. They wanted to decide whether the cat belonged to the western house or to the eastern one. All nonsense—especially for monks! Poor Nansen was too well known, so there were many insincere monks who gathered around him, simply attracted by his reputation as a teacher. The poor fellow was thus bothered by many worthless monks.

On the day of the quarrel, he happened to pass by the foolish group on the lawn. Suddenly he seized the cat and said, "If any of you can say a word, you will save the cat." He meant, "You fellows gather here to study

Zen. Now say a word of Zen for the life of this cat. If it is good, I will let the cat go; otherwise I must kill it." No one answered. None of the monks present had attained any Zen, so Nansen cut the cat in two. Some of the monks had thought Nansen's threat was a joke, and some could not believe that Nansen would dare kill the cat, breaking the first precept: kill not any living thing. Nansen had the sword that could either kill or save. He sacrificed his karma to teach the monks. How many of the monks learned Zen at that moment, I do not know.

Those who have studied this koan know clearly that Zen allows for no hesitation. Wasting time is wasting life. Our study of this koan has nothing to do with the stupid monks who fought over the cat. Even the poor cat that lost its life is not actually involved. Simply watch Nansen's swift action, which turns the wheel of Dharma. The world greatly needs such action to avoid its troubles, because most of our misfortunes are caused by hesitation. One's first instinct can indicate the right action, but humans foolishly rely on second thoughts, thus making their lives an uncertain gamble.

Nansen did not regret what he had done, and told Joshu, his senior disciple, about the incident. Joshu removed his sandals and, placing them on his head, walked out. Nansen said, "If you had been there, you could have saved the cat." Nansen had thought the cat was the cause of the trouble, and had cut it in two, but Joshu knew the remote cause of all trouble.

The monastery should not have kept so many monks. The greater the crowd, naturally the more troubles arise. Nansen should have taught them beforehand not to have any idea of possession, as even their bodies were not their own. After all, either blaming the monks or blaming the cat would have been entirely wrong. Nansen should have blamed himself. Joshu saw that everything in the monastery was topsy-turvy, and rather than using words with which he might have accused his teacher, he immediately expressed his understanding through a topsy-turvy action— putting his sandals on his head and walking out.

MUMON'S COMMENT

Why did Joshu put his sandals on his head? If you can answer this question, you will understand exactly how Nansen enforced the edict. If not, you'd better watch your own head.

It's no use to cry over spilt milk. No matter what Joshu might have said, he could not have brought the cat back to life. If Joshu had said, "Master, you were right," he would have committed an act against the precepts. If he had said, "Master, you were wrong," he would have been unkind to the slow-witted monks, denying them an opportunity to learn Zen.

I admire Joshu's action, yet I would act differently. I would crawl on my hands and knees, and cry, "Mew, mew!" This would bring back the poor cat, and save Nansen from acquiring a reputation as a killer. There is no individual cat separate from other animals or from the universe— the deluded view that sees an individual cat is the same as that which stamps certain monks as impossible Zen students. Nansen may have failed to enlighten them, but Joshu, his disciple, did not fail to encourage them.

Age after age, generation after generation, countless bodhisattvas are working to save all sentient beings. You, too, are joining in this Buddhist endeavor, a bloodless war against the delusions of all sentient beings. Be brave and march toward enlightenment—not only for yourself, but for all living things.

Mumon's poem is a sort of war cry:

MUMON'S VERSE

Had Joshu been there
He would have enforced the edict differently.
Joshu snatches the sword,
And Nansen begs for his life.

You see, the soldiers of bodhisattvahood have no time to waste. They march straight forward, and never hesitate for an instant. This is the spirit of our seclusion in commemoration of Buddha's realization.

Case Fifteen
Tozan's Three Blows

Tozan went to Ummon, who asked him where he had come from. Tozan said, "From Sato village." "In what temple did you stay for the summer?" "The temple of Hoji, south of the lake," Tozan replied. "When did you leave there?" asked Ummon, wondering how long Tozan would continue giving such factual replies. "The twenty-fifth of August," answered Tozan. Ummon said, "I should give you three blows of the stick, but today I will spare you."

The next day, Tozan bowed to Ummon and said, "Yesterday, you spared me three blows of the stick. I do not know why you thought me wrong." Ummon, rebuking Tozan's spiritless responses, said, "You good-for-nothing! You just wander around from one monastery to another." Before Ummon had finished speaking, Tozan was enlightened.

BODHISATTVAS: When Ummon asked Tozan, "Where did you come from?" he was not asking for his last address, as a policeman would. He was testing the newcomer's Zen. Tozan said, "From Sato village," probably a place no more than a day's journey on foot from the monastery. This was a stupid reply: a bodhisattva travels from eternity to eternity. There is no beginning, and so no ending. He comes from nowhere and goes to nowhere. It was a foolish question to ask Tozan where he had come from, too. If I had been Tozan then, I would have said, "Master Ummon, I see you now," and would have bowed to him politely. Why should I tell him of my last lodging? I have forgotten it, and have no time for reminiscences. Tozan, however, was a greenhorn, with whom Ummon was patient, then asking him, "In what temple did you stay for the summer?" He meant, "How did you polish your Zen mirror during the summer?" Tozan uncomprehendingly said, "The temple of Hoji, south of the lake." The big fool! This was not an examination in geography! "When did you leave there?" continued Ummon, wondering how long Tozan would keep on with such prosaic answers. "The twenty-fifth of August," answered Tozan. Whereupon Ummon declared, "I should give you three blows of the stick, but today I will spare you."

Similarly, many people come to this zendo from remotely related movements such as Vedanta, Theosophy, and so on. They talk of their peregrinations, but show no attainment. Do they not also deserve three blows?

When Tozan went to Ummon the next day and asked why he deserved three blows, the poor teacher could restrain himself no longer, crying out, "You good-for-nothing! You just wander around from one monastery to another." Before Ummon had finished speaking, Tozan was enlightened. My only comment is this: "Honesty is the best policy."

Mumon's comment

Ummon fed Tozan good Zen food; if Tozan could have digested it, Ummon would have added another member to his family. In the evening, Tozan was swimming in a sea of good and bad, but at dawn, Ummon threw him a life-preserver.

Now I ask you, "Did Tozan deserve the three blows?" If you say yes, not only Tozan but everyone everywhere deserves them. If you say no, you make Ummon a liar. If you answer this question clearly, you can eat the same food as Tozan.

All I have to say is that Ummon, Tozan, Mumon, and all of you are cordially invited to our next monastic dinner. Boiled rice cooked with peas, stewed vegetables, and radish and carrot salad will be served abundantly.

MUMON'S VERSE

The lioness teaches her cubs roughly:
When they jump up, she knocks them down!
Ummon's first arrow barely touched Tozan,
But the second arrow went deep.

Case Sixteen
The Bell and the Ceremonial Robe

Ummon said to his disciples, "You monks live in such a wide world. Why do you put on your seven-piece robe when you hear the bell calling for services?"

BODHISATTVAS: In India, a monk had three kinds of robes—an undergarment of five pieces sewn together; a formal robe made of seven pieces; and an outer cloak made of nine pieces. They were each just a simple oblong cloth. When Buddhism entered China, the climate did not allow the monks to wear the same clothes as in India. Chinese monks wore their native clothes and then put the formal Indian robes over them. Thus, the plain raiment of an Indian monk became the official robe of Chinese Buddhism. In Mumon's time [and today as well], monks would put on their seven-piece robes when they heard the morning bell, and assemble in the chapel to recite sutras. It was the unwritten rule of a monastery, just as it was once the custom here for boarders to put on their sportcoats when they came down to the dining room at the sound of the dinner bell.

Ummon asks his disciples why, when the world is so wide, they confine themselves to such a narrow path. Why do you get up in the morning, when the twenty-four hours have no beginning and no ending? Why do you say good morning when some of you are experiencing a very bad "morning after"? The smooth working of the mental mechanism can never be recognized by one's consciousness. The minute you observe your inner datum, your mind jerks, and you lose the harmony of mind and body. Why do you stop your car at the signal of a red light, and why do you make it start at the sight of the green light? A law-abiding citizen will not raise even the shadow of such a question.

When you train yourself in meditation, your mind has no trace of unnecessary thought. It is as empty and clear as a mirror. When a flower comes in front of that mirror, its delicate color reflects on the silvery face instantly. As soon as the flower passes, that reflection vanishes. There is no trace of the flower. If a bird comes in front of that mirror, the reflection is of a bird, and nothing else.

Ummon is testing the monks to see how many of them have such empty mirror minds. "Why do you put on your ceremonial robe when you hear the bell?" Such a foolish question! You call, and I answer. Voice is not an entity, nor is its echo. Ummon's words, "such a wide world," are to catch you. Do not pay any attention to the words, and then you will be peacefully and naturally at home in "such a wide world." Inspiration for an artist comes the same way. A Japanese swordsman forgets the sword and wins the battle. If your every movement is made without self-consciousness, your action will be perfect, physically and morally; it will be the unrecognized merit of your constant meditation.

MUMON'S COMMENT

When you practice Zen, you need not follow sound, color, or form. Even though some have attained insight when hearing a voice or seeing a color or form, that is very ordinary. It is not true Zen. If you are a real Zen student, you are the master of sound, color, and form, and you actualize the truth in your everyday life. Does the sound come to the ear, or does the ear go to the sound? When you see with your ears, and hear with your eyes, you will pass this koan.

Now I ring the bell—did the sound come to you? Or did the ear go to the sound? When you recognize the sound, there is nothing but sound.

When you recognize the ear, there is nothing but the ear. Zen teachers always use "catch words." Don't be hooked by their words. Just deal with the original source.

MUMON'S VERSE

> *With realization, you belong to the family;*
> *Without realization, you are a stranger.*
> *Without realization, you belong to the family;*
> *With realization, you are a stranger.*

The universe is our great home, and we belong to the same family. Your realization will prove it to you. For those who wander around in the world of discrimination, each is a stranger to the other. When those who do not understand look at the whole, they belong to the same family, whether they realize it or not. There is, however, no such entity as a whole; therefore, you are as strangers to each other in the world of phenomena.

Case Seventeen
The Three Calls of the Emperor's Teacher

Chu Kokushi,[28] *teacher of the emperor, called Oshin, his attendant.*[29] *Oshin answered, "Yes." To test him, the master called again, "Oshin." Oshin replied, "Yes." Once again, Chu Kokushi called, "Oshin." And, once again, Oshin replied, "Yes." Chu Kokushi then said, "I guess I ought to apologize to you, but really you should apologize to me."*

BODHISATTVAS: Zen monks are not only the friends of paupers and beggars, but also the teachers of emperors. Yet whenever a monk is called by an emperor, he usually makes some excuse, declining to see him. Why? Because fame and glory are a bother to him. Chu Kokushi had resided on a mountain for forty years, hiding himself from the world. But he was at last discovered by the emperor of his time, and was obliged to have a crowned pupil. In Chinese Zen, when a national teacher is mentioned without qualification, it refers to Chu Kokushi, the first and best of the emperor's teachers.

At the time of this anecdote, the teacher was over one hundred years old, and his attendant, Oshin, was a well-trained Zen monk, still young, yet able to receive the lamp of Dharma. When his teacher called "Oshin," and Oshin answered, "Yes," the dialogue of Zen came to an end; why then did the teacher call his disciple again and again? He was an old man, and wanted to make sure of his pupil's attainment. The disciple knew this, answering his teacher each time patiently. Chu Kokushi then declared, "I guess I ought to apologize to you for all this calling, but really you ought to apologize to me." Some Japanese teachers say that Oshin was too stupid to understand Zen, that the teacher was demanding an apology. But they forget the age of the teacher, and interpret the dialogue as if it were their own.

When a Zen teacher calls the name of his disciple, he means to knock at the inner door of the student's buddha-nature. If the teacher had only everyday business in mind, he would not have called a second time. He might say, "Bring me a cup of tea," or "Give me my cloak, as I feel chilly." In Zen, neither master nor disciple should waste time, materials, words, or thought. If Oshin had no Zen, the teacher might have hit him before calling a second time. If it had been merely ordinary business between them, it would have been dealt with before the second call.

When I was in charge of a kindergarten, I used to play with the children and allow myself to be defeated in a game of wrestling. I had no wish to cheat them, but simply enjoyed being defeated to encourage the children. Japanese wives always make their husbands believe that men are strong and wise, and that no woman can surpass them. They are not pretending inferiority, but simply enjoying thus the harmony of home life. After all, in Japan the women are the winners of peace, not the men.

In this koan, the teacher is an old man, and wants to make sure of the attainment of his disciple, like an old woman who checks the lock on the door two or three times before she leaves the house. Oshin, the disciple, joins the teacher's efforts, and answers his calls again and again. Is it not a beautiful picture of beloved ones? If you want to learn Zen, you must understand how to give in.

MUMON'S COMMENT

When old Chu Kokushi called Oshin three times, his tongue was rotting, as he did a most unnecessary thing. *When Oshin answered three times his words were brilliant,* for he knew how to appreciate his old teacher's kindness. *Chu Kokushi was old and lonesome. He held the cow's head to feed it clover. Oshin did not trouble to show his Zen, either.* If he had shown it outwardly, he would have failed to express his appreciation. *His stomach was full; he had no desire to feast.* Do we not envy him? *In a prosperous country, people are indolent; in a wealthy home, the children are spoiled. Now I want to ask you, which one should apologize?* No one should do anything. The show is over, the curtain is down. Let us go home.

MUMON'S VERSE

> *When the iron yoke has no hole for the head,*
> *The prisoner and the descendants are in double trouble.*
> *If you want to hold up the gate and the door of a falling house*
> *[You must climb a mountain of swords with bare feet.]*[30]

This koan is very hard to digest, tinged with the delicate flavor of Zen. When reason dominates the mind, Zen becomes too stiff, yet when emotions rule, it is bound to become too soft. "If you want to hold up the gate and the door of a falling house"—of Zen—you will have to pass through dire difficulties.

Case Eighteen
Tozan's Three Pounds

A monk asked Tozan, "What is Buddha?" Tozan, who was engaged in weighing some flax, replied, "This flax weighs three pounds."

BODHISATTVAS: Tozan lived in a locality where people cultivated flax. The soft fiber obtained from the flax plant was sold as the raw material to weave linen. Tozan lived like those around him: he raised plants and made filaments. His labor was his Zen, and his Zen was his labor. When the monk came to him and asked, "What is Buddha?" the questioner meant the true body of Buddha, "Buddhakaya," which fills the world. Perhaps he remembered the famous gatha:

> The Buddha-body fills the world,
> Universally immanent in all things;
> It manifests wherever and whenever conditions are mature,
> Though it never leaves the seat of Bodhi.

He reasoned that Buddha is superior to a mere object of worship, but he could not see it clearly as yet. I am reminded of Johann Heinrich Pestalozzi, who was one of the world's greatest educators of the eighteenth century. When he was a young schoolteacher, he was talking to his class about a window, so he drew a picture of a window on the blackboard. But one pupil raised his hand and asked, "Teacher, why do you take such trouble, drawing a picture of a window? Can't you see we have a real window in this classroom?" It is said that Pestalozzi's new system of pedagogy was inspired by this child.

Yes, the child was right. Why do you draw a picture of a window when you are in a room with many windows? Some of you may say that the Buddha exists everywhere, and yet in all honesty you do not see it clearly. So you ask continually, "What is Buddha?" And why? Because you are trying to draw a picture of the everlasting Buddha on the blackboard of your dualistic mind. Look at the real window—the real Buddha resides in you. But do not think that it is confined within you—within your body or your mind. You have no such lodging place in your possession. You are floating on the ocean of Buddhakaya, and there is nothing but Buddha within and without. The so-called "you" is a piece of ice, which is another form of water in the ocean of Buddhakaya. In your introspection, it is your buddha-nature. Objectively, it includes all sentient beings. In your postulation, it is the Buddha, the Enlightened One. Therefore it is said that mind, Buddha, and all sentient beings are one.

Tozan lived Buddha's life, day and night. His meditation was the life of Buddha, and so his labor was also Buddha's life. He said, "This flax weighs three pounds." It was nothing more and nothing less. If the questioner failed to realize the truth at that moment, he must have been deaf and blind. However, since it is very clear that he attained enlightenment, the text says nothing more. In the original Chinese, it goes, "The flax, three pounds"—the simpler, the better. The Japanese read it, *"Ma san gin,"* and modern Chinese, *"Ma san chin."*

"What is Buddha?"

"Ma san gin."

"What is Buddha?"

"Ma san chin."

"What is Buddha?"

"The third stick of incense has just burned down."

MUMON'S COMMENT

Old Tozan's Zen is like a clam: the minute the shell opens you see the entire interior. However, I want to ask you, do you see the real Tozan?

Tozan had no wish to preach about Zen or answer questions. He just lived in Zen. Until you have lived as Tozan did, you will never meet him squarely. It is not necessary to cultivate flax to live in Zen: no matter what your everyday task may be, it will turn into Zen if you quit looking at it with a dualistic attitude. Just do one thing at a time, and do it sincerely and faithfully, as if it were your last deed in this world.

There is a pleasing Japanese Zen poem that applies here:

> Buddhism is practiced on the doorknob,
> On the pine tree of yonder hill,
> On the matches and cigarette,
> And in the songs of spring birds.

When you open the door, you hold only the doorknob in your hand. After you open the door and see the pine tree on yonder hill, you think no more of the doorknob. Then you take some matches and a cigarette from your pocket and enjoy a smoke, and you no longer have the pine tree in your mind. Then, when you hear the songs of the spring birds, you forget about smoking, even though the cigarette is still held between your lips. This whole process shows you the secret of Buddhist happiness.

MUMON'S VERSE

> *Three pounds of flax are right in front of your nose.*
> *You are close enough, yet mind is still closer.*
> *Whoever talks about affirmation and negation*
> *Lives in the region of right and wrong.*

Here is a freer translation:

> *Ma san gin* in front of your nose.
> See it before you hear the words.
> Realize it before you see it.
> Whosoever comes to you and says right or wrong
> Lives in the region of right and wrong
> And is a stranger to Zen!

Case Nineteen
Everyday Life Is the Path

Joshu asked Nansen, "What is the Path?" Nansen said, "Everyday life is the Path." Joshu asked, "Can it be studied?" Nansen said, "If you try to study it, you will be far away from it." Joshu asked, "If I do not study it, how can I know it is the Path?" Nansen replied, "The Path does not belong to the world of knowing, nor does it belong to the world of not-knowing. Knowing is delusion and not-knowing is confusion. If you want to reach the true Path beyond doubt, place yourself within the same freedom as that of the sky. How can it be called good or not-good?" At these words Joshu was enlightened.

BODHISATTVAS: The Buddhist Path is eightfold and psychological. Let me name the eight—right view, right resolution, right speech, right action, right mode of life, right effort, right awareness, and right concentration. It is eightfold, but combined, it is the manifestation of one's purified mind. It is psychological, and therefore it can be practiced by all humankind, regardless of race, ancient or modern.

In this koan, Joshu asked Nansen, "What is the Path?" Joshu was still young at that time, probably twenty years old, and the teacher, Nansen, was about fifty—a well-matured Zen teacher. Joshu was not satisfied merely to be an ideal man of Confucianism, fulfilling his obligations to family and society, but wanted to purify his mind and reach the enlightenment that is the origin of the Eightfold Path. He was an earnest seeker, but he did not realize that his desire to see was shutting his inner door. Nansen said, "Everyday life is the Path." He did not mean that Zen is naturalism and doesn't aim at the advancement of the mind. He intimately saw the brilliance of buddha-nature in this actual everyday life, while young Joshu overlooked it, postulating a Path beyond his own being.

Lao-tzu said, "The path that can be known is not the changeless path. The name that can be spoken is not the changeless name." Lao-tzu was a teacher of Confucius, and his wisdom is the mother of Zen in China and Japan. I recommend this koan to the Jews and Christians of the world with the sincere hope that they may meet the nameless God within themselves, and find the changeless Path in their everyday life.

Poor Joshu could not understand as yet, and asked, "Can it be studied?" Nansen said, "If you try to study it, you will be far away from it." See how kind and patient the teacher was! Joshu was still blind, and asked, "If I do not study it, how can I know it is the Path?" If a few years later Joshu were asked such a foolish question, he would have said, "Then you had better not study at all." Nansen was a kind-hearted gentleman and replied, "The Path does not belong to the world of knowing, nor does it belong to the world of not-knowing. Knowing is delusion and not-knowing is confusion. If you want to reach the true Path beyond doubt, place yourself within the same freedom as that of the sky. How can it be called either good or not-good?" Joshu, at these words, was enlightened. When you recognize the Eightfold Path, you are not on it. When you have nothing to do with the Path, you are a senseless corpse. A fish does not recognize water, but has much to do with it. If a fish is conscious of the water, the fish will not be happy in it. Forgetting the water and living in it—this is the secret of a happy life.

MUMON'S COMMENT

Nansen melted Joshu's ice at once when Joshu asked his questions. I doubt, though, that Joshu reached the point of Nansen's understanding. He needed thirty more years.

Zen is not a study. It is life itself. I wish all of you to take good care of your health and live at least sixty years more and accomplish your Zen. Joshu lived for 120 years.

MUMON'S VERSE

> *In spring, hundreds of flowers; in autumn, a harvest moon;*
> *In summer, a refreshing breeze; in winter, snowflakes accompany you.*
> *If useless things do not clutter your mind,*
> *Every season is a good season for you.*

I would be a big fool to comment on such a poem. Let us sip our tea and exchange the greetings of the season in silence.

Case Twenty
The Man of Great Strength

Shogen asked, "Why is it that the man of great strength cannot pick up his own leg and stand?" and he also said, "Opening the mouth has nothing to do with the tongue."

BODHISATTVAS: This koan is not referring to a man of great physical strength, but to a man of accomplishment in his meditation. It is a two-fold aphorism—one is to wake up those who are stuck in the formality of meditation, and the other is to reprove those who are running around after preachings.

So-called Zen masters of Japan nowadays will give you this koan and say, "Hold up your leg and raise up your whole body, or else, open your mouth and say something without using your tongue." They think that koans must always be something about which we can make neither heads nor tails. Nonsense! It proves their ignorance of Chinese idioms and slang. "Pick up the leg and stand" means "pick himself up" or "brace himself." And "opening mouth" means "speech" or "preaching." The whole two-fold aphorism should be, "Pick yourself up and do something, if you are a man of great strength, and remember that speech does not necessarily come from your mouth." Now you see some sense in this koan.

Some people pay a good sum of money to teachers from India in order to learn diverse methods of meditation. Some of them give imaginary names to their own bodies, and believe that each part of them develops, meditation after meditation, until the kundalini, the highest stage, is attained. It is like a card game of solitaire. You can play it by yourself for as long as you like. However, your physical organs, your stomach and other parts, go to work constantly, whether you name them or not. When your husband returns from work, if you do not prepare dinner for two, meditation or no meditation, some "kick" may be coming to you just the same. In such an instance you may use this koan and say, "Pick yourself up and stand."

The monks of the Soto School of Zen used to meditate for long hours. They would say, "We meditate, not seeking enlightenment; this is enlightenment itself." They needed sharp remarks every once in a while, like this koan—"Why doesn't the enlightened man stand on his own two feet and explain himself?" Nowadays, many Soto Zen novice monks are promoted to the rank of priest after just a few years, before they truly learn how to meditate, and then they have to preach to earn their own living. I must remind each of them of this koan and say, "It is not necessary for speech to come from the tongue." They should become farm hands and work in the field, or else clean the parks and squares while other people are sleeping, in the midnight hour. But the saddest part now is that all priests have families to support and they cannot give up their job of priest-craft—easy work and fair pay.

I appreciate the fact that you are trying to learn Zen meditation. I will join you in studying it, with pleasure. Every once in a while I must warn you with this koan, saying, "Brace yourself and stand up," as your purpose in coming here is not to become stone buddhas. I appreciate your enthusiasm in copying my lectures and keeping them, but remember that I speak them with shame and tears. I do such a dirty job (this talking on Zen) because nobody else has done it here before me. Please do not show my lectures to any outsiders and say that they are a part of my Zen. I have no such funny business as preaching Zen. Whatever I say passes away before you record it. You only catch my yawns and coughs.

Shogen said in this koan, "Opening the mouth has nothing to do with the tongue." Thus, he is canceling what he said before. What do you know about that?

MUMON'S COMMENT

Shogen spoke plainly enough, but how many will understand? If you think you do, come here and test out my big stick. Look! If you want to test real gold, you must see it through fire.

The big stick is not only to be found in the hand of Mumon. Life is, after all, a great furnace to test your real gold.

MUMON'S VERSE

If the leg of enlightenment moved, the great ocean would overflow,
If that head bowed, it would look down upon the heavens.
Such a body has no place to rest....
Let another continue this poem.

Mumon wrote only three lines in the original Chinese, and then said, "Let another continue this poem." It is your koan at the end to make your own line—the fourth line of this poem—and complete it.

I can hear the water boiling, I can smell the roasting *bancha* in the kitchen. "Let us pour the hot tea, just one-third of a cup, and sip it slowly." What? Do you say I made the fourth line?

Zen students should not repeat what they hear.

Case Twenty-one
Dried Dung

A monk asked Ummon, "What is Buddha?" Ummon answered, "Dried dung."

BODHISATTVAS: The monk asked, "What is Buddha?" He did not say, "Who is Buddha?" The historical Buddha, Siddhartha Gautama, who was born in India in 565 B.C.E. and passed from there in 485 B.C.E., has nothing to do with this question. The monk was asking for a God-conception of Buddhism, if I were to express it in Christian terminology. The religious experiences of Buddhism, however, are quite different from those of Christianity, and the term God is not adequate to interpret any of them. In philosophy, pantheism identifies the universe with God, but Buddhism sees both of them as a whole. You can call it the universe or you can name it God. When you recognize the universe, there is no God. When you recognize God, there is nothing but God. A German scholar coined the term *panentheism* to express such an idea. According to panentheism, God is all and one, and also more than the totality of existence. The Buddhist notion of ultimate being is, thus, absolute and transcendent. It is called Dharmakaya or Buddhakaya, or merely "Buddha" for short.

The monk in this koan was asking about this Buddha. We cannot presume duality between this Buddha and the world. Buddhism is not a matter of going to the Buddha by forsaking the world, but of finding the Buddha in the world. Our faith is to believe in our essential oneness with

Buddha. "Buddha in us and we in Buddha" is the fundamental faith of Buddhism. The monk in this koan had been taught to believe this oneness, but he had never experienced it for himself. When he asked Ummon, "What is Buddha?" he was more likely expecting to get some guidance from the great teacher, so that he could actualize his faith as his own inner experience. Ummon answered, "Dried dung," which is another Chinese slang term meaning "good-for-nothing." "What is Buddha?" "Good-for-nothing." Can you beat that?

Zen teachers never give anything to their pupils. Instead of giving, they take away whatever the pupils are attached to. When the Dharmakaya is most concretely understood, it becomes the Buddha, or Vairochana, or Amitabha. Buddha means "the enlightened one," and this may be understood to correspond to "God is wisdom." Vairochana is "coming from the sun," and Amitabha "infinite light," which reminds us of the Christian notion, "God is light." Now, Zen teachers crush this postulated wisdom and blow away such an illusory light, in order to have pupils look within. There is a saying in Zen, "If you say the word 'Buddha,' you must wash your mouth three times." American students of Zen speak too often of the term "realization." Remember that the minute you say the word you are surely not in the mind that the word stands for. We serve tea to wash such an unclean mouth and purify the inner treasure in silence. "What is Buddha?" Throw away such an idea, and reflect your inner self.

MUMON'S COMMENT

It seems to me Ummon was so poor he could not distinguish the taste of one food from another, or else he was too busy to write legibly. He tried to uphold his school with dried dung. His teaching was just as useless.

In his comment, Mumon seems to be attacking Ummon's way of teaching, but I take it as high praise. Zen teachers live in this world to take off the burdens from their pupil's shoulders, not to leave beautiful records or romantic anecdotes. The koans are like medicines. Some of them have ugly colors, and some bad odors. In so far as they cure the sickness of delusion, their mission is fulfilled, and each of them is as sacred as the poetical gathas in the sutras of old.

As I said before in another lecture, my ideal life is to become one useless mushroom, with no attractive flowers or bothersome stems or leaves. When you start liking me too much, I will disappear from you. I am not like some priests who send out reports to the cathedrals and to fellow workers, and advertise how splendidly they are doing. In fact I have no cathedral to which I belong. This little group is my own cathedral, and I am quite contented with it. I have no fellow workers, as non-work is the work of Zen. Most of the so-called religious workers are working for propaganda purposes, not for the true teaching. I want them to count me out from their groups. A professor of the University of Theosophy always invites me to attend his lectures when he comes to this city. He probably thinks the mushroom has plenty of time to waste. A woman who devotes herself to a worldly peace movement asks me to work for her. If a person cooperates with all the movements of which he approves, how can he do his own work? This useless mushroom wants to be left alone. It is busy with its own task, minute after minute. Mumon's poem proves it.

MUMON'S VERSE

> *Lightning flashes.*
> *Sparks shower.*
> *In the blink of an eye*
> *You have missed it.*

Case Twenty-two
Kashyapa's Preaching Sign

Ananda asked Mahakashyapa, "Buddha gave you the golden-brocade robe of successorship. What else did he give you?" Mahakashyapa called, "Ananda!"

"Yes, Brother," answered Ananda. Mahakashyapa said, "Knock down my preaching sign and put up your own."

BODHISATTVAS: Before you study this koan, I encourage you to look at the sixth koan, "Buddha Twirls a Flower," in which Buddha gave Mahakashyapa the golden-brocade robe of successorship. Here, Ananda asks what else Mahakashyapa received from Buddha. He knew the robe was only a symbol of revelation, which Buddha named the eye of the true teaching, the heart of nirvana, the true aspect of non-form, and the ineffable gate of Dharma. Ananda had studied under Buddha for twenty-six years, and after the Buddha passed, continued for twenty years more under Mahakashyapa. He had a wonderful memory, and repeated Buddha's sermons almost word for word before the remaining disciples when they assembled to compile the complete teachings of their deceased master. Yet his "eye of the true teaching" had not opened, and the heart of nirvana had not been revealed to him. The true aspect of non-form, and the ineffable gate of Dharma were, as yet, beyond the reach of Ananda. Mahakashyapa wanted to wake him up, and called, "Ananda!" Ananda, like an echo, answered, "Yes, Brother." The voice that called had no trace of ego or personality, and the answering voice also had none. There was no caller who claimed to be a caller, and there was no one who established himself as the respondent.

The original Chinese records the words of Mahakashyapa as, "Knock down my preaching sign," and ends right there. I should have presented the words as they were, but I wanted to show readers the transmission of Dharma from Mahakashyapa to Ananda, so I wrote, "Knock down my preaching sign and put up your own." I have depicted snakes with feet, and rabbits with horns. I deserve a scolding from Mahakashyapa.

MUMON'S COMMENT

If you understand this, you will see that the old assembly is still gathering; if not, even though you have sought the truth since the ages before the buddhas, you will not attain enlightenment.

I hope that none of you will get the wrong impression from Mumon's words, "if you understand this." You all know very well that Zen realization is not mere intellectual understanding. Each of us must experience it as the resurrection of our life, crushing our ego-shell and freeing our true nature. It will not come to us by luck, as in a lottery. We must work hard for it, taking Ananda as our example. He studied twenty-six years under Buddha, and then twenty more years under Mahakashyapa.

Japan was once called the mecca of Buddhism, but there is no more gathering of the old assembly there. One New Year's Day I wrote a Chinese poem, which may be rendered as follows:

> One hundred thousand *bonzes* of Japan are intoxicated
> with sake on this New Year's Day.
> Alone, Brother Soen is sober—nothing is able to tempt him.
> I light a lamp on my windowsill, and pine for him
> from this side of the ocean.
> He must be very happy when the plum blossoms herald the
> coming of spring!

This monk is my discovery, being of the same first name, by pronunciation, as my teacher Soyen Shaku, but written differently in Chinese characters. He is in Mishima, Japan, these days. His full name is Soen Nakagawa.[31] He will come to America in the future, gather the old assembly around him, and tear Mahakashyapa's preaching sign into rags.

MUMON'S VERSE

> *The point of the question is dull, but the answer is intimate.*
> *How many who hear it will open their eyes?*
> *The elder brother calls, and the younger brother answers.*
> *This spring is the eternal one—no ordinary season.*

Case Twenty-three
Think Neither Good, Nor Not-Good

In confirmation of his realization, the Sixth Patriarch received the bowl and robe from the Fifth Patriarch. They had been given from the Buddha to his successors, generation after generation. An envious monk named Myo pursued the Sixth Patriarch, intending to take this great treasure away from him. The Sixth Patriarch placed the bowl and robe on a stone in the road and told Myo, "These objects just symbolize the faith. There is no reason to fight over them. If you wish to take them, do so now." When Myo tried to lift the bowl and robe, they were as heavy as mountains, and he could not budge them. Trembling in shame he said, "I came for the teaching, not for material treasures. Please teach me." The Sixth Patriarch said, "Think neither good, nor not-good. Now, what is your true self?" At these words Myo was illuminated. Perspiring all over, he wept and bowed, saying, "You have given me the secret words and secret meaning. Is there a deeper teaching still?" The Sixth Patriarch replied, "What I have told you is no secret at all. When you realize your own true self, the secret belongs to you." Myo said, "I trained under the Fifth Patriarch for many years, but could not realize my true self until now. Through your teaching, I have found the source. It is like a person who drinks water and knows whether it is cold or warm. May I call you my teacher?" The Sixth Patriarch replied, "We studied together under the Fifth Patriarch. Let us call him our teacher. Just treasure what you have attained."

BODHISATTVAS: The kernel of this koan is, "What is your true self?" The title of this koan, "Think neither good, nor not-good," is showing you the way to meet your true self. The whole story tells you how the mind of Myo was cornered by the situation. He could do nothing else but turn inward and face his own buddha-nature squarely.

There is a prologue to this story, and it opens a very important and quite interesting page in the early history of Zen in China. There is a faithful translation of a book from Chinese into English by Wong Mou-lam, titled the *Sutra Spoken by the Sixth Patriarch on the High Seat of the Treasure of the Law.*[32] According to this text, the Fifth Patriarch assembled all his disciples one day and said to them, "Go and seek for Prajna (wisdom) in your own mind, and then write me a stanza about it. He who understands what the Essence of Mind is will be given the robe (the insignia of a Patriarchate) and the Dharma (i.e., the esoteric teaching of the Dhyana School), and I shall make him the Sixth Patriarch." The chief monk of the monastery wrote his stanza on the wall, hoping it would comply with the teacher's request. The stanza read:

> Our body may be compared to the Bodhi-tree,
> While our mind to a case of bright mirror
> Carefully we wipe and sweep them hour by hour.
> And let dust fall on them not.[33]

The Fifth Patriarch called the chief monk to him privately and said, "Your stanza shows that you have not yet realized the Essence of Mind. So far you have reached only the border of the door of enlightenment, but you have not entered it." Eno,[34] a newcomer to the monastery, also did not approve of the stanza of the chief monk, and he wrote his own stanza on the next part of the wall, as follows:

> Neither is there Bodhi-tree,
> Nor case of bright mirror,

> Since intrinsically it is void,
>
> Where can the dust alight?

The Fifth Patriarch saw the stanza and admitted the attainment of
Eno, the newcomer, but he rubbed off the stanza with his sandal, lest jeal-
ous ones should cause any trouble. At midnight, Eno was called by the
Fifth Patriarch, and the Dharma was transmitted, from heart to heart.
Eno became the inheritor of Zen, receiving the robe and the bowl. The
Fifth Patriarch escorted his successor across the river and said to him,
"Three years after your departure from me, I shall leave this world. You
may start on your journey now. Go as fast as you can toward the South.
Do not preach too soon, as Buddhism is not so easily spread."

Many monks went in pursuit of Eno, now the Sixth Patriarch, with the
intention of stealing back the robe and the bowl. Among them was a
monk named Myo who had been a general of the fourth rank in lay life.
His manner was rough and his temper hot. Of all the pursuers, he was the
most vigilant in search of Eno. Now the account reaches the point where
our present koan begins. I will follow Mumon's description, changing a
little here and there.

Overtaken by Myo, the Sixth Patriarch placed the bowl and the robe
on a stone in the road and said, "Such treasures are nothing but a testi-
monial. What is the use of taking them away by force?" Myo went to take
the objects on the rock, but they were as unmovable as a mountain. He
trembled in shame, and said, "I came for the Dharma, not for the robe and
bowl. Please teach me." The Sixth Patriarch said, "Since the reason for
your coming is the Dharma, now just refrain from thinking anything, and
just keep your mind empty. I shall then preach to you." When Myo had
done this for a considerable time, the Sixth Patriarch said to him, "Thinking neither good nor not-good, at this very moment, what is your real
nature?" At these words, Myo was enlightened. Perspiration broke out all
over his body. He further asked, "Apart from this truth, handed down
from generation to generation, are there still other esoteric teachings?"

The Sixth Patriarch replied, "What I have told you is not esoteric. If you realize your own true self, you will find what is esoteric within you." Then Myo said, "In spite of my staying in the monastery for many years, I did not realize my real self. Now, thanks to your guidance, I know it in the same way as one who drinks water knows whether it is cold or warm. You are now my teacher." The Sixth Patriarch said, "This may be the case; however, you and I are fellow disciples of the Fifth Patriarch. Just treasure what you have attained." The story ends here, and your business of digesting this koan also ends here, without any awkward explanation from me.

MUMON'S COMMENT

The Sixth Patriarch certainly was kind in such an urgent situation. It was as if he removed the skin and seeds from the fruit, and then put it into the pupil's mouth, so that all he had to do was swallow it.

MUMON'S VERSE

> *You cannot describe it, you cannot picture it.*
> *You cannot admire it, you cannot imagine it.*
> *It is your true self; it has nowhere to hide.*
> *When the world is destroyed, it will not be destroyed.*

Mumon is like a foolish father who exaggerates the beauty of his newborn baby, using the terms of physiognomy. A wise mother does not say much about the features of the baby, but just loves it as a whole, without praising the details. Mumon says, "When the world is destroyed, it will not be destroyed." Do not follow him carelessly. If you do, you may tangle yourself up again with ideas of a Supreme Being. I say, "The world is destroyed; it will also be destroyed." It is the destroyer, and also it is the creator. Eternity does not mean stillness. The changeable phenomena themselves are the noumenon itself. Therefore, in Buddhism, we say "Suchness" instead

of "Divine Being" and "Thusness" instead of "the Creator and Creatures."
"When the world is destroyed, it will not be destroyed." What a foolish
remark!

Case Twenty-four
Without Speech, Without Silence

A monk said to Fuketsu, "Speech becomes less and less until it reaches the limit, which is called ri, *yet it is unable to express reality. Silence becomes deeper and deeper until it reaches the limit, which is called* bi, *yet it is not able to express reality. There must be a way to express reality beyond both* ri *and* bi. *Will you please show me the way?" Fuketsu said, "I always remember springtime in Southern China—the birds singing among innumerable kinds of fragrant flowers."*

BODHISATTVAS: *Fuketsu* means "windy cavity." It was the name of a deserted temple that this master came across in Juchou, in the vicinity of modern Hunan. There he resided for some time. His real name was Ensho, but the monks of his time called him Fuketsu, the master of the windy hole. The temple was afterward known for its humbleness and poverty. Its master was the Fourteenth Patriarch.

In condensed form, the monk's question is, "Without speech, without silence, how can you express the truth?"

Fuketsu reminisced fondly, "I always remember springtime in Southern China—the birds singing among innumerable kinds of fragrant flowers." The words of the master were from an old T'ang dynasty poem written by Tutzumei. It was quite popular among the Chinese even in the time of Fuketsu, two centuries after the poet had passed. The poem depicted a beautiful scene on the southern shore of Yongtsukiang. Thus the master invited the troubled monk across the great river, and there let him forget his disturbing preoccupation, lost in the coolness of a moonlit night. In Japan we say that a poet can visit all the famous places while sitting in his own room. The master, however, did not mean to interest the monk in geography, as of course you already know. But it is doubtful whether the monk followed the master's meaning.

Do you remember Tennyson's "Maud?" Let me quote part of it:

> Come into the garden, Maud,
> For the black bat, night, has flown;
> I am here at the gate alone;
> And the woodbine spices are wafted abroad,
> And the musk of the rose is blown.

Now, you are not in Europe! Neither are you in Asia or America. This is my way, this evening, to express Zen without speech, without silence. Walt Whitman sang:

> Logic and sermons never convince;
> The damp of the night drives deeper into my soul.

Who said that Zen must be written in Chinese characters? English is good enough to express it!

Mumon's comment

Fuketsu had lightning Zen; whenever he had the opportunity, he flashed it. But this time he failed to do so, and just borrowed from an old Chinese poem. Never mind Fuketsu's Zen. If you want to express the truth, throw away your words, drop your silence, and tell me your Zen.

I hope all of you will study Fuketsu's Zen, and express your own attainment without speech, without silence, and then offer it to the Buddha.

Following Fuketsu, I will repeat an old poem, my gatha from the Parinirvana retreat of last year. It may help you to solve this koan:

> Under the Sala trees, Buddha stretched out on his death bed and said to
> his disciples, "Those who say that the Tathagata enters into nirvana
> are not my disciples.
> Yet those who say that the Tathagata does not enter into nirvana also are
> not my disciples."
> Like the last saying of a father to his beloved children,
> Buddha emphasized these words of Zen.
> It is not only a narrative of two-thousand-five-hundred-and-twenty years
> ago, but is also our concern this very day.
> Look! The bushes outside this humble house stretch their young leaves,
> and the golden flowers are blooming here and there.
> The spring breezes nurse gently the whole body of Tathagata, which does
> not come from anywhere and which does not depart to any place.

MUMON'S VERSE

> *Without revealing his own understanding,*
> *He offered another's words, not his to give.*
> *Had he chattered on and on,*
> *His listeners would have been embarrassed.*

I, too, should cease my chattering and join you in a cup of tea.

Case Twenty-five
Preaching from the Third Seat

In a dream Kyozan went to Maitreya's Pure Land. He saw himself in the third seat in Maitreya's abode. A monk announced, "Today, the one who sits in the third seat will preach." Kyozan arose and, hitting the podium with the gavel, said, "The truth of the Mahayana teaching transcends words and thought. Understand! Understand!"

BODHISATTVAS: Kyozan was born in China, in 814 C.E., and died there in 890. He was a native of Canton and preached in a monastery in Hunan. Kyozan's first teacher, Isan, gave him the secret book of Zen,[35] which had all the important records of Zen, together with accounts of the experiences of ancestral masters. It was a symbol of successorship, but Kyozan instantly burned the book and reduced it to ashes. The teacher said, "How dare you destroy the treasury of our teaching?" Kyozan said, "If you want it so badly, I will give it back to you." Then he wrote page after page in front of the teacher and completed the book from memory.

Kyozan's second teacher (the first one passed when Kyozan was quite young) told him one day, "The last preaching of the Buddha was recorded as the *Mahaparinirvana Sutra*. It was translated into Chinese. There are forty volumes of that work. I consider half of them the Buddha's teaching, but the other half is the preaching of devils. What do you say about this?" Kyozan said, "All of them are the devils' preachings." He was such an iconoclast. Not only the *Mahaparinirvana Sutra*, but all the sutras of Buddha's teachings—5,048 volumes—were mere trash to him. And so we come to the present koan.

One day in a dream Kyozan went to Maitreya's Pure Land. Buddhists who cannot build a Pure Land in this world always dream of it beyond this life. They only see the illusions of paradise. Filled with emotional pining, they close themselves off from their inner wisdom. Kyozan's dream was his everyday life, and his daily task was nothing but his dream. He recognized himself seated in the third seat in the abode of Maitreya. His first teacher had passed, but his second teacher was with him at the time. He always considered himself seated in the third seat, during his actual days in the monastery as well as in his dreamland of Maitreya, the future Buddha.

Someone announced, "Today the one who sits in the third seat will preach." Kyozan arose and, hitting the podium with the gavel, said, "The truth of the Mahayana teaching transcends words and thought. Understand! Understand!" He would say the same thing if he were in the paradise of God or Allah. He would not change his tune even if he were living in our time in the Western Hemisphere. Kyozan is not only telling what the Mahayana teaching is, but also showing it to everyone openly in broad daylight. Some say that the scriptures written in Pali are Theravada teachings and those in Sanskrit are Mahayana teachings. Our Kyozan would laugh at such statements. If you open your own third eye, you can read the whole of the Mahayana teachings in a glance at the blue sky, but if you close yourself off from your inner wisdom, both the scriptures written in Sanskrit and in Pali are nothing but papers smeared with nonsense.

Mumon asks you urgently to have your own experience, passing through the samadhi of meditation, not to linger on the superficial level of cognition.

Mumon's comment

I want to ask you monks, "Did he preach or did he not?" If you open your mouth, you are lost. If you do not open it, you are lost. Whether you seal your mouth or not, you are 108,000 miles from the truth.

Mumon's verse

> *In the light of day,*
> *Still in a dream, he speaks of a dream.*
> *A monster among monsters,*
> *He intends to deceive the whole assembly.*

In a Chinese record it says that the assembly in Maitreya's hall scattered and vanished like smoke when they heard the preaching of Kyozan. Another record says that Kyozan's second teacher praised him highly when he was told this dream story. I deny the facts in these two records, because we are going to have an assembly of *bancha* this evening, and none of us is awed at all by Kyozan's words.

Case Twenty-six
Two Monks Roll Up the Screen

Hogen of Seiryo monastery was about to give a talk before the midday meal. The bamboo screen, which had been lowered for meditation, had not been rolled back up. He pointed to it. Two monks arose from the assembly and rolled it up. Hogen said, "One gains, the other loses."

BODHISATTVAS: In monasteries they use heavy drapery in winter and bamboo screens in summer to divide the hall or room into sections. Sometimes corridors or verandas are shut by the screens to prevent monks from coming or going for certain periods, or else to regulate the amount of sunshine or wind. I imagine that the case in this koan refers to a screen that was hung along the veranda. Master Hogen pointed to the bamboo screen, through which the spacious sky could be seen. Anyone who had clarity of sight could have seen it. It would not have mattered if there were drapery or a screen for those with penetrating eyes. Good monks probably did not even nod at the lesson, but got it in a flash. However, two monks arose from the audience and rolled up the bamboo screen clear to the top. Hogen, observing this, said, "One gains, the other loses." Perhaps one monk arose first and the other followed him. Perhaps the first monk knew that his teacher liked to give lectures in a well-ventilated room. Of course he got the implication of vastness and enjoyed his teacher's sparkling wisdom, but at the same time he understood the physical component.

The other monk just followed his brother, thinking about keeping the lecture hall in the proper condition. The teacher saw this at a glance, and said, "One gains, the other loses." In our life we waste many thousands of minutes that could be devoted to useful thoughts and actions. Hesitation and discontinuity are enemies of Zen, and imitations are the worst. Zen students must devote their lives to actualization of truth. They have no time to spare in consideration of their teacher's preferences. Real Zen teachers should only consider their students' realization, sacrificing every comfort of their own. Nothing can please them better than the constancy of their pupils' meditation. The pupils should pay strictest attention to their main work, and go straight ahead, without thinking of anything else. Suppose the first monk was the only one who rolled up the screen and there was no other monk to follow. The master would have said just the same, "One gains and also loses."

I reject any second-hand answer in sanzen. The fruit of meditation never spoils, even if one postpones sanzen until the next time. Thus what is green may ripen.

MUMON'S COMMENT

I want to ask you, which monk gained, and which one lost? If any of you has an eye to see, you will know where the teacher failed. This has nothing to do with gain and loss.

Mumon's comment is too late for this meditation gathering. We have investigated the minds of the two monks, and we are not praising even the one who supposedly may have gained. Hogen was kind enough in pointing to the bamboo screen, and his remarks about the two monks were not necessary at all. He failed because he was too kind in teaching the monks; he had forgotten to keep his own dignity. He broke his silence and spoke of gain and loss, which are not words of Zen at all.

MUMON'S VERSE

With the screen rolled up, the vastness of the sky pervades.
Yet even vastness is not the teaching of Zen.
Forget the great sky.
Do not allow even a puff of wind to come and disturb it.

You see, it is not necessary to roll up the screen. The drapery may be needed instead, to keep the teaching hidden. Most teachings lose their richness when they have many followers. Buddhism, especially Zen Buddhism, should be kept among a few students, who should take heed to prevent dissolution.

Let me take this opportunity to tell you the story of Tosui. Tosui was a well-known Zen master of the Tokugawa era. He lived in several temples and taught in various provinces. The last temple accumulated so many adherents that Tosui told them he was going to quit lecturing entirely. He advised them to disperse and to go wherever they desired. After that no one found any trace of Tosui.

Three years later, one of his disciples discovered him living with some beggars under a bridge in Kyoto. He at once implored Tosui to teach him. "If you can do as I do for even a couple of days, I might," Tosui replied. So the former disciple dressed as a beggar and spent a day with Tosui. The following day, one of the beggars died. Tosui and his admirer carried the body off at midnight and buried it on a mountainside. After that they returned to their shelter under the bridge. Tosui slept soundly the remainder of the night, but the disciple could not sleep. When morning came, Tosui said, "We do not have to beg for food today. Our dead friend has left some over there." But the disciple was unable to eat a single bite of it. "I said you could not do as I do," Tosui rebuked him. "Get out of here, and do not bother me again." Thus, Tosui guarded his teaching secretly, without any disciples at all.

Case Twenty-seven
It Is Not Mind, It Is Not Buddha,
It Is Not Things

A monk asked Nansen, "Is there a teaching no master has ever preached?" Nansen said, "Yes, there is." "What is it?" asked the monk. Nansen replied, "It is not mind, it is not Buddha, it is not things."

BODHISATTVAS: The teachings can only describe or explain what Truth is by referring to its attributes or to relationships that distinguish it from untruth. Master or no master, that is all that can be done. All masters describe or explain Truth, but none of them can make you realize it. You must open your own inner gate by yourself. This monk asked Nansen, "Is there a teaching no master has ever preached?" Nansen replied, "Yes, there is." The answer is honest and true.

A master never preaches the inner, or esoteric, teaching. But the kind of preaching that merely entertains listeners is rather harmful. It gives them the burdens of delusion, endlessly. A master speaks abruptly, and cuts off the road of thinking in the mind of the listener. The simpler the better for Zen teaching. No word is best of all. Joshu said "Mu," and Tenryu said nothing, but simply raised his finger. The monk in this koan asked Nansen, "What is it?" Stupid! He is asking Nansen to feed him a dish of ice cream. When the ice cream melts it is no longer ice cream. When Zen is answered by words it is no longer Zen. I would like to grab hold of his chest and say, "Speak! Speak!" If it were Rinzai, he would give the monk a slap and push him away. Nansen was gentle enough to say, "It is not mind, it is not Buddha, it is not things." I doubt that the monk attained realization at these words of Nansen, yet they are quite interesting for us to investigate.

The idealist thinks everything is a phenomenon of mind, but does not know the essence of mind. The materialist believes in the existence of all matter, but when it comes to the theory of electrons, there is the dilemma of self-contradiction. Buddhist realism explains very well that the noumenon is the phenomenon, and the phenomenon is the noumenon, but to actualize what reality is, one has to pass the gateless gate. The reality is called Buddha, but the name is only a shadow, not the essence. In pointing to the esoteric or inner teaching, therefore, Nansen could only say, "It is not mind, it is not Buddha, it is not things." If you add a word to Nansen's answer, you spoil his Zen. If you take a word from the answer, you break the completeness of his Zen. Just enter into the realm of golden silence through this gate of no-thing. When you emerge from your samadhi, you see everything, and you may say, "Masters preached this, and nothing else. It is mind, it is Buddha, and it is all things."

Biographically speaking, the words of Nansen in this koan were the actual transmission from his teacher, Baso. Baso used to answer the question, "What is Buddha?" with the words, "This mind of yours is Buddha." Another time, when he was asked that question, he said, "This mind of yours is not Buddha" [see Cases Thirty and Thirty-three]. A monk asked Baso, "Why did you say, 'This mind of yours is Buddha,' when you were asked, 'What is Buddha?'" Baso said, "I wanted the children to stop their crying." He was giving candy to those crying baby monks. The questioner continued, "When the children stop crying, what would you say?" Baso answered, "Then I would say, 'This mind of yours is not Buddha.'" The questioner said, "Suppose one neither cries nor wishes candy, then what would you say?" Baso said, "Then I would say, 'There is no thing.'" The questioner continued, "If there comes one who does not cry, who needs no candy, and who does not cling to nothingness, what would you propose?" Baso said, "Such a person is a master, and can handle all situations. Why should I say anything?" This anecdote will give you the key to open the gate, and also it will teach you how to practice Zen in your everyday life.

MUMON'S COMMENT

Old Nansen gave away his treasure. He must have been greatly upset.

Nansen had the purity of heart of a young lover. His blushing and his awkward words are admirable. According to another record, the monk who asked the question was Hosho, who afterward became a successor of Hyakujo, and lived in the mountain temple where the story of the fox was told [Case Two]. Even though the monk could not receive the family treasure at the time of this koan, he became a nephew of Nansen in the teaching line. So the words of Nansen were not wasted after all.

MUMON'S VERSE

Too much attentiveness caused him to lose his dignity.
Only silence would bring real merit.
Even if the mountain were to become the sea,
Words could never open another's mind.

Case Twenty-eight
Ryutan Blows Out the Candle

BODHISATTVAS: For this case, I will read the text for you, inserting my comments here and there, for the text is quite long. *Tokusan came to Ryutan at night and asked many questions.* Beginners always think they can attain Zen by asking questions. A student who asks a question and gets Zen as the answer is one lucky dog. The teacher answers the question by throwing a bone, but not the meat. Most of the students bite the bone. Tokusan was a hungry dog and tried to jump at one bone after another. *The teacher said, "It's getting late. Why don't you retire?"* You see, the dog was driven out with a big stick by the teacher. A night gets late mercilessly. Why should we waste precious moments in vain? We serve tea after meditation, and after the third cup we collect the empty cups. It means, "The night is getting old. Why don't you retire?"

Tokusan bowed and opened the screen to go out. Turning, he said, "It is very dark outside." His insight was pitch-dark also. *Ryutan offered Tokusan a lighted candle so that he could find his way.* Can't you see the dull face of Tokusan, receiving a lighted candle that illuminated only a few feet around him? The good-hearted teacher had no more patience. *Just as Tokusan received it, Ryutan blew it out. At that moment, Tokusan's mind was illumined.* The hungry dog suddenly turned into a lion. *Ryutan asked, "What have you attained?"* An old farmer always knows a good potato at a glance. The attainment of Tokusan was recognized by the teacher in a flash. *"From now on," said Tokusan, "I will not doubt the renowned teacher's words."* He did not say such nonsense as, "I understand Buddhism," or "I realized Zen." He only said, "From now on I will not doubt the renowned teacher's words." I admire this expression.

During his lecture the next day, Ryutan told the monks, "I see a monk among you whose teeth are like a sword tree, whose mouth is like a bowl of blood. If you hit him hard with a big stick he will not so much as look back at you. Some day, this monk will mount the highest peak and carry on my teaching there." Ryutan was too proud of his newly captured lion to keep his mouth shut, so he described Tokusan's Zen for the monks. We humans may use weapons to crush our enemies, but the lion has no sword, no hammer; the lion only uses mouth, teeth, and paws. Shingon Buddhism may use rituals, and Tendai Buddhism may require the speculation found through book knowledge, but Zen crushes all delusions with this very body given to us by our parents.

Tokusan brought his commentaries on the Diamond Sutra *to the front of the lecture hall and burned them, saying, "However abstruse the teachings are, compared to this enlightenment they are like a single hair floating in the great sky. However profound all the truths are in the world, compared to this enlightenment, they are like a drop of water in the great ocean."* These were roars of the lion. *Then he left Ryutan's monastery.*

Johann Tauler, the fourteenth-century mystic who was a disciple of Meister Eckhart, had an experience like Tokusan's. He wandered in *"Die Welt in der Wuste"*—"the world of wilderness"—and passed through *"Finsternizs,"* that is, "absolute darkness," and *"Abgrund,"* "the bottomless abyss." Then suddenly he entered into the realm of inner truth and declared, *"Gott ist Nichts,"* that is, "God is Nothingness." You may have your own experience of this. Zen students, however, do not tarry in the realm of nothingness. They pass through the darkness and see that "God is Everything." Until that moment, candles and torches are blown out in vain.

MUMON'S COMMENT

When Tokusan was in his own region, he had heard about Zen, and objected to it. He thought, "Those southern monks say they can teach Dharma out-side the scriptures. They are all wrong. I must correct them." So he traveled south. He stopped for refreshments at a teashop near Ryutan's monastery. An old woman who was there asked him, "What is in that heavy bundle you are carrying?" Tokusan replied, "These are commentaries I have made on the Diamond Sutra, *after many years of study." The old woman said, "I read that sutra, and it says, 'Past mind cannot be held, present mind cannot be held, future mind cannot be held.' You wish some tea and refreshments. With what mind will you have them?" Tokusan was dumbstruck. Finally he asked the woman, "Do you know of any good teacher around here?" The old woman referred him to Ryutan, not more than five miles away. In all humility, feel-ing quite different from the way he had when he started his journey, he went to Ryutan, who was so kind he forgot his own dignity. It was like pouring muddy water over a drunken man to sober him up. What an unnecessary comedy!*

MUMON'S VERSE

> *Hearing cannot surpass seeing.*
> *You saw the teacher, and now seeing cannot surpass hearing.*
> *Your nose is very high,*
> *But after all, you are blind.*

In this poem, Mumon is warning his monks not to follow the way of Toku-san. Tokusan should have stayed at Ryutan's monastery and meditated for a while. Instead, excited about his attainment, he burned his commentaries on the *Diamond Sutra*, declared his words of Zen realization, and left. It was dramatic enough, but it leaves a bad taste—not at all the taste of Zen. He heard about Master Ryutan, and was able to meet him. Then he gave up his teacher, after one glance. First he trusted his ears, and then turned his confidence to his eyes. Clinging to his superficial attainment, he then went off to other teachers, despite Ryutan's praising words. He must have been trusting his ears again. The whole trouble was his nose, which was raised as high as the heavens. After all, he was blind.

Case Twenty-nine
Not the Wind, Not the Flag

Two monks were arguing about a flag. One said, "The flag is moving."
The other said, "The wind is moving." The Sixth Patriarch happened
to be passing by. He told them, "Not the wind; not the flag; your mind
is moving."

BODHISATTVAS: The flag never moves by itself, but it looks as though
it is moving, according to the movement of the wind. One monk, therefore, said, "The wind is moving, not the flag." Now, the wind has neither
color nor form. Without the flag, one cannot recognize the movement of
the wind. Therefore the other monk said, "The flag is moving, not the
wind." Yet the wind is the movement of the air, therefore the flag is not
guilty of moving at all. The fish balloon floats in the air and looks as
though it is swimming because of the force of the wind, but the living
goldfish swims by itself in the water. The children of our day will not have
an argument as foolish as that of those two monks. The Chinese mind of
1,262 years ago was quite different. One monk was a materialist, and he
said that the flag was moving, since he actually witnessed the fact. The
other monk was a fatalist, believing in the invisible cause of things, and he
said that the wind was moving, not the flag.

The Sixth Patriarch, aiming to hit two birds with one stone, said, "Not
the wind; not the flag; your mind is moving." He thus struck the two birds
of sophistry, and instead of killing them, turned them loose among the

phoenixes of the holy land. If you merely think of his words, "Mind is moving," as an expression of idealism, you will fail to catch even a glimpse of him.

Let me quote here from the writings of William James:

Some years ago, being with a camping party in the mountains, I returned from a solitary ramble to find everyone engaged in a ferocious metaphysical dispute. The corpus of the dispute was a squirrel—a live squirrel supposed to be clinging to one side of a tree trunk, while over against the tree's opposite side a human being was imagined to stand. This human witness tries to get sight of the squirrel by moving rapidly around the tree, but no matter how fast he goes, the squirrel moves as fast in the opposite direction, and always keeps the tree between himself and the man, so that never a glimpse of him is caught. The resultant metaphysical problem now is this: Does the man go around the squirrel or not? He goes around the tree, sure enough, and the squirrel is on the tree; but does he go around the squirrel? In the unlimited leisure of the wilderness, discussion had been worn threadbare. Everyone had taken sides, and was obstinate; and the numbers on both sides were even. Each side, when I appeared, therefore, appealed to me to make it a majority. Mindful of the scholastic adage that whenever you meet a contradiction you must make a distinction, I immediately sought and found one, as follows: "Which party is right," I said, "depends on what you practically mean by 'going around' the squirrel. If you mean passing from the north side of him to the east, then to the south then to the west, and then to the north of him again, obviously the man does go around him, for he occupies those successive positions. But if on the contrary, you mean being first in front of him, then on the right of him, then behind him, then on the left of him, and finally in front again, it is quite obvious that the man fails to go around him, for by the compensating movements the squirrel makes, he keeps his belly turned toward the man all the time, and his back turned away. Make the distinction and there is no occasion for further dispute. You are both right and both wrong according as you conceive the verb 'to go around' in one practical fashion or the other....The pragmatic method in such case is to try to interpret each notion by tracing its respective practical consequences. What difference would it practically make to anyone if this notion rather than that notion were true? If no practical difference whatever can be traced, then the alternatives mean practically the same thing, and all dispute is idle."

If the two monks had been students of William James, they would have been convinced by the professor's lecture and their argument would have ceased, but they would never have gained the wisdom of Zen. The Sixth Patriarch said, "Not the wind; not the flag; your mind is moving."

Now, show me how your mind moves.

MUMON'S COMMENT

The Sixth Patriarch said, "Not the wind; not the flag. Your mind is moving." What did he mean? If you understand this intimately, you will see two monks intending to buy iron and gaining gold. The Sixth Patriarch could not bear to see those two dullards, so he struck such a bargain.

One must be very careful when buying goods at a bargain sale. The wind and flag are no staple goods in this zendo. A chick that has hatched from an egg grows to be a hen, and that hen lays an egg from which a chick will be hatched. Now tell me, which is first and which is last—egg or chick? If William James were living in our time, perhaps he would be able to answer the question.

MUMON'S VERSE

> *Wind moves, flag moves, mind moves—*
> *The same misunderstanding.*
> *When the mouth opens*
> *All are wrong.*

If I say, "Wind moves as mind, and flag also moves as mind," the statement is true as far as it goes, but the old-timers in this zendo will be disgusted with my bad manners, and will cut me off for good from the family of Zen Buddhism. The mouth is the gate of all troubles.

I will not say a word. I will not say a word.

Case Thirty
This Mind Is Buddha

Daibai, a Zen monk, asked Baso, "What is Buddha?"
Baso replied, "This mind is Buddha."

BODHISATTVAS: "What is Buddha?" This is the first and last question in Buddhism. As a beginning student you occupy yourself with it, and when you have resolved it, you spend your time teaching it to other students. You study Buddha's lectures, the sutras, and you strive to live like Buddha. Step by step you may advance in the understanding of Buddhist scriptures, but not until you have attained realization through your own efforts can you answer the question, "What is Buddha?" In living like Buddha you will be many times disappointed, for the model is so great, and the imitator so small. But you should persevere, for the Buddha himself said, "I am the present Buddha, the accomplished one; and you are future buddhas, bodhisattvas on your way to buddhahood."

Daibai had thrown off all worldly burdens, but still carried this question, "What is Buddha?" He came to Baso, the great teacher of his time, for instruction.

Baso's answer, in the original Chinese, has four letters, *Tsi Sin Tsi Fu*, or in the Japanese pronunciation, *Soku Shin Soku Butsu*. *Tsi* means, "It is one, not two." *Sin* means, "Mind," and *Fu*, "Buddha." Therefore Tsi Sin Tsi Fu means, "Mind and Buddha are one, not two." I would like to phrase it in English as, "The actual mind is the actual Buddha."

An American student once went to Japan and studied this koan, expressing his attainment to the master through an interpreter. The master covered the interpreter's mouth with his hand and looked at the American student, who promptly shouted, "Soku Shin Soku Butsu!" So the master passed the student on that koan. I am no master of Zen, but I can at least guard the gate and refuse to admit anyone on a stolen ticket. Now answer me, what is Buddha? No, no, don't shout. What? "Tsi Sin Tsi Fu?" It is Chinese all right, but it is not the answer. Better close your mouth, stop your flow of thinking, and tell me: What is Buddha?

Daibai, the monk in this koan, having attained realization at the words of Baso, journeyed to a distant mountain and remained in seclusion for many years. One day a monk from his old monastery came to visit him. Daibai asked the monk, "What answer does our teacher give these days when he is asked, 'What is Buddha?'" The visitor said, "Our teacher changed his answer recently, saying, 'This mind is not Buddha.'" Daibai responded, "No matter what our old teacher says, I say, 'This mind is Buddha.'" When the visiting monk returned to the monastery, he related the exchange to Baso, who was very pleased. Baso declared, "I see now that the big fruit has ripened." The name Daibai means Big Plum in Chinese.

Mumon's comment

If you thoroughly understand this, you wear Buddha's clothing, eat Buddha's food, speak Buddha's words, and behave as Buddha. In fact you are Buddha. This anecdote, however, has weighed down many a student. If you understand, you will wash out your mouth for three days after saying the word "Buddha," and will cover your ears and run for your life when you hear, "This mind is Buddha."

The comment ends here, but let me continue it. A true student, not clinging to formality, may be an American woman. She need not shave her head and live in poverty, begging for a living. She can keep her hair and curl it fashionably.

MUMON'S VERSE

Under the blue sky in the bright sunlight,
One should leave off searching.
To ask, "What is Buddha?"
Is like hiding the loot in one's pocket and declaring oneself innocent.

Case Thirty-one
Joshu Investigates

A traveling monk was on his way to a certain very popular temple at Taizan that was supposed to confer wisdom upon those who worshipped there. At a fork in the road there was a tea-house. The monk stopped and asked the old woman who ran it for directions to the temple. The woman told him, "Go straight ahead." When he had proceeded a few steps, he heard her mutter under her breath, "He too is just a common churchgoer." Someone related the incident to Joshu, who decided to look into the matter. So the next day Joshu went and asked the same question, receiving the same answer and the same comment afterward. Joshu later remarked to his monks, "I have investigated that old woman for you."

BODHISATTVAS: Taizan is an abbreviation of Gotaisan, which is the name of a mountain in the state of Shan-Hsi, where a statue of Manjushri Bodhisattva has been enshrined since ancient times. Chinese Buddhists believed that whoever climbed this mountain and paid homage to the statue would be endowed with wisdom. Even Zen monks would sometimes be found there, hoping that a miracle would save them the work required to emancipate themselves. The old woman in this koan probably set up her tea-house at the intersection with the express purpose of intercepting visitors on their way to the shrine. Most of the pilgrims would naturally stop for tea and ask the way to the temple. But her direction, "Go straight ahead," was more than it appeared to be—for she was a bodhisattva, one who has a compassionate heart and longs to enlighten others. Her expression was also a key to open the inner gate of Zen; but all of the pilgrims, even the Zen monks, had minds that were closed to her kindness. When a stupid fellow proceeded a few steps without insight, she would say regretfully to herself, "He too is just a common churchgoer." Did she make a mistake when she applied her formula to Joshu?

MUMON'S COMMENT

The old woman knew how to plan strategy, but forgot that a spy might sneak in behind her tent. Old Joshu played the spy's part and turned the tables on her, but he was not an able general. Both had their faults. Now, tell me, what did Joshu find out in his investigation?

Once when Joshu, too, was a common churchgoer, he planned to climb the mountain, Gotaisan, and pay homage to the statue of Manjushri, so that he might be endowed with wisdom. But an old monk wrote a poem for him:

> *All mountains are equally good.*
> *Blue ones afar, and a green one near,*
> *Each one has a Manjushri enshrined*
> *So why go to Gotaisan in particular?*

> *The sutras depict Manjushri riding on a lion.*
> *You may see many illusions like that*
> *In the mountain clouds.*
> *It is not real to the eye of a Zen monk;*
> *It is not the happiness a Zen monk seeks.*

So Joshu didn't go to Gotaisan after all. After many years of hard practice, Joshu became a Zen teacher. One day he saw a monk paying homage to a statue of the Buddha.

"What are you doing?"

"I am paying homage to the Buddha," replied the monk.

"What is the use of that?" inquired Joshu.

The monk said, "Is it not a good thing to pay homage to the Buddha?"

Joshu declared flatly, "A good thing is not better than nothing."

Another time a monk drew a picture of Joshu and showed it to him. Joshu said, "Does it really look like me or not? If it does, you had better kill me. If it does not, you must burn such trash." A very different Joshu from the common churchgoer!

MUMON'S VERSE

> *When the question is common*
> *The answer is common.*
> *When the question is sand in a bowl of rice,*
> *The answer is a stick in the soft mud.*

The old woman may swallow a mouthful of rice without noticing the sand, but she will feel the stick if she walks through soft mud in her bare feet. After all, the iconoclast school is as dense as the common churchgoer.

Case Thirty-two
A Philosopher Asks Buddha

A non-Buddhist philosopher came to Buddha and said, "I do not ask for words; I do not ask for no-words." The Buddha kept silence. The philosopher bowed and thanked the Buddha, saying, "Your loving-kindness has cleared away my delusions and allowed me to enter the true Path." After he had gone, Ananda asked the Buddha what the philosopher had attained. The Buddha replied, "A good horse runs even at the shadow of the whip."

BODHISATTVAS: In the original Chinese the questioner was described as an "outsider." In the time of the Buddha there were ninety-six schools of philosophy besides Buddhism. One of the students of a certain school came to the Buddha and said, "I do not ask for words; I do not ask for no-words." The truth can neither be described by words nor by no-words. Words are shadows of assertion, and no-words are those of negation. Both are unreal. I can imagine the philosopher standing in front of the Buddha, his whole being a question mark.

Buddha could see that the conceptual mind of the philosopher was losing its grip, and that he was about ready to enter into Buddha-Mind. Therefore Buddha kept silence, like the great ocean that receives all streams and rivulets. The Tibetan Buddhist recites a formula, *"Om mani padme hum,"* and observes, "The sunrise comes, the dewdrop slips into the shining sea." He should meet the Buddha of this koan at that moment.

The philosopher bowed and thanked Buddha, saying, "Your loving-kindness has cleared away my delusions, and allowed me to enter the true Path." He was not an outsider any more. After he had gone, Ananda asked the Buddha what the philosopher had attained. The Buddha replied, "A good horse runs even at the shadow of a whip." Ananda was educated under the Buddha for many years, and he knew the ways his teacher used to guide pupils gradually. He witnessed here an abrupt method to enlighten another for the first time. He was a donkey who needed whipping all the time.

MUMON'S COMMENT

Ananda was a disciple of the Buddha, but his comprehension did not surpass that of the outsider. I want to ask you monks how much difference there is between a disciple and an outsider.

Buddhists in Ceylon think a shaved head is the most important thing in qualifying as a monk. I admire their obedience to the old Buddhist custom. I suppose all the monks in Ceylon look like Ananda, as far as heads are concerned. A monk who wears white hair like Senzaki would not be allowed to enter any monastery in the lands of Theravada Buddhism. I have no attachment to my hair. I would shave off my hair, should I go on a pilgrimage to the southern lands. However, I would ask the monk who guards the gate there to show me the way to the monastery without words and without the wordless. If he did, I would consider him a disciple of Buddha even though he is living 2,500 years after Buddha's time. If he did not, I would have to tell him that he is an outsider, even though he sits inside the gate.

MUMON'S VERSE

Walking along the sharp edge of a sword,
Running over smooth ice,

One need not follow in anyone's footsteps.
Just walk over the cliffs with hands free.

The poem is not describing an acrobat on the skating rink. It is admiring a bodhisattva who is free from all formalities and does unselfish work to save other beings. We say in Zen, "A true student should not follow even the footsteps of Buddha." The poem says, "One need not follow in anyone's footsteps; just walk over the cliffs with hands free." This is the way to study koans. This is the way to be free from words and from the wordless.

An American footnote to "walks over the cliffs with hands free" can be found in a quotation from a discussion on American philosophers by Will Durant:

> Consciousness is not an entity, not a thing, but a flux and system of relations; it is a point at which sequence and relationship of thoughts coincide illuminatingly with the sequence of events and the relationship of things. In such moments it is reality itself, and no mere "phenomenon," that flashes into thought: for "phenomena" and "appearances" there is nothing. Nor is there a going beyond the experience-process to a soul; the soul is the sum of our mental life, and the "noumenon" is simply the total phenomena, and the "absolute" the web of the relationships of the world.

I will add a footnote to that footnote, from *The Central Conception of Buddhism,* by Theodor Ippolitovich Stcherbatsky:[36]

> The conception of a dharma is the central point of the Buddhist doctrine. In the light of this condition Buddhism discloses itself as a metaphysical theory developed of one fundamental principle, viz. the idea that existence is an interplay of a plurality of subtle, ultimate, not further analyzable elements of Matter, Mind, and Forces. These elements are technically called dharmas, a meaning which this word has in this system alone....

But although the conception of an element of existence has given rise to an imposing superstructure in the shape of a consistent system of philosophy, its inmost nature remains a riddle. What is dharma? It is inconceivable! It is subtle! No one will ever be able to tell what its real nature, *dharma-svabhava,* is! It is transcendental!

Case Thirty-three
This Mind Is Not Buddha

A monk asked Baso, "What is Buddha?"
"This mind is not Buddha," replied Baso.

BODHISATTVAS: This koan seems the exact opposite of the thirtieth, "This Mind Is Buddha." While the questioners are different in each case, it was the same master, Baso, who answered both times. So Daibai, one of Baso's disciples, said, "The dear old teacher misleads others endlessly. No matter what he says, I still say, 'This mind is Buddha.'"

But whatever Baso said was merely the finger pointing at the moon. When you see the moon, the finger is forgotten. If a student were to seek Buddha outwardly, Baso would say, "This mind of yours is Buddha," pointing to the inner understanding of the student. If the student were to picture Buddha within, the master would say, "This mind is not Buddha," crushing the inner image, to reveal the formless and independent mind of the student. Thus the words of Zen are medicines to cure sickness. If there were no sickness, there would be no use for medicine. If there were no delusions, buddhas and masters would not say a word of Zen. Baso sent his first medicine, "This mind is Buddha," out into the market, but soon had to issue a new formula for an antidote when people began taking overdoses of the medicine.

The original Chinese of Baso's answer has four characters that are pronounced *Fei Sin Fei Fu* in modern Chinese. Now, *Fei* means "not right" or "mistake," in a rather scornful sense. *Sin* means mind, and *Fu* is Buddha. If he were living in our day, Baso might have said, "The true Buddha is neither within nor outside your mind. There exists no such thing to be called 'mind.' When you say 'mind,' you are wrong. When you say 'Buddha,' you are quite mistaken. Now, shut your mouth; block your road of thinking, and tell me—what is Buddha?"

What can we do with such an unreasonable Chinaman? I will make a bed for him and let him sleep quietly in the next room while we modern Zen students keep on meditating here. "Fei Sin Fei Fu"—what a noisy language the fellow speaks! Let us forget what he said, and let us also forget where he is.

MUMON'S COMMENT

One who understands this is a graduate of Zen.

There is no graduation in Zen. Each of us takes a vow to enlighten all sentient beings and, as these are countless, so our vow is endless. From eternity to eternity, Buddhists work to enlighten others, all for one and one for all. "A graduate of Zen"—Mumon, Mumon, don't talk such nonsense.

MUMON'S VERSE

If you meet a swordsman on the road,
You may present a sword.
If you meet a poet, you may offer him a poem.
When you speak to others, say only part of what you intend,
Never give all of it at once.

The Buddhist who preaches all of it at once, with no regard for the listener's understanding of what is said, is a poor follower of Buddha. Such a one should not carry the sword of Dharma, nor compose a poem of Zen.

In this respect, you will see clearly that sectarian Buddhism—whether Mahayana or Theravada—adulterates the pure teaching of Buddha. Zen holds the threadbare garment inherited directly from the Buddha by the masters, generation after generation. These words of Baso, "This mind is not Buddha," prove it precisely.

Case Thirty-four
Wisdom Is Not the Path

Nansen said, "Mind is not Buddha. Wisdom is not the Path."

BODHISATTVAS: We have studied in the twenty-seventh koan what Nansen said, "It is not mind, it is not Buddha, it is not things." Nansen was a disciple of Baso. We have discussed what Baso said, "This mind is not Buddha." Both of them—the teacher and the disciple—expressed the truth in such a negative way to prevent their listeners from attachment to words. Do you remember what Buddha said in the *Diamond Sutra*? He said, "A bodhisattva who retains the thought of an ego, a person, a being, or a soul is no more a bodhisattva." This case shows the true path of a bodhisattva: "Mind is not Buddha. Wisdom is not the Path."

Here is a sermon by Baso on the Path, translated by D.T. Suzuki and included in his *Manual of Zen Buddhism*:

> The Path in its nature is, from the first, perfect and self-sufficient. When a man finds himself unceasing in his management of the affairs of life, good or bad, he is known as one who is disciplined in the Path. To shun evils and to become attached to things good, to meditate on Emptiness and to enter into a state of Samadhi—this is doing something. Of those who run after an outward object, they are the farthest away from the Path. Only let a man exhaust all his thinking and imagining he can possibly have in the Triple World. When even an iota of imagination is left with him, this is his Triple

World, and the source of birth and death in it. When there is not a trace of imagination, he has removed all the source of birth and death, he then holds the unparalleled treasure belonging to the Dharma-raja. All the imagination harbored since the beginningless past by an ignorant being, together with his falsehood, flattery, self-conceit, arrogance, and other evil passions, are united in the body of one Essence, and all melt away.

This mind is Buddha and no other, but one who clings to words and postulates an idea of it is far away from the Path. If you meditate on empti-ness, you can never empty your mind. If you aim to enter samadhi, you will never reach it. Buddhist wisdom comes directly from one's own buddha-nature. It is not like so-called knowledge, which is merely the psycholog-ical result of human experiences. We Buddhists do not discourage ourselves from learning things and accumulating knowledge. We can have as much worldly knowledge as we need, in dealing with the world in a dualistic way. We do not forget, however, that we have our own home which is, from the first, perfect and self-sufficient. Baso said, "If a man is of superior character and intelligence, he will, under the instruction of a wise director, at once see into the essence of things and understand that this is not a matter of stages and processes. He has an instant sight into his own original nature." What Baso said here is the penetrating wisdom that Nansen had attained under his guidance. It is not learning. It is not mere knowledge.

Alexis Carrel wrote the following conclusion to his book *Man, the Unknown*:

The day has come to begin the work of our renovation. We will not estab-lish any program. For a program would stifle living reality in a rigid armor. It would prevent the bursting forth of the unpredictable, and imprison the future within the limit of our Mind. We must arise and move on. We must liberate ourselves from blind technology and grasp the complexity and the wealth of our own nature. The sciences of life have shown to humanity its goal and placed at its disposal the means of reaching it. But we are still immersed in the world created by the sciences of inner matter without any respect of the laws of our development. In a world that is not made for us, because it is born from an error of our reason and from the ignorance of our true self. To such a world we cannot become adapted. We will, then, revolt against it. We will transform its values and organize it with reference to our true needs. Today, the science of man gives us the power to develop all the potentialities of our body. We know the secret mechanism of our physiological and mental activities and the causes of our weakness. We know how we have transgressed natural laws. We know why we are punished, why we are lost in darkness. Nevertheless, we faintly perceive through the mist of dawn a Path which may lead to our salvation. For the first time it has at its disposal the gigantic strength of science. Will we utilize this knowledge and this power? It is our only hope of escaping the fate common to all great civilizations of the past. Our destiny is in our hands. On the new road we must now go forward.

The demarcation between science and philosophy, or knowledge and wisdom, is vanishing naturally and happily in the writing of this noted thinker. Nansen said, "Wisdom is not the Path," in the old days in China, but I say here in America, in our time, "Wisdom is the Path, and none other."

MUMON'S COMMENT

Nansen was growing old; he forgot to be ashamed. Speaking out with bad breath, he exposed the scandal of his own home. However, there are a few who appreciate his kindness.

When in Rome, do as Romans do. If Nansen and Mumon lived in our day and the former said what we read in the text, the latter would not make such a comment. For the very truth Nansen spoke of is in common with the advanced thought of modern thinkers. Those who call themselves Zen masters and keep a cheap "home remedy" as a secret formula are out of date now.

MUMON'S VERSE

When the sky clears, the sun appears,
When the earth is parched, rain will fall.
He opened his heart and spoke out fully,
But it was useless to talk to pigs and fish.

There are in our era educated pigs, and also a fish who takes sunbaths. Mumon, Mumon, what do you know about them?

Case Thirty-five
Two Souls

Goso said, "Seijo, the Chinese woman, had two souls. One was always sick at home, and the other was a married woman with two children, living in another province. Which was the true soul?"

BODHISATTVAS: In Lafcadio Hearn's translation of the story, Hearn named the girl Ts'ing, using Peking Mandarin. His interest was in the exotic nature of the story, while Goso, the Zen master, and Mumon, the author of the *Gateless Gate*, picked up the story as a pointing finger to show the moon of realization. Here is the story:

There lived in Han-yang a man called Chang-kien, whose young daughter, Ts'ing, was of peerless beauty. He also had a nephew called Wang-chau, a very handsome boy. The children played together and were fond of each other. Once Kien jestingly said to his nephew, "Some day I will marry you to my little daughter." Both children remembered these words, and thus they believed themselves betrothed.

When Ts'ing grew up, a man of rank asked for her in marriage; her father decided to comply with the demand. Ts'ing was greatly troubled by this decision. As for Chau, he was so much angered and grieved that he resolved to leave home and go to another province. The next day he got a boat ready for his journey, and after sunset, without bidding farewell to anyone, he proceeded up the river.

But in the middle of the night he was startled by a voice calling to him,

"Wait!—It is I!"—and he saw a young woman running along the bank of the river toward the boat. It was Ts'ing. Chau was unspeakably delighted. She sprang into the boat; the lovers found their way safely to the province of Chuh.

In the province of Chuh they lived happily for six years; they had two children. But Ts'ing could not forget her parents, and longed to see them again. At last she said to her husband, "Because in a former time I could not bear to break the promise made to you, I ran away and forsook my parents, although knowing that I owed them all possible duty and affection. Would it not now be good to try to obtain their forgiveness?" "Do not grieve about that," said Chau, "we shall go to see them." He ordered a boat to be prepared, and a few days later he returned with his wife to Han-yang.

According to custom, the husband first went to the house of Kien, leaving Ts'ing alone in the boat. Kien welcomed his nephew with every sign of joy and said, "How much I have longed to see you! I was afraid that something had happened to you." Chau said respectfully, "I am distressed by the undeserved kindness of your words. It is to beg your forgiveness that I have come." But Kien did not seem to understand. He asked, "To what matter do you refer?" "I feared," said Chau, "that you were angry with me for having run away with Ts'ing. I took her with me to the province of Chuh."

"What Ts'ing was that?" asked Kien. "Your daughter Ts'ing," answered Chau, beginning to suspect his father-in-law of some malevolent design. "What are you talking about?" cried Kien with every appearance of astonishment, "My daughter Ts'ing has been sick in bed all these years—ever since the time that you went away."

"Your daughter Ts'ing," returned Chau, becoming angry, "has not been sick. She has been my wife for six years and we have two children and we have both returned to this place only to seek your pardon. Therefore, please do not mock me!" For a moment the two looked at each other in silence. Then Kien arose and, motioning to his nephew to follow, led the way to an inner room where a sick woman was lying. Chau, to his utter amazement, saw the face of Ts'ing—beautiful, but strangely thin and pale. "She cannot speak," explained the old man, "but she can understand." And Kien said to her, laughingly, "Chau tells me that you ran away with him, and that you gave him two children." The sick daughter looked at Chau and smiled, and remained silent.

"Now you come with me to the river," said the bewildered visitor to his father-in-law. "For I can assure you—in spite of what I have seen in this house—that your daughter Ts'ing is at this moment in my boat." They went to the river; and there, indeed, was the young wife, waiting. And seeing her father, she bowed down before him, and besought his pardon. Kien said to her, "If you are really my daughter, there is something which I cannot understand—come with me to the house."

The three proceeded toward the house. As they neared it, they saw that the sick daughter, who had not left her bed for years, was coming to meet them, smiling as if much delighted. The two Ts'ings approached each other. But then—nobody could ever tell how—they suddenly melted into each other, and became one body, one person, one Ts'ing—even more beautiful than before, and showing no sign of sickness or sorrow. Kien said to Chau, "Ever since the day of your going, my daughter was dumb, and most of the time seemed like a person who had taken too much wine. Now I know that her spirit was absent."

Ts'ing herself said, "Really I never knew that I was at home. I saw Chau going away in silent anger and the same night I dreamed that I ran after his boat—but now I cannot tell which was really I—the I that went away in the boat, or the I that stayed at home." Story ends.

MUMON'S COMMENT

When you understand this, you will know it is possible to come out from one shell and enter another as if you were a traveler staying at an inn. But if you cannot understand, you will be like a crab thrown into boiling water and struggling with many arms and legs.

"When you understand this"—the essence of mind—"you will know it is possible to come out from one shell and enter another..."—Mumon does not here mean that a soul migrates from one body to another. He only emphasizes that the shell, envelope, or lodging cannot particularize the universal body or eternal traveler. For instance, while I am talking to you, I never recognize my individuality. I only use the term "I" in contrast to "you." My whole being is passing transiently through this body, these clothes, and this house. There is no such animal steadily labeled Senzaki. This monk you call Senzaki is passing minute after minute, from one envelope to another. Tomorrow you may see a man who looks like Senzaki, thinks like Senzaki, and speaks or acts like Senzaki, but that fellow will not be the Senzaki you recognize this minute. Liking him or disliking him are altogether your illusion.

"But if you cannot understand"—the truth of no-self—"you will be just a crab thrown into boiling water, struggling with many arms and legs"—you will whine, "Oh, what shall I do? I have to die now." Big fool! There is no individual life, and therefore there is no personal death. In such a predicament, you may say, Mumon did not tell me where to go! But it will be too late then.

MUMON'S VERSE

> *The moon above the clouds is the same moon,*
> *The mountains and rivers below are all different.*
> *All are blessed, in unity and diversity.*
> *This is one; this is two.*

If the story had originated in Japan, the young woman who was sick in bed would have been a friend who had taken Ts'ing's place in sympathy, and sacrificed her days, months, and years in silence. She would have happened to look like the real Ts'ing, and would have fooled the father and other members of the family, keeping her mouth shut like a dummy.

When the real Ts'ing returned home with her husband and her two children, the sick woman would have disappeared, fulfilling her friendship.

There is a koan, "Avalokiteshvara has one thousand eyes. Which is the real eye?" If an actress in the movies could pass this koan, she would be able to turn every role she played into a masterpiece, and also lead her private life ethically and intelligently. Then I would say, as Mumon did, "This is one; this is two."

Case Thirty-six
Meeting a Master on the Road

Goso said, "When you meet a Zen master on the road, you cannot speak, you cannot remain silent. What will you do?"

BODHISATTVAS: Master Hoyen was called Goso by the monks of his time, as he lived on Mount Goso. There was a saying among the monks, "On your way, if you meet one who has reached the way, neither speak nor remain in silence." Zen monks in China used to travel during the summer vacation, and they often met good teachers on the road. One who speaks usually bores another. One who remains silent loses the opportunity to receive instruction. Monks at that time, therefore, warned each other to avoid extremes and to walk the path of the middle way. Goso brought up this saying as the subject of Zen, and demanded his monks tell him what they would do in an actual case.

Rudyard Kipling wrote a story about words. Let me read it for you:

There is an ancient legend which tells us that when a man first achieved a most notable deed he wished to explain to his tribe what he had done. As soon as he began to speak, however, he was smitten with dumbness, he lacked words, and sat down. Then there arose—according to the story, a masterless man, one who had taken no part in the action of his fellow, who had no special virtues, but afflicted —that is the phrase—with the magic of the necessary words. He saw, he told, he described the merit of the notable deed in such a fashion, we are assured, that the words became alive and walked up and down in the hearts of all his hearers. Thereupon, the tribe, seeing that the words were certainly alive, and fearing lest the man with the words would hand down untrue tales about them to their children, they took and killed him. But later they saw that the magic was in the words, not the man.

Do you remember what Mumon said in his poem in the first koan, "Joshu's Dog"? He said, "If you say yes or no, you lose your own buddha-nature." From the ancient times of simple language to the modern age of radio broadcast, we humans endanger ourselves by the use of words. We do not know that words are mere shadows of thought, and never will they be the thought itself. The magic of words has killed many people and spoiled many sorts of business. Zen students, therefore, never depend on words, and warn each other to escape from the danger of this magic. Silence is their safeguard.

According to Madame Guyon, there are three kinds of silence. She said:

Silence from words is good, because inordinate speaking tends to evil. Silence or rest from desires or passions is still better, because it prompts quickness of spirit. But the best of all is silence from unnecessary and wandering thoughts, because that is essential to internal recollection and because it lays a foundation for a proper regulation and silence in other respects.[37]

Zen not only admires silence, but lives in it. When one lives in silence, one does not recognize silence. Thomas Carlyle admired silence, and said, "Looking around on the noisy insanity of the world—words with little meaning, actions with little worth—one loves to reflect on the great Empire of Silence, higher than all stars; deeper than the Kingdom of Death! It alone is great; all else is small." A beautiful expression! But he spoke too much, and broke the silence. I rather prefer Cicero, who

COMMENTARIES ON THE *GATELESS GATE* 165

said that there is not only an art but an eloquence in silence. He must have experienced the true silence, otherwise he would not have used such a word.

Goso said, "When you meet a Zen master on the road, you cannot speak, and you cannot remain silent. What will you do?" You can speak if you are not clinging to words. You can remain silent if you are free from silence. How do you know the one you meet is a Zen master? In Japan, these days, some Zen priests carry their cards printed with the title "Zen master." It proves that they are not Zen masters at all. If you have Zen in you, whomever you meet, and whatever you see, will be your noble and beautiful associate without exception. Why pick out a particular individual and call that one a Zen master?

MUMON'S COMMENT

In such a case, if you can answer intimately, your realization will be beautiful, but if you cannot, you should look around without seeing anything.

Each person walks the road of life. If one clings to the things one has seen, one cannot advance along the path. Mumon says, "Look around without seeing anything." This is the secret of Buddhist meditation.

MUMON'S VERSE

Meeting a Zen master on the road,
Respond neither with words nor with silence.
Give him an uppercut
And you will be one who understands Zen.

Give the uppercut to your own dualistic ideas. There is nobody to meet. There is no Zen to be understood by you.

Case Thirty-seven
The Cypress Tree in the Garden

A monk asked Joshu, "Why did Bodhidharma come to China?" Joshu said, "The cypress tree in the garden."

BODHISATTVAS: D.T. Suzuki translates the name of the tree in this koan as cypress. I think he is right. The Chinese character of the name was commonly understood by Japanese as the oak, but no Chinese person, ancient or modern, takes it for that. The koan has, however, nothing to do with the name of the tree.

Bodhidharma came to China to actualize Zen, and to guide others in that land to realize it. Those who lived with him witnessed precisely the real objective of his coming east. Those who received the lamp of Zen from him, directly or genealogically, lived the same way he did. The question "Why did Bodhidharma come to China?" was the same expression as "What is Zen?"

According to another record, the dialogue was as follows: "Why did Bodhidharma come to China?" asked the monk. Joshu answered, "The cypress tree in the garden." Then the monk said, "Don't tell me about it objectively. My question is beyond objectivity." Joshu said, "I am not telling you objectively." Then the monk asked again, "Why did Bodhidharma come to China?" Joshu said, "The cypress tree in the garden." Joshu's answer transcended both objectivity and subjectivity. The monk failed to catch a glimpse of Zen at Joshu's first answer. I doubt if he attained anything even at the second answer. Mumon shortened the dialogue and kept the question and the answer in his *Gateless Gate*. "Why did Bodhidharma come to China?"—"The cypress tree in the garden." Here is your task for the evening.

A Zen student in China once said, "Bodhidharma never came to China." This student was not refusing objectivity. D.T. Suzuki translates another dialogue beautifully. Let me quote it for you.

> Tesshikaku was a disciple of Joshu. When he visited Hogen, another great Zen Master, after Joshu's death, Hogen asked him where he had been. Tesshikaku replied that he had come from Joshu's place. Said Hogen, "I understand that a cypress tree once was the subject of his talk; is that really so?" Tesshikaku was positive in denial, saying, "He gave no such talk." Hogen protested, "All the monks coming from Joshu's place lately speak of his reference to a cypress tree in answer to a monk's question, 'What was the real objective of Bodhidharma's coming east?' Why do you say that Joshu made no such reference to a cypress tree?" Whereupon Tesshikaku roared, "My late master never gave such a talk—make no slighting allusion to him, if you please!" Hogen greatly admired this attitude on the part of this disciple of the famous Joshu, and said, "Truly you are a lion's child!"

Joshu's response in this koan is obviously gentle, but it contains a secret power that can steal away all your delusions before you recognize it. Kanzan, a Japanese Zen master, therefore said, "The koan of the cypress tree steals everything from you." Ingen, who came to Japan in the Tokugawa era (1603–1868) from China, visited the monasteries on the islands and investigated the remaining works of the founders, the masters of old Japan. He was told at Myoshin-ji Monastery that the founder, Kanzan, kept no records of lectures or Zen poems. He left just one saying, "The koan of the cypress tree steals everything from you," which still survives among the monks. Ingen appropriately spread his bowing cloth on the ground and paid deep homage to the statue of Kanzan, despite the nearly 300 years between the master's time and his own.

MUMON'S COMMENT

If you see Joshu's answer clearly, there is no Shakyamuni Buddha before you and no Maitreya Buddha after you.

At the time of Mumon, both in China and in Japan it was believed that the era belonged to the declining age of Buddhism, in which all the moral and ascetic precepts given to monks would be neglected, and no one would be able to attain supreme wisdom. Here in this comment Mumon crushed such a foolish idea, and declared that anyone could become a buddha in any era. He gave the assurance that this koan alone, "A cypress tree in the garden," could prove it for those who worked honestly. True Buddhism has nothing to do with belief in a legend, after all.

MUMON'S VERSE

> *Words cannot express it.*
> *Words cannot deliver the heart's message.*
> *If you take words literally, you will miss it.*
> *If you try to explain it with words, you will remain deluded.*

This was originally a poem by Tozan, but Mumon borrowed it happily and brought it up here appropriately. You Americans need not worry about why Bodhidharma came to China. Let the old story be buried in the past. The most important business for you is to practice your Zen in your everyday life. The shrubs in our garden are growing fast, and the streetlight comes through sparsely. When you leave to go home through the shadowy path, watch your step. Don't bump your head on the Candana tree[38] in the garden!

Case Thirty-eight
A Buffalo Passes through an Enclosure

Goso said, "It is like a buffalo that gets out of his enclosure. His horns, his head, and his hoofs all pass through. Why can't his tail also pass through?"

BODHISATTVAS: Buffalo on the old continent were the same as those in the New World. They liked their freedom, and would fight for it. The Chinese people caught the beasts, and tried to tame them to be useful for farm work. The male buffalo were, however, quite wild, and often ran away. Each one, therefore, had to be kept in a barn, facing toward a window. The back door of the barn would be latched firmly, and blocked on the outside with millstones and other heavy things. There would also be a deep ditch under the window. If a buffalo broke through and tried to run away, he would fall into the ditch and be caught again.

A Zen monk renounces the world and breaks the bondage of physical and mental attachments. He may pass a number of koans. He may understand the meaning of the scriptures. He may even preach as a teacher. He is like the escaping buffalo. His horns, head, and hoofs are all free, but a tail—some little thing—is caught by something, and he has not yet gained full emancipation. A monk may have been accumulating the gold pieces of meditation for twenty years, yet he might lose them overnight at the beautiful smile of a woman. Others may live together for many seasons as a harmonious Sangha, but a storm of anger may sweep away the peace and make them enemies of each other. Vanity, pride, self-conceit, envy, jealousy, and other emotions—each looks so small that one usually does not notice it. You Zen students talk of delusions and illusions collectively, and may think that you are free from all obstacles to enlightenment. Each of you, however, is forgetting your own tail.

Master Goso saw this fact clearly, and warned his monks with this koan. He said, "Your horns, head, and hoofs are out of the enclosure, but how about that tail?" I can almost see the monks shrinking into themselves like turtles at the words of the master. Humanity is declared quite civilized now. Yet modern anatomy proves that there is still a trace of a tail. No wonder men still fight according to their selfish desires, the same as their cousins from ancient times, the monkeys.

There is a sutra that was translated into Chinese in which a king asks Buddha to interpret a dream. The king dreamed that an elephant escaped from an enclosure. Its nose, ears, body, and feet were out, but the tail was caught by something. The Buddha tells the king, "This dream predicts that monks in later periods may renounce the world, but they will not be able to free themselves from desires, passions, and attachments to fame and glory." Master Goso modified this story to teach his monks. The sutra emphasizes the moral precepts, while the koan warns of the danger of self-certification, both morally and intellectually. There is no enclosure when you are not craving escape. Horns, head, and hoofs—you are not partially out. Your whole body, including the tail, walks freely between heaven and earth.

Some Japanese Zen teachers ask their students about the buffalo that passes through a window. "His horns, his head, and his hoofs have already passed through," say the teachers, "so why can't the tail also pass?" Those teachers are trying to mystify Zen teachings. They do not read the original Chinese carefully. They do not study the derivation of koans from the sutras. They are proclaiming themselves Zen masters, just because they passed several hundred koans in the secret rooms of their teachers. They teach their students in their own secret rooms and produce similar Zen teachers. It is a sort of school for magic and tricks. It has nothing to do with the understanding of Buddha Shakyamuni and Bodhidharma. The whole matter is nothing but a joke. No wonder most Zen teachers in Japan now have wives and children. They drink and smoke, and accumulate money for the comfort of themselves and their families. They certainly have long, bushy tails, like foxes.

MUMON'S COMMENT

If you can open your one eye at this point and say a word of Zen, you are qualified to repay the four obligations, and you will be able to save all sentient beings in the realms beneath you. But if you cannot say such a word, you should turn back to your tail.

The four obligations are to one's parents, to the peacemakers of the land, to all sentient beings, and to the three treasures—Buddha, Dharma, and Sangha. "Turn back to the tail" means to be watchful about desires and passions, and endeavor to keep the moral precepts. When Theravada Buddhists try to advance themselves toward the attainment of Prajna Paramita, true wisdom, and Mahayana Buddhists keep the precepts strictly to emancipate themselves fully, the brilliance of Buddhadharma will illuminate humankind, despite that prediction of Buddha in the old scripture.

MUMON'S VERSE

If the buffalo gets out, he will fall into the trench.
If he turns back, he will be butchered.
That little tail
Is a very strange thing.

The explanation I gave you in the beginning will help you to see the poem clearly. It is a bad dream to think that we have tails, after all. Look and see if you have one.

Case Thirty-nine
Ummon's Off the Track

A monk said to Ummon, "The brilliance of Buddha illuminates the whole universe—" Before he could finish, he was interrupted by the master: "You are quoting the poem of Cho, the candidate, are you not?" The monk answered, "Yes." Then the master said, "You are off the track." More than one hundred years after Ummon's passing, Master Shishin told his students about this and said, "Tell me, monks, at what point did the monk go off the track?"

BODHISATTVAS: Here is the background to this koan. A young scholar paid homage to Sekiso, a Zen master. The master asked, "What is your name?" "I am Setsu, of the Cho family," answered the young man. *Setsu* means "awkwardness." Then the master said, "There is neither absolute skillfulness nor unconditional awkwardness. How can you keep such a name for the rest of your life?" The scholar was fortunate enough to catch a glimpse of the mind-essence at the words of the master. He wrote a poem expressing his attainment. My prose translation of it goes as follows:

"The brilliance of Buddha illuminates the whole universe. Sages and mediocrities, animals and insects, all belong to the same family. If no thought of discrimination arises, the universe is revealed in full. If the six sense organs make even the slightest movement, the clouds of discrimination cover the essence. If one tries to wipe away delusions, one will suffer endlessly. If one tries to reach the essence, one is going in the wrong direction. One should live one's life without hindrances. Enlightenment and delusion, both are illusory flowers in the air."

The young scholar was on his way to take the examination for government service, but first he passed the examination of Zen. His poem was known among the monks as "the poem of Cho, the candidate." Master Sekiso was born in 807 and passed away in 888; Ummon, the master of our koan this evening, was born forty-five years later than the former, and survived him by sixty-one years. The poem was quite popular among the monks of Ummon's time, and it was quoted and evaluated everywhere.

No one knows the motive of the monk who began quoting, "The brilliance of Buddha illuminates the whole universe—." He probably expressed the phrase as his own, or perhaps he was going to ask the master to evaluate the poem. In either case, he was not showing his Zen. Ummon saw this at a glance and interrupted, saying, "You are quoting the poem of Cho, the candidate, are you not?" The monk replied meekly, "Yes," as if he had been caught trying to pass a counterfeit.

Zen words are the treasures of the world. No one can monopolize them. If the monk had been expressing his own Zen, he should have been able to repeat the words without fear. The words may have been similar to those of Cho's, but if they had come from the essence of the monk's mind, they would have been his creation, and no one else's. The monk could have covered Ummon's mouth with his hand before the master finished his question. He had no such Zen alertness, however, but said "Yes," apologetically. Ummon must have been quite disappointed with him. "You are off the track," said the master. Even if the monk had recited the poem with a clearer voice, if he had no Zen, the poem he recited would never be the same as that which Cho, the candidate, had written. How, then, could anyone recognize or evaluate it?

When Sir Henry Irving played Hamlet, I was told, he had nothing to do with Shakespeare. His acting and his words were altogether his own creations. Some said that Ellen Terry's Portia was also performed that way.

I did not attend the plays featuring these two artists, but I saw Margaret Anglin and another actor, whose name slips my memory, and until the curtain fell at the end of the play I never thought of Shakespeare—poor Bill! He was forgotten by everyone, and he would be proud of that. The monk in our koan was like the workers in the talkies.[39] He was probably thinking of the drum that announces dinner, and could not fully concentrate on the Zen poem. In the talkies, I can often hear an imaginary voice alongside the words from the screen, saying something like "How much do we get?" or "When do we eat?" Talkies ought to have a bit of Zen, too.

Shishin, at a later date, asked his monks what was wrong with this student. Our text says, "At what point did that student go off the track?" From the very beginning, Cho, the candidate, was sidetracked when he wrote the poem as a message from the Great Silence. Ummon really meant this when he said, "You are off the track." From the very beginning, the monk should not have mentioned such a poem. Mumon's comment is the answer to Shishin's question.

Mumon's comment

If you recognize Ummon's particular skillfulness, you will know at what point the student was off the track, and you will be a teacher of humans and devas. If not, you cannot even recognize yourself.

Mumon's verse

When a fish meets the fish-hook
If it is greedy, it will be caught.
When its mouth opens
Its life is already lost.

Case Forty
Tipping Over a Water Vessel

Hyakujo wanted to choose a monk to open a new monastery. He told his pupils that whoever could best answer his question would be appointed. Placing a water vessel on the ground, he asked, "Who can say what this is without using its name?" The head monk said, "No one can call it a wooden shoe." Isan, who was the cook monk, kicked over the vessel and went out. Hyakujo smiled and said, "The head monk loses." He appointed Isan to become the master of the new monastery.

BODHISATTVAS: It is impossible to determine the exact date of this event. Isan, the cook in this koan, entered Hyakujo's monastery in 793. He was twenty-three years old, and Master Hyakujo was seventy-four at the time. Twenty-one years later, Hyakujo passed from the world. The date of the event, therefore, must be the early years of the ninth century, in the T'ang dynasty in China.

There was a man named Shiba Zuda who was a traveling psychic. He was a true friend of many monks, often calling at one monastery or another and associating with Zen teachers and their pupils. He told Hyakujo that he had found a good site on a mountain in the state of Tan where a great monastery should be established. He suggested Hyakujo send a good disciple there to start the work. Hyakujo called the head monk and introduced him to Shiba. "Show me how you cough," Shiba said. "Hmmm... now show me how you walk...hmmm...you won't do."

Shiba thus rejected the head monk. Isan, the cook, happened to pass by. "Here is a good one," the traveler said to the master. The head monk was very indignant, and said, "No one can say that the cook is better than the head monk in this monastery." So Hyakujo told his pupils that whoever answered a question most ably would be appointed. Placing a water vessel on the ground, Hyakujo asked, "Who can say what this is without calling its name?" This is not just a question of olden times. This is not only a question for the monks of Hyakujo's monastery.

Alfred, Lord Tennyson sang:

Flower in the crannied wall,
I pluck you out of the crannies,
I hold you here, root and all, in my hand,
Little flower—but if I could understand
What you are, root and all, and all in all,
I should know what God and man is.

Lao-tsu said, "The Tao that can be known is not the changeless Tao. The name that can be spoken is not the changeless name."

A true Zen student knows all in all. He must be able to call the changeless name of the water vessel. What do you think of the head monk's words, "No one can call it a wooden shoe"? Poor potato! He clung to the name. He could not see the essence of things. A Zen monk carries a water vessel to wash his hands before he starts meditation. Sometimes he uses fragrant water and purifies his hands before he sits on the seat of meditation.

The dramatic scene of this koan happened in the living quarters of the master, and his wooden shoes were in front of his seat. The master looked at Isan, the cook. Isan kicked over the vessel with his foot, and went away. He answered the question. He declared what it was without calling its name. He kicked all in all, and exposed the changeless Tao. Hyakujo smiled and said, "The head monk loses." Of course he did. From the very beginning he could not pass the examination of Shiba Zuda, the traveler. He always carried the sign "head monk" pasted on his forehead.

Isan went to the mountain to prepare for the establishment of his monastery. He stayed there many years, with no monks, but only monkeys and rabbits as company. It was in the year 820 C.E. that the monastery of Isan was finally built. Eventually 1,500 monks gathered there to study Zen under his guidance. Just as Rome was not built in a day, that monastery required many years to be established.

MUMON'S COMMENT

Isan was brave enough, but he could not escape Hyakujo's trap. After all, he gave up a light job and took on a heavy one. Can't you see, he took off his comfortable headband and placed himself in an iron yoke.

Isan was a successor of Hyakujo. He was destined to carry the lamp of Dharma through many difficulties. Mumon's comment is praising him somewhat ironically. Zen teachers are hard workers, and they cannot quit the job until all sentient beings are emancipated. I cannot understand why the so-called Zen masters of modern Japan do not take off their comfortable hats and place themselves in iron yokes. They dislike hard jobs; they enjoy staying in the fog of glory and wealth. They smoke. They drink. They accumulate money and treasures. They cling to position. Something is the matter with their feet. Why do they not kick all in all, and expose the nameless name?

MUMON'S VERSE

> *Giving up cooking utensils,*
> *Defeating the chatterbox—*
> *Though his teacher sets a barrier for him*
> *His feet will kick everything over, even the Buddha.*

Case Forty-one
Bodhidharma Pacifies the Mind

Bodhidharma sat facing the wall. His future successor stood in the snow, cut off his arm, and presented it to Bodhidharma. He cried, "My mind is not pacified. Master, please, pacify my mind." Bodhidharma said, "If you bring me your mind, I will pacify it for you." The future successor said, "When I search for my mind, I cannot find it." Bodhidharma said, "There, I have pacified your mind."

BODHISATTVAS: I will tell you the life story of Bodhidharma, according to *The Religion of the Samurai*, by Kaiten Nukariya.[40] The book was published in the early days, before the writings of our Daisetsu Suzuki were well known among English readers. I wish you to read it once, and pay respect to the author as the pioneer scholar of Japanese Zen in Western countries.

In this koan, Mumon condensed the story and dramatized it, to emphasize how Bodhidharma pacified the mind of his disciple. I must tell you, however, the historical details of the story, borrowing from the book and adding my comments here and there. It may help you in your study of the koan.

Bodhidharma came to China from southern India, in 520 C.E. He passed through the South Sea Islands; it took him three years to reach the land of his destination. On the first of October, he met with the emperor of southern China, who was an enthusiastic Buddhist and quite a scholar.

Bodhidharma saw that his Zen was beyond the understanding of the emperor. The elephant, he mused, can hardly keep company with rabbits. The orthodox Buddhism of the emperor could not keep pace with the elephantine stride of Bodhidharma's Zen.

Bodhidharma then left not only the palace of Emperor Wu Ti, but also the kingdom of Liang. Crossing the river Yang-tsu-chiang, he went to the northern Wei. He found a deserted temple, Shao-lin-szu, and stayed there, mostly sitting silently in meditation, with his face to the wall.

On the night of November 9 of that year, there came a learned man, Shen-kuang by name, for the purpose of solving a problem that troubled him greatly. He was far from being one of those half-hearted visitors who knock at the door of a teacher only out of curiosity. But the silent master was cautious enough to try the sincerity of the newcomer before admitting him. Shen-kuang was not allowed to enter the temple, and had to stand in the courtyard, deep with snow. His firm resolution and earnest wish kept him standing continually in one spot until dawn, beads of frozen teardrops on his breast. At last, with a sharp knife he cut off his left arm and presented it, showing his resolution to follow the master even at the risk of his life. Thereupon, Bodhidharma admitted him into the order as a disciple, fully qualified to be instructed in the teaching of Zen. A new name was given to the disciple by the master. It was Huiko, which is pronounced Eka by the Japanese.

Huiko said to the master, perhaps with a sigh, "I have no peace of mind. Might I ask you, sir, to pacify my mind?" Bodhidharma answered him, "Bring the mind that troubles you so much here before me, right this minute. I shall pacify it." Huiko said, "It is impossible for me to find my troubled mind." The teacher exclaimed, "There, I have pacified your mind." The disciple was instantly enlightened. Bodhidharma had a few other disciples, but Huiko was the one who received the bowl and the robe from him, becoming the second patriarch of Chinese Zen.

Let us look at our koan of this evening again, and see how we can pacify our minds.

Buddha told Subhuti in the *Diamond Sutra*, "Subhuti, thoughts of the past cannot be grasped, thoughts of the present cannot be grasped, and thoughts of the future cannot be grasped." In his *Manual of Zen Buddhism*, Suzuki said the word "thoughts" is a translation of the Sanskrit word *citta*. He wrote, "*Citta* stands for both mind and thought. The idea expressed here is that there is no particularly determined entity in us which is psychologically designated as mind or thought. The moment we think we have taken hold of a thought, it is no more with us. So with the idea of a soul, or an ego, or a being, or a person, there is no such particular entity objectively to be so distinguished, and which remains as such eternally separated from the subject who so thinks. This ungraspability of a mind or thought, which is tantamount to saying that there is no soul-substance as a solitary, unrelated 'thing' in the recesses of consciousness, is one of the basic doctrines of Buddhism, Mahayana and Hinayana."[41]

Huiko must have studied the *Diamond Sutra*, but he had never understood the words of Buddha to describe his own case until Bodhidharma actually cornered him. He was brave enough to cut off his left arm, but he did not have the nerve to use the knife upon his own mind and thought. Bodhidharma said, "Bring the mind that troubles you so much here before me, right this minute." He was like a good surgeon, who uses his knife as quick as a flash. He said, "There, I have pacified your mind." The operation was finished before the nurse could give any anesthetic to the patient. Who was sick? What was the trouble? It was merely illusory; unreal. Your mind is already pacified.

Mumon's comment

That broken-toothed old Hindu, Bodhidharma, came thousands of miles across the sea from India to China as if he had something wonderful. It can be said that he was raising waves where there was no wind. Although he remained for years in China, he only had one successor, and that one lost his arm and was deformed. Ever since he has had fools for disciples.

Bodhidharma came to China when he was 150 years old. He stayed in the Shao-lin monastery for nine years, and then he passed from the world. Nukariya writes, "He came to China to introduce his Zen, not the dead scriptures, as was repeatedly done before him, but a living Buddha-Hridaya, Buddha's mind. He was very severe to his disciples as well as to himself. He would not smile at every face, as modern ministers do, but would stare with large glaring eyes that penetrated to the innerliness of the man. He was entirely indifferent to his apparel being always clad in a faded yellow robe. He would sit as silent as a bear, and kick one off, if one should approach him with idle questions. Bodhidharma's method of instruction was entirely different from that of ordinary instructors of learning. He would not explain any problem to the student, but simply help him to get enlightened by putting him an abrupt but telling question."

Mumon also describes the quaintness of his ancient master, but he really means to praise him. Those "queer birds," the Zen masters, struggled for their existence, generation after generation, carrying the teaching among a few monks, distinguishing themselves from ordinary earthworms. Yet they did not do anything more than uncover the truth, and they rather discouraged wise thinking and smart chattering. They were certainly deformed and brainless disciples.

MUMON'S VERSE

> *Why did Bodhidharma come to China?*
> *For years monks have wrestled with this.*
> *All the troubles ever since*
> *Are due to that teacher and his disciple.*

Case Forty-two
The Woman Comes Out from Meditation

BODHISATTVAS: For this case, I shall weave my comments into the text. *In the time of Buddha Shakyamuni, Manjushri,* who was thus named for his attainment of great wisdom, *went to an assembly of buddhas.* According to a sutra, the assembly was held in the land of another buddha. Buddha Shakyamuni went there, and his disciple, Manjushri, followed him. Manjushri was not allowed to enter the hall, as he had not enough compassion to balance his wisdom. He tried his best to accomplish his virtue, and went back there again. *When he arrived there the conference was over, and all the buddhas* except his teacher, Shakyamuni, *had returned to their own buddha-lands. Only a young woman remained, sitting in deep meditation. Manjushri asked Buddha Shakyamuni how it was possible for this young woman to reach a state that even he could not attain. "Bring her out from samadhi and ask her yourself," said the Buddha. Manjushri walked around the young woman three times and snapped his fingers. She still remained in meditation. So with his miraculous powers, Manjushri transported her to a high heaven. He tried his best to bring her out, but in vain.* A true meditation embraces all heavens. There would be no difference whether she was in the land of a buddha or in a heaven. *Buddha Shakyamuni said, "Even a hundred thousand Manjushris would not be able to bring her out from samadhi. But below this place, past twelve hundred million lands, is the bodhisattva Momyo ("Seed of Delusion"). If he comes here, she will come out."* No sooner had the

Buddha spoken than that bodhisattva sprang up from the earth and bowed,
paying homage to the Buddha, who directed him to rouse the young woman.
The bodhisattva went in front of her and snapped his fingers, and instantly
she was roused from her deep meditation.

The story of this koan was reproduced from a sutra that exists only in
two translations, Chinese and Tibetan. Japanese read the name of this
sutra *Sho Butsu Yo Ji Ko,* while Chinese call it *Chu Fo Yao Chi Ching.* The
sutra was translated by Dharmaraksha, who lived from 266 to 313 C.E. In
Mumon's time it was one of the most popular readings among the monks,
giving them a dramatic thrill. Mumon changed the story to express his
Zen. He was not as faithful to the original as Charles Lamb was in writing tales from Shakespeare.

The original sutra named the bodhisattva who came out of the earth
"Pure White Bodhisattva," but Mumon changed it to Momyo, "Seed of
Delusion." Here you can see the creative art of Mumon's Zen. One comes
out from deep meditation to save all sentient beings. One moves with
sympathy and grief for the delusions of other beings, and wishes to save
them from their endless suffering. This koan simply emphasizes the noble
power of compassion, which must go hand in hand with great wisdom.
The sutra named him "Pure White" because true buddhahood must have
a balance of spotless wisdom and colorless compassion. Both the sutra and
Mumon abused Manjushri too severely.

MUMON'S COMMENT

Old Shakyamuni put on a very poor theater piece. I want to ask you monks
why Manjushri, who was supposed to be the teacher of seven buddhas,
could not bring this young woman out of meditation, and why a bod-
hisattva who was a mere beginner could do it. If you understand this inti-
mately, you yourself can enter samadhi while living in the world of
delusion.

Buddhism is a religion of enlightenment. Therefore, wisdom is self-salvation. Manjushri, the symbol of wisdom, is for this reason called the teacher of all the buddhas. Buddha Shakyamuni used to speak about seven buddhas before him, using that number to represent countless buddhas of the past. Momyo, "Seed of Delusion," was an innocent bodhisattva, like a child in kindergarten. Mumon, therefore, calls him a mere beginner.

MUMON'S VERSE

> *One could not awaken her, the other could.*
> *Neither was a good actor.*
> *One wore a god-mask, one a devil-mask.*
> *Had both failed, the drama would still be a comedy.*

Manjushri appeared on the stage wearing a god-mask, and succeeded in playing the part of a failure, while Momyo in the devil-mask won applause for his acting. Until all sentient beings are enlightened, comedy or melodrama will be a failure, notwithstanding the combined work of the old sutra and Mumon, the author of this koan. This is the answer to Manjushri's question about why the young woman was able to enter into such a deep meditation in the land of a buddha.

Case Forty-three
Shuzan's Short Staff

Shuzan held out his short staff and said, "If you call this a short staff, you oppose its reality. If you do not call it a short staff, you ignore the fact. Now, what will you call it?"

BODHISATTVAS: Shuzan Shonen, 926–993 C.E., was a successor of Fuketsu Ensho. Do you remember the master of the windy hole in the twenty-fourth koan? Shuzan, our teacher of this evening, is the monk who received the lamp of Dharma from the master of humbleness and poverty. Shuzan Shonen is the fifteenth ancestor after Bodhidharma.

Zen teachers carry a short staff called a *shippei* while preaching to the monks or giving them personal guidance. It is like the rod of a school-teacher with which she points to a map or to the writing on a blackboard. Since Zen has nothing to point out, Zen teachers use the staff to strike their monks' shoulders. A shippei is a short bow-shaped stick made of two pieces of bamboo, usually an inch-and-a-half wide by fifteen inches long, tied firmly with rattan. Its shape is like that of a stringless bow or an Australian boomerang. Originally it was used in the Chinese Imperial Court to punish misdemeanors. Japanese children use two fingers, index and middle, to punish the loser of a game. That action is also called "shippei."

Master Shuzan held out his shippei and said, "Now, monks, tell me, what is this? If you call it a shippei, you oppose its reality. If you do not call it a shippei, you ignore the fact. What will you call it?" You can see the glaring eyes of the master, and also visualize the uncomprehending faces of the dumbfounded monks. This is not a typical schoolroom. We are not playing a child's game. It does not matter whether one holds out a shippei or any other kind of staff. This iron *nyoi*[42] would do just as well as the shippei. Now tell me what this is, without opposing the reality, without ignoring the fact. This is your koan for the evening.

H.G. Wells said, "The forceps of mind were clumsy forceps and crushed the truth a little when grasping it." I admire the keen observation of Wells. He knows that the grasping mind is the main trouble, worse than empty verbalism. He only needs a touch of Zen.

Forty years ago I was working on this koan under the master of a neighboring monastery. Our teacher was absent at the time. I entered the sanzen room, and saw a very stout monk sitting cross-legged like a stone buddha. He put the shippei on his thighs, holding it with two hands. He was old, and quite hard of hearing. He said, "Come near me and repeat your koan." I approached him and did so. Before I could finish speaking, he struck me with the shippei and rang the bell, chasing me out of the room. The next time, as soon as I finished my bows, I jumped on him and seized his shippei. Before I presumed to strike him with the captured staff, he shrieked, "Ouch, you hurt me," and rang the bell again, so I had to "beat it."

Mumon, in his comment on this koan and in his poem, is drawing feet on a snake, but I will read them:

Mumon's comment

If you call this a short staff, you oppose its reality. If you do not call it a short staff, you ignore the fact. It cannot be expressed with words and it cannot be expressed without words. Now, tell me at once: What is it?

Mumon's verse

Holding up his short staff
He gave an order to kill and to give life.
When positive and negative interweave,
Even buddhas and patriarchs cannot escape this attack.

Case Forty-four
Basho's Staff

Basho said to his disciples, "If you have a staff, I will give it to you. If you have no staff, I will take it away from you."

BODHISATTVAS: This Basho is not the *hokku*[43] poet of Japan. He was a native of Korea and preached in Eishu, China, in the T'ang dynasty, some ten centuries before the poet of the same name. The mountain where the monastery was established was called Basho, "Banana Tree." Probably it was named so on account of the trees that grew there. The hokku poet of that name was very fond of banana trees. He had them in his garden, and he took the name as his *nom de plume*. Of course bananas have nothing to do with this koan.

The staff in the last koan was short, but the one mentioned here is quite long—a sort of alpenstock for a Zen monk. One carries it when climbing mountains, and keeps it even in one's home temple, as a souvenir. It is called a *shujosu*, and is often used as a symbol of Zen. Ummon said, "My shujosu turned into a dragon and swallowed the whole universe" [Case Sixty of the *Blue Rock Collection*]. Such a trick is not a big surprise for American Zen students. Why, one of you picked up Ummon's shujosu on the cashier's counter of the cafeteria and seized it with your teeth! Tai-I Botetsu said, "If you have a shujosu, I will take it from you. If you have no shujosu, I will give it to you." His meaning was, "If you have Zen, I will take it from you. If you have no Zen, I will give it to you."

Our koan expresses this in reverse. "If you have a staff, I will give it to you. If you have no staff, I will take it from you." You might interpret the words as follows: "If you have Zen, I will give you more of it. You can never have too much of it. If you have no Zen, what is the use of giving it to you? I will take away the Zen that I intended to give you." I am not satisfied with such interpretations. You cannot give others your Zen. You cannot take Zen from others. My Zen is mine, and never will be yours. You have to dig deep down into your own inner being and flush your Zen up from the bottom of the gash.

In Matthew 13:12 there is a similar expression, "For whosoever hath, to him shall be given, and he shall have more in abundance; but whosoever hath not, from him shall be taken away even that which he hath." This koan aims at Zen realization, not the mysteries of the kingdom of heaven. Our age's so-called civilization has forgotten the true meaning of the scriptures, and interprets the words according to its own selfish desires. Nations that have in abundance want more and more, and countries that have not enough are losing even what they have. If you show the full moon to a hungry child, he will take it for a hot cake; what can you do with the poor fellow?

MUMON'S COMMENT

When there is no bridge over the river, the staff will help me cross. When I return to my village on a moonless night, the staff will accompany me. But if you call this a staff, you will enter hell with the speed of an arrow.

Zen can be a helpful companion on the dark side of life, or on the verge of dangerous curves. Mumon described it beautifully. He then warned Zen students. The nobility of Zen is its hidden power. If its merits are too openly exposed, it will be so ugly that Buddha Shakyamuni and Bodhidharma cannot look at it squarely. It is a pity to have any association with churches and cathedrals. Properly speaking, they are in opposition to Zen in every respect. There should be no bishops or archbishops in Zen. They all carry clumsy old sticks that were never used to climb mountains, but are merely symbolic imitations. They have no shujosu. They have no Zen. If Basho were alive today he would again say, "If you have no staff, I will take it away from you." They will, as Mumon said, enter hell like an arrow, no doubt about it. You are chosen as Zen students. You have shujosu in your hands. Strive constantly, and keep the lamp of Dharma burning in this zendo. Let Basho repeat, from his deep meditation, "When you have a staff, I will give it to you." This is my sincere wish to you in this seclusion in memory of Bodhidharma. Three days of the week have passed already; precious opportunity has gone forever. You must not waste any more of your days. Make what remains of them your golden epoch of Zen meditation.

MUMON'S VERSE

With this staff in my hand
I can measure the depths and shallows everywhere.
The staff supports the heavens, and makes firm the earth.
Wherever it goes, the true teaching is spread.

Case Forty-five
Who Is It?

The patriarch of the Eastern Mountain, Master Hoen, said, "Shakya-muni Buddha and Maitreya Buddha are both servants of that one. Now tell me, who is it?"

BODHISATTVAS: The master in this koan is Goso Hoen, the same as in the thirty-fifth koan, "Two Souls," the thirty-sixth, "Meeting a Master on the Road," and the thirty-eighth, "A Buffalo Passes through an Enclosure."

The mountain where the Fifth Patriarch lived was called Gosozan or Tozan. The latter means "Eastern Mountain," and the former "The Mountain of the Fifth Patriarch." Maitreya is the future Buddha, who will appear in the world five billion six hundred seventy million years after the death of Buddha Shakyamuni.

All Zen questions ask for buddha-nature, and nothing else. All answers must come, therefore, directly from it, that is to say, from the inner being of one's own self. Buddha means accomplishment of wisdom and virtue, and is not the proper name of an individual. The term should be understood objectively, as it is an ideal that is common to each of us. A true Buddhist, especially a Zen student, must first of all crush the idea of God, personal or non-personal. You have no Zen unless your mind turns within and examines itself. You cannot postulate even the shadow of a single hair in front of your mind-mirror. Just shake off all kinds of ideas, and meet that one within you. That one is the master of all masters. Shakyamuni and Maitreya are the servants of that one.

Two years ago I drew up my will, and left you my last words. I said, "Friends in Dhamma, be satisfied with your own heads. Do not put any false heads above your own. Then, minute after minute, watch your step closely. Those are my last words to you." I still insist these words be my last will. The head of each one of you is the noblest thing in the whole universe. No god, no buddha, no sage, no master can reign over it. Rinzai said, "If you are the master of your own situation, wherever you stand is the land of truth." How many of our fellow beings can prove the truthfulness of Rinzai's words through their actions?

Henri Bergson said, "The spectacle of what religions have been in the past, of what certain religions still are today, is indeed humiliating for human intelligence. What a farrago of error and folly! Experience may indeed say, 'That is false' and reasoning 'That is absurd.' Humanity only clings all the more to that absurdity and that error. *Homo Sapiens*, the only creature endowed with reason, is also the only creature to pin its existence to things unreasonable."

You see, this Frenchman was quite indignant with those who put false heads above their own. Bodhisattvas, you are the only group in the Western lands to show this French philosopher how to shut his mouth. But to do so, you must live in Zen. To live in Zen, you must watch your step closely, minute after minute. As I have always told you, you should be mindful of your feet, not of your head or chest, in your meditation as well as in your everyday life. Keep your head cool and your feet warm. Do not let your sentiments sweep you off your feet. This means that you should forget about your lungs and only be conscious of your feet while breathing. The head is the sacred part of your body. Let it do its own work, but do not make any "monkey business" with it. The master in this koan asks you, "Shakyamuni Buddha and Maitreya Buddha are both servants of that one. Who is it?" Just stamp your feet and tell me who that one is.

MUMON'S COMMENT

If you realize clearly who that one is, it is like meeting your own father on a busy street. There is no need to ask anyone whether or not your recognition is correct.

Do you remember the baby we kept here every afternoon during the springtime of this year? I took care of him while his mother taught school in the neighborhood. That little fellow seemed to take his fingers as something else, not his own. He used to suck them in the same way as he did the rubber nipple on his milk bottle. He was then only four months old. The other day, his mother sent me his picture from Japan. He is now a full year old. I suppose he has discovered that his fingers are his own by this time.

MUMON'S VERSE

> *Do not fight with another's bow and arrow.*
> *Do not ride another's horse.*
> *Do not discuss another's faults.*
> *Do not meddle in another's business.*

The founder of a religion does not suggest that others worship him. He worships God or Allah and expects others to do the same. Then the foolish followers begin to worship the founder. The foxy preachers pretend that they themselves are the agents of either the founder, or of a Supreme Being. They don't know how to turn their own minds within and examine them.

Case Forty-six
Proceed from the Top of the Pole

Sekiso asked, "How will you proceed on from the top of a hundred-foot pole?" Another Zen teacher said, "One who sits on the top of a hundred-foot pole has attained something, but is still not handling Zen freely. One should proceed on from there and manifest one's whole body throughout the ten directions."

BODHISATTVAS: Mumon brings forth two Zen teachers in this koan: Sekiso and another Zen teacher, Chosha Keishin, who lived in the early part of the ninth century, T'ang dynasty. There are seven monks named Sekiso in the history of Chinese Zen, and no one knows which Sekiso it is who appears in this koan. Sekiso means "Frost on a Stone." I say, it's just as well to sweep away the name and the saying altogether from this koan. Mumon repeats the same question in his comment, and it seems better situated there than in the koan.

If I were to rewrite the koan, it would be like this:
Chosha Keishin showed his poem to a disciple:

> *One who sits on the top of a hundred-foot pole*
> *Has attained Zen partially, not in whole.*
> *One should proceed on from there,*
> *For the universe is one's own real body.*

A Chinese acrobat climbs up a hundred-foot pole and at the top does all sorts of stunts. Some Zen monks have been watching the act, their mouths hanging open foolishly. A monk who has attained something may think reaching the top of a hundred-foot pole is like getting to the goal in a modern athletic game.

A monk asked Nansen, "When one has reached the top of a hundred-foot pole, then where should one go?" Nansen said, "Proceed on, one more step." Tosetsu said, "One should aim to reach the top of a hundred-foot pole in one's meditation." Tosetsu, in this statement, is like modern Zen teachers in Japan who give a koan as an object of Zen. When a monk passes a certain number of koans, he might consider that he has reached the top of a hundred-foot pole, and he might ask the teacher the same question as that monk of olden times asked of Nansen: "When one reaches the top of a hundred-foot pole, then where should one go?" A poor teacher might say, "You are a graduate of Zen. You can teach others now." Such a teacher can thus produce an acrobat but not even a single Zen student (much less a teacher). Nansen's answer was, "Proceed on, one more step." Our koan of this evening tries to illustrate the words of Nansen.

Chosha Keishin was a disciple of Nansen. He showed the poem that I have quoted above to a monk who asked, "How can one proceed on from the top?" Chosha Keishin answered, "The mountain in Lang Chou and the water in Li Chou." The monk did not understand, and said, "Please tell me again." The master said, "Four seas and five lakes are under the reign of the emperor." I could change the expression "the mountain in Lang Chou and the water in Li Chou" to "the hills of San Francisco and the bridges of Portland." Instead of "Four seas and five lakes are under the reign of the emperor," I would say, "This is a free country. You can go wherever you wish. No one will hinder you."

Mumon changed the last line of Chosha Keishin's poem, saying, "One should proceed on from there and manifest one's whole body throughout the ten directions." I prefer the original phrase: "One should proceed on from there, for the universe is one's own real body." In fact, there is no such pole of Zen measuring one hundred feet, or any specific height. Like a magician from India, you can extend your own rope and climb up it or come down along it. Since the whole universe is your own real body, there are no ups and downs after all. You seek wisdom higher and higher, but your influence of loving-kindness should be wider and wider. You come to this zendo to meditate. After you finish your meditation, next you will have your tea. After the third cup, you will go home. Now, are you thus proceeding or retreating on the road of Zen?

MUMON'S COMMENT

If you step forth and turn your body freely about, you will be worthy of respect. I want to ask you monks, however: How will you proceed on from the top of that pole?

MUMON'S VERSE

> *One who lacks the third eye of insight*
> *Will cling to the measure of one hundred feet.*
> *Such a one will jump from there and be killed,*
> *A blind person leading the blind.*

The old-timers in a religious group consider themselves to have reached the top, and then jump from where they are, leaving the very principles of that religion. They are poor fish who cannot swim in the water.

Case Forty-seven
The Three Barriers of Tosotsu

Tosotsu erected three barriers and made the monks pass through them. The first is, in studying Zen, the aim is to see your own true nature. Now, where is your true nature? Secondly, when you realize your own true nature, you will be free from birth and death. Now, when the light is gone from your eyes and you become a corpse, how can you free yourself? Thirdly, when you free yourself from birth and death, you should know where you are. Now your body separates into the four elements. At this moment, where are you?

BODHISATTVAS: All koans in the *Gateless Gate* deal with one's own true nature. They begin with Joshu's "Mu." Gutei's finger, Zuigan's inner master, the Sixth Patriarch's true self, and Bodhidharma's pacified mind— each leads the student directly into the region of buddha-nature. Anyone who has experienced turning inwardly can actualize the same, with ease, at any time. It is not confined in a thing; therefore, it will be discovered in everything. It is not excluded from a place; therefore it will be exposed at any place. The first barrier of Tosotsu is, "Now, where is your true nature?" At the moment of your hesitation, you are far away from it, ten thousand miles afar.

The second barrier of Tosotsu is, "When you realize your own true nature, you will be free from birth and death. Now, when the light is gone from your eyes and you become a corpse, how can you free yourself?"

Kukai, a ninth-century Japanese Shingon monk, said, "When death comes, I am not there. While I am here, death cannot claim me. Why should I be afraid of death?" The statement is quite logical. Dualistic consciousness and death have no opportunity to meet each other. People simply fear death due to their habit of dualistic thinking. In fact, they are threatened by the idea of death, not by death itself.

Dogen, a thirteenth-century Japanese Soto teacher, said, "In the region of buddha-nature, there is no birth, and accordingly, there is no death. Life never begins; therefore, it never ends. Birth and death are simply psychological demarcations." This is my free translation. In this koan of Tosotsu, to pass through the second barrier, you must eliminate not only the fear of death, but death itself, birth itself. Some of you come to sanzen and show me your own last moment, shutting your eyes and playing a corpse. You are dead, sure enough, but where is your buddha-nature? Until you can prove yourself in real freedom beyond birth and death, you are just a bad actor, after all.

The third barrier: "When you free yourself from birth and death, you should know where you are. Now your body separates into the four elements. At this moment, where are you?" Some of you stretch your arms and legs out on the floor. I never blame the manner in which you present your koan in sanzen, as long as you express Zen from the bottom of your heart. If you mean, however, to indicate the four elements—earth, water, fire, and air—by means of such acrobatic stunts, you simply make me laugh. To represent the elements of modern chemistry, your fingers and toes are not enough, in any case. Now what are you going to do? A good physician knows about the health of a patient's blood from a glance at the face, even before laboratory work is done. Now show me the four elements, which move on as vividly as the ebb and surge of the sea of buddha-nature.

MUMON'S COMMENT

If you can pass these three barriers, you will be a master wherever you are. Whatever happens around you will be nothing but the essence of Zen. Otherwise, you will be living on poor food, and will not have enough of it to satisfy yourself.

Years ago, a Japanese woman worked on this koan. She worked hard, day and night. At the end of the third seclusion, she came to sanzen and expressed her Zen in silence, folding her hands, palm to palm. I said, "The first barrier is passed. How about the second barrier?" She kept herself in the same pose. I said, "Come on, now, tell me, when the light is gone from your eyes and you become a corpse, how can you free yourself?" She went on in the same pose, folding her hands palm to palm. I said, "You are quite stubborn. Never mind the second barrier. How about the third? Now your body separates into the four elements. Where are you?" She did not change her pose at all. I said, "Come on, come on, where are you?" She still stood, folding her hands palm to palm, without a word. I said, "Such monotonous Zen! What is the use of it? Get out." Before I rang the bell to call the next student, she bowed to me and got out of the last barrier gracefully. I know it is useless to bring up a canceled check here. I only wanted to suggest to you that the answer in Zen is not necessarily shown by gesture, or by words. When one can master oneself wherever one stands, one can turn whatever happens into true and living Zen. Of course I am not praising stubbornness or uniformity at all.

Case Forty-eight
One Path of Kempo

A Zen pupil asked Kempo, "All buddhas in the ten directions enter the one Path to nirvana; where does that Path begin?" Kempo, raising his walking stick and drawing the figure "one" in the air, said, "Here it is."

The pupil went to Ummon and asked the same question. Ummon, who happened to have a fan in his hand, said, "This fan will reach the thirty-third heaven and hit the nose of the presiding deity there. It is like the dragon carp of the Eastern Sea, tipping over a rain cloud with its tail."

BODHISATTVAS: Kempo, the master of this koan, was a disciple of Tozan Ryokai, the founder of the Soto school. His biography is not known by scholars of Zen history, but this koan alone made him famous among the monks of his time. Mumon lectured about this koan 327 years after the master's death, and put it as the last of his forty-eight koans of the *Gateless Gate*. I do not think, however, that it is particularly profound, in comparison with the others. Its most admirable point is to present a very common question in Zen, "Where does the Path begin?" Do you remember what was said in the *Shinjinmei*?[44]

> In being "not two," all is the same,
> All that is comprehended in it;
> The wise in the ten quarters,
> They all enter into this absolute Reason.

Yes, the wise in the ten quarters know because they are the wise, but there are millions of the "not-wise" who must ask the question, "Where does the Path begin?" Modern German scholars classify our knowledge into three divisions:

1. *Arbeitswissen*, scientific knowledge. It is also called *Leistungswissen*. We know that we must go along with this knowledge because it is practical and profitable for us.

2. *Bildungswissen*, philosophical knowledge. With this knowledge we convince ourselves that all sentient beings have the same nature. Cornered by logic, we surrender ourselves within the limits of cognition. The monk in this koan knows clearly, "all buddhas in the ten directions enter the one Path to nirvana," because it is very comfortable to think that way; that is, his scientific knowledge, or Arbeitswissen, or Leistungswissen, can allow for the statement. Furthermore, his philosophical knowledge admits that the statement is theoretically correct. He is correlating his idea with his Bildungswissen. But the poor fellow has never experienced entering the one Path to nirvana. Therefore, he is still an outsider, and wonders, "Where does that Path begin?"

3. *Erlosungswissen*, knowledge of emancipation. With this knowledge we can throw off all unnecessary burdens from our minds and feel lighter and happier. Kempo, raising his walking stick and drawing the figure "one" in the air, said, "Here it is." The walking stick had nothing to do with it, after all. The figure "one" is even a nuisance. Look! I say. Here it is.

This pupil of Kempo then went to Master Ummon and asked the same question. Ummon, who happened to have a fan in his hand, said, "This fan will reach the thirty-third heaven and hit the nose of the presiding deity there. It is like the dragon carp of the Eastern Sea tipping over a rain cloud with its tail." Poor monk! I do not think that even then he realized the entrance to the Path. The poor devil was certainly "up against it"; therefore, he asked for a loan. Ummon tinkled the gold pieces in his pocket, but had no wish to give a loan. If I had been the monk, I would have covered my nose with my hand and said, "Master, you hit me too hard. Please tell your fish to behave in the monastery."

MUMON'S COMMENT

One teacher enters the deepest sea, scratches the earth, and raises dust. The other goes to the highest mountain and raises waves that almost touch the heavens. One holds fast, the other lets go. Each supports the profound teaching with a single hand. Kempo and Ummon are like riders, neither of whom can pass the other. It is very difficult to find the perfect person. Frankly, neither of them knows where the Path begins.

Here is another clown who disturbs the magic performance and nevertheless makes the show go on. Not only Kempo and Ummon, but also Mumon himself does not know where the Path starts. Buddha Shakyamuni and Bodhidharma do not know the Path; if they did, they would be neither Buddha nor Patriarch.

MUMON'S VERSE

Before the first step is taken, the goal is reached.
Before the tongue moves, the speech is finished.
More than brilliant intuition is needed
To find the origin of the right Path.

Amban's Addition

The text that Saladin Reps and I translated and published in 1934 has Amban's Addition as the last chapter. Let me read it for you.

Amban, a lay Zen student, said, "Mumon has just published forty-eight koans and called the book the Gateless Gate. *He criticizes the old patriarchs' words and actions. I think he is very mischievous. He is like an old doughnut seller grabbing customers and forcing doughnuts into their mouths until they can neither swallow nor spit them out. Mumon has annoyed everyone enough, so I think I shall add one more as a bargain. I wonder if he himself can eat this bargain. If he can eat it in one bite, and digest it well, it will be fine, but if not, we will have to put it back into the frying pan with his forty-eight, and cook them again. Mumon, you eat first, before someone else does."*

BODHISATTVAS: Amban was a high official in the Imperial Court of the later Sung dynasty. He was also a man of letters, and wrote sixty books. His Zen, however, was the work of a mere amateur. These remarks are nothing but an imitation of Mumon's way of "knocking down." In Japan, a modest mother complains to her visitor that her boy is not as smart as she might have wished. She knows in fact that the boy is quite smart, and she admires him in her heart. She would refrain from saying so to her visitor. If the visitor takes the words of the mother and offers her his condolences, what do you think would be the result? Never again would he be welcomed into her home. Zen aims at harmony in life. One raps and the other soothes, and the whole affair becomes peaceful.

Monks have no monopoly on Zen. Zen belongs to the world. Laymen and laywomen adherents should study Zen—even children in kindergarten should be trained in the Zen way. The shrubs and grasses around this humble house also study Zen. They show the color of Zen through their own natural green. In fact, they are better Zen students than this Amban person who imitates a Zen master and loves to preach Zen; he does not belong to the real Sangha at all. Zen monks are like street cleaners. They do their work so that others can go their different ways. In Japan these days the work of giving Zen lectures and receiving sanzen is considered honorable. It shows that true Zen is disappearing from the country. There are many Ambans giving lectures on Zen or writing Zen essays. They carry on their own work besides, in their particular fields of politics, economics, or industry. True monks who guard the lamp of Dharma are becoming fewer and fewer. It is like issuing too much currency or minting too many coins with no consideration for the real wealth of a nation. There was an old saying in Europe, "Children should be seen, but not heard." I must say the same thing about Zen in the world. Those who digest Zen well should do their work in the world without displaying any trace of Zen. Zen should be preserved among those who love silence more than anything else, yet break that golden lock whenever the world badly needs the teaching.

All religions are corrupted after the death of their founders because of two kinds of followers: the clergy and worldly lecturers. My teacher gave me strict orders not to speak on Zen, but just to live in it and then die in this foreign land, like a mushroom on an unknown mountain.

Amban should have used the very best of his flowery language to praise Mumon for being the wonderful Zen teacher he was. That would have fixed the chattering monk for good. But Amban thought he, too, could reproduce a koan, setting forth one from the *Saddharma-pundarika*

Sutra and then making a comment. There is nothing wrong with that, but nothing good either. Let me read them for you and be finished with them!

THE KOAN

Buddha, according to a sutra, once said, "Stop, stop. Do not speak. The ultimate truth is not even to think."

AMBAN'S COMMENT

Where did that so-called teaching come from? How is it that one could not even think of it? Suppose someone did speak about it—then what became of it? Buddha himself was a great chatterbox, and in this sutra he contradicted himself. This is why people like Mumon appeared later in China, making their useless doughnuts and annoying people. What shall we do after all? I will show you. (Amban puts his palms together.) "Stop, stop. Do not speak. The ultimate truth is not even to think." And now I will make a little circle on the sutra with my finger, and declare that five thousand other sutras and Vimalakirti's gateless gate are all here!

AMBAN'S VERSE

If anyone tells you fire is light,
Pay no attention.
When two thieves meet, they need no introduction.
Unquestionably they recognize each other.

In giving you some talks on Zen, I have no desire to get followers for this dirty job, but to have you digest what I have said and apply the wisdom in your everyday life, with no stink of Zen. This is the only way in which you can be worthy of having the *Gateless Gate* in your home for the rest of your life.

This series of lectures was started on September 21, 1937, and finishes this evening, July 6, 1939. Upasika Chogetsu typed the original copy, and Upasaka Dairin and Upasika Keirin made the distributing copies from the first copy. The copies are scattered in San Francisco, Oakland, and in Los Angeles, and also in Dayton, Ohio; Houston, Texas; and Honolulu, Hawaii. In Japan, my two brother monks, Sohaku Ogata and Soen Nakagawa, have copies. My crude English was polished by Upasakas Zoso, Dairin, Yuzan, and other Zen friends in the Sufi group. In the Zen home of Tetsugen and Gyokugan the copies were reproduced and distributed among their friends. Before I finished the last chapter, I had to repeat the former parts all over again for the newcomers. That is one of the reasons why the work was delayed. Upasika Kindo attended every lecture from beginning to end, keeping up her sanzen during the process. In the Japanese group, Upasaka Hakukan and Upasika Shubin [Tanahashi] kept up their sanzen, using koans from the *Gateless Gate*. These students encouraged me a great deal.

The Chinese and Japanese publications of the *Gateless Gate* contain the following articles in addition to what we have translated: the Three Gates of Oryu, with Comments in Verse by Muryo Soju; the Motto of Zen by Mumon; the Last Remarks of Mumon; a Preface by Shuan Chinken; a Letter to the Emperor [Riso, of the Southern Sung dynasty] by Mumon; and an Epilogue by Mokyo.

Among them, I plan to translate the Three Gates of Oryo with Comments in Verse by Muryo Soju, and the Motto of Zen by Mumon, each as an independent article. You may consider them as a supplement to this series if you like. As for the rest of them, I do not see any necessity for translating them.

Our Kato-san cooked udon, Japanese noodles, for us this evening. Let us invite Master Mumon to our party in the tearoom. I recited a *dharani* to express our thanks to Mumon for his teaching.

September 21, 1937–July 6, 1939

PART II
COMMENTARIES ON
THE *BLUE ROCK COLLECTION*

Case One
I Know Not

Emperor Wu-tei asked Bodhidharma, "What is the first principle of the holy teaching?" Bodhidharma answered, "In the boundless universe there exists nothing to be called 'holy.'"

The emperor then asked, "Then whom am I facing?" ("Are you not a holy man?")

Bodhidharma replied: "I know not." The emperor could not understand the patriarch. Bodhidharma then crossed the Great River and went to another empire of Wei.

Afterward, Emperor Wu-tei told the anecdote to Shiko, one of the Buddhist scholars of the court. Shiko asked the emperor, "Did His Majesty know that person or not?" The emperor replied, "I know not." (The same words Bodhidharma had used, but with quite a different meaning.) *Shiko told him, "That was Avalokiteshvara, who carries the seal of the Buddha-Mind!" The emperor then very much regretted the incident, and wanted to send a messenger to call Bodhidharma back to his realm. Shiko informed him, "Please do not do so, Your Majesty. Even if all the people of our country were to go after him, he would not return."*

SETCHO'S VERSE

Boundless universe,
Nothing "holy."
Then who knows the true thing?
"I know not!"
Slipping out from the palace
He crossed the Great River;
This caused all kinds of trouble.
All the people of the country
Would go after him in vain.
In vain! From ancient to modern times
The regret still lingers.
Oh! Stop regretting!
The spring breeze fills the world!
Setcho looked around and said,
"Can you find Bodhidharma around here?"
Answering himself, he replied, "Yes."
Then again he muttered,
"Call him back to me. I will let him wash my feet."

Case Two
The Ultimate Path

Joshu said to his monks, "The ultimate Path is not difficult to reach. One who walks on it must not make any preferences. If one says a word, one is stuck either in preference or non-preference. I do not linger even at non-preference. Can you follow me?"

A monk then stood up and asked, "If one has no preference, what does one follow?"

Joshu answered, "I know not!"

The monk argued, "If you do not know, why do you say that you do not even linger at non-preference?"

Joshu said, "This business of asking questions is finished. You had better make a bow and retire."

A real Zen teacher does not answer a student's question intellectually, but only shows the way to live Zen. Here in America, many so-called spiritual teachers gather students who bring many questions; they then patiently try to entertain them with favorable answers. They should follow Joshu's way every once in a while and say, "This business of asking questions is finished. Why don't you go home and take a rest?"

SETCHO'S VERSE

> *The ultimate Path is not difficult to reach.*
> *Word or no-word*

Walking is never disturbed.
One is many,
Many are one.
Sun rises and moon sets.
Water is icy cold
In the remote mountains.
Dried skull is not separate
From living head.
Decayed trees rustle in the wind,
Their life has not yet ceased.
Hard, hard.
Preference or non-preference—
To experience this,
One must work it out for oneself.

Equality without discrimination is wrongly conceived equality. Discrimination without equality is wrongly conceived discrimination. We see the rising sun and falling moon on this side of the earth, while people who live on the other side see the moon rising and the sun setting! Is the water icy cold in the remote part of the mountain, or are we entering the remote mountain and therefore feeling icy cold? A skull could never be a skull without having been a living person. "Decayed tree" is another name for living tree. You put out your hand, and it is a combination of "palm" and "back of hand." I call it "hand" for convenience. If I call it "foot," no one can blame me!

In the original Chinese, Joshu said, "Preference is the colorful part, and non-preference is the white part. I am not even proceeding along the white part!"

Here on American highways, we see many white lines, but if you cling only to the white lines and do not know how to use them appropriately, you will be in danger.

Case Eight
Suigan's Eyebrows

At the end of the summer seclusion, Suigan said to his monks, "During this seclusion I spoke to you frequently. Now look and see if I still have my eyebrows."

Three of his brother monks were staying at the same monastery at the time. One of them, Hofuku, said, "A thief always tells a lie." The second one, Chokei, remarked, "They are growing now." The third, Ummon, responded, "Look out!"

In India, Buddhist monks had to stay in one place during the rainy season, meditating and studying together, because they were unable to beg for food due to the difficulties of travel during that period. Chinese Buddhists follow the same custom, even though they do not have a rainy season like that of the Indian climate. Monks usually stay in one temple from April 15 until July 15, a period of ninety days. After this interval, they are free to travel, to go to another monastery, or to do as they wish. During the seclusion no one may go into the monastery and no one may leave. The monks remain under one teacher. The master of the monastery devotes himself to teaching the monks, giving sanzen, delivering lectures on certain days, and encouraging all to live together in harmony, making an ideal Sangha. Sometimes, monks who are quite advanced in Zen join together, taking the place of the senior monks, or even substituting for the master when this is necessary.

A Zen legend says: "If one speaks in error and fails to guide one's monks properly, one's eyebrows will fall off as punishment."

Suigan really meant, "Did I speak in a way that helped you monks, or did I fail you in your Zen practice?" No student answered quickly enough, so his three brother monks spoke up. Hofuku's "A thief always tells a lie," strangely enough, was meant as praise. Zen teachers remove people's tightly held delusions the way a pickpocket swiftly "lifts" his treasure. Hofuku meant, "The master of this monastery did wonderful work in removing stubborn delusions, without the monks even knowing it." The second brother, Chokei, in saying, "They are growing now," meant, "You may slip a few steps in guiding some monks, and could lose your eyebrows, but since your intention is loving-kindness, yours are still growing!" Ummon's praising response was, "Look out!" He was warning not only the master of the monastery, but his two brother monks who had opened their mouths, about how dangerous speech is. Ummon's response is written in one Chinese character. In Japanese it is read as *kan*, which is similar in meaning to *kwatsu*. Kan carries deep significance, even though it is Chinese slang. In America we would say, "Look out!"

It is said that an Englishman who did not understand American slang was riding on a train and leaning out the window. His seat companion, seeing this, said to him, "Look out!" The Englishman, not understanding, leaned farther out the window and was struck on the head by a signal pole as the train sped by.

Setcho's verse

> *Suigan's words to his monks*
> *Are beyond comparison in Zen history.*
> *Ummon's one character hits the mark,*
> *But he is like a man who, losing his money,*
> *Is punished by the law.*
> *Does Hofuku praise Suigan or slander him?*

No one knows!
Suigan talked too much,
But he stole something, no doubt about it.
These brothers praise a crystal ball
That has no crack.
Who knows which is true or untrue?
Chokei knew well, and said,
"Now, eyebrows growing!"

In China, if a person loses his currency and reports it to the authorities, he has to pay the government the sum lost and he also receives a fine for not taking care of government property. Ummon said, "Look out!" But I say to the poet Setcho, *"Kan!"*

Case Twelve
Tozan's Three Pounds of Flax

A monk asked Tozan, "What is Buddha?" Tozan said, "Three pounds of flax."

Tozan lived in a locality where people cultivated flax. The soft fibers from flax plants were sold as the raw material from which linen was woven. Tozan's work was similar to that of the people around him. He raised flax plants and turned the fibers into filaments. His labor was his Zen and his Zen was his labor. When the monk came to him and asked, "What is Buddha?" he was asking about "the true body of Buddha"—Buddhakaya, which fills the world. He reasoned that Buddha, in that sense, must be superior to a mere object of worship, but he could not see it clearly as yet.

Tozan was weighing flax at the time. Reading the number on the scale, he said, "Three pounds of flax." Continuing his work, he piled up one bundle after another. This was expressing Buddhakaya actively, instead of in the quiet sitting position. If the questioner failed to realize the truth at that moment, he must have been deaf and blind. It is not necessary to cultivate flax to live in Zen. No matter what your everyday task may be, it will turn into Zen if you quit looking at it from a dualistic attitude. Just do one thing at a time, and do it sincerely and faithfully, as if it were your last task in this world.

SETCHO'S VERSE

Time passes without hesitation.
There is no gap between
The question and the answer.
To meet Tozan in this way
Never will happen again.
That lame turtle is blind
Wandering in the wilderness.
One flower after another
Bursts from a spring branch.
One design joins another in a beautiful brocade.
Bamboo sprouts south of the river,
Timber grows in the north.
Officer Riku and monk Chokei—
Why criticize laughing or crying!

When Nansen passed away, one of his lay disciples, Officer Riku, approached the coffin and laughed. The attending monk reprimanded him severely for his impolite manner. The officer said, "What should I do?" The monk could not answer. Then the officer wept for a while. When Chokei heard about this anecdote, he said, "Laughter is good. Why cry?" Each action is correct at the moment, if there is no gap between thought and action.

Case Twenty-two
Seppo's Cobra

One day Seppo said to his monks, "There is a cobra on Southern Mountain. You monks ought to see it." Chokei, one of his disciples, replied, "We have heard about it, and some of us are already frightened to death of it." Another monk repeated this conversation to Gensha, also a disciple of Seppo. Gensha looked at his brother monk and remarked, "Brother Chokei is the one who should go see the cobra, not me." The tale-bearing monk then asked, "But why not you?" Gensha answered, "I am tired today, and do not feel like walking to Southern Mountain."

In the original Chinese of the *Blue Rock Collection*, the story continues thus: "Ummon, another disciple of Seppo, stretched out his cane toward Seppo and gestured as though being frightened by a snake." This sentence should have been inserted even before the remarks made by Chokei and the rest of the unnecessary conversation by the tell-tale monk and Gensha. I suppose that Setcho, the compiler of the *Blue Rock Collection*, wished to save the faces of those monks, which were not really worth saving.

Bunsen Ikegami, a well-known Japanese Zen artist, drew a picture of Ummon holding a snake twined around his staff. This picture is a total failure for a Zen artist to have made. Ummon never had a snake on his cane.

Seppo did not mean to pretend to be a cobra, but since he belonged to the "cobra family," he expected some young cobras to be born in his monastery. He must have been very happy to have seen Ummon's response the minute after his words were uttered. As for Chokei and Gensha, they were like the Japanese artist who later drew the picture configuring a snake, or else they were trying to dream up some brilliant Zen action for the future.

SETCHO'S VERSE

> *Seppo lives on the rocky mountain.*
> *One cannot reach it easily.*
> *Cobras hide there*
> *Under trees, among the bushes.*
> *Only snake charmers can climb that steep mountain.*
> *Chokei and Gensha were young at the time*
> *So they joined the ranks of others who were frightened*
>   *by these stories.*
> *Ummon quickly went to search out the cobra,*
> *South, north, east, west,*
> *And still could not find it.*
> *So he made himself a cobra*
> *With head raised toward Seppo,*
> *Opening wide its poisonous mouth*
> *And shooting out lightning.*
> *The action was so momentary*
> *That others did not see it.*
> *That cobra is in my monastery.*
> *Have you monks any method of finding it?*

After reciting his own poem, Setcho cried out loudly,

> *"Monks, watch your feet!"*

undated

PART III
COMMENTARIES ON
THE *BOOK OF EQUANIMITY*

Introduction

Wanshi (1090–1157), a Zen master of the Southern Sung dynasty, wrote one hundred poems inspired by anecdotes and sayings of the old masters. Later, Bansho, another Zen master, gave one hundred lectures to his monks using Wanshi's manuscripts as the text. Each of his lectures consisted of an introduction, or preliminary remarks; Wanshi's illustrative case or background for each poem, with a sharp critique by Bansho after each sentence; Wanshi's poem, again followed by Bansho's response; and Bansho's lecture.

I could not get Bansho's complete text, but I was able to find a copy of an extract without his critiques on Wanshi's case and poem, and without his lecture. This translation, therefore, includes the introduction by Bansho, the case by Wanshi, and the verse by Wanshi.

I added my own notes to clarify the meaning of the original, and to suggest to you, Wanshi's intimate fellow students, how to practice Zen in your everyday life.

This·is perhaps a peculiar attempt to renew our old meditation class, because I am now living within barbed-wire fences in a relocation center for so-called "Japs."

You may read or copy the writings the same as you did before, among your old classmates, but you should not show the manuscript to outsiders, or publish it in any magazine or periodical.

The dates of Bansho's birth and death are not known exactly, but he lived in the time of the Southern Sung and Kin dynasties in China. He taught in the Southern Sung dynasty, and later was invited to court by the emperor of the Kin dynasty, and gave lectures to him in the year 1194. After that he must have met Yeh-lüch'u Ts'ai (H.G. Wells, in his *Outline of History*, spells his name Yeliu-chutsai), who was an administrator of the Kin government. When the Kin dynasty was conquered by the Mongols, this man, Yeh-lüch'u Ts'ai, was forced to work for Genghis Khan, who conquered the northern part of China, that part held by the Kins, which included Korea and Kharezm. Wells described Yeh-lüch'u Ts'ai as "one of the great political heroes of history," saying that he "tempered the barbaric ferocity of his masters, and saved innumerable cities and works of art from destruction." This Tartar statesman asked his teacher, Bansho, to send him his lectures on Wanshi's poems. After seven years, at last he received the complete manuscript from his teacher. He then immediately published its first edition. He wrote to Bansho, "For many years I had to accompany Genghis Khan on his warfare in the western countries. Now, at last, having received your manuscript, I feel like a man who is sober after having been intoxicated. I am like a person who returns to the world from the valley of death. I was so happy when I received the manuscript that I almost danced by myself. I paid homage to you, bowing toward the East, where you live. I rubbed the manuscript with my hands and said, 'Here is my teacher, who has come back to me, into the western countries.'"

Genghis Khan died in 1227, and his son, Ogdai Khan, took his place. Kin was altogether subdued by the Mongols in 1234, and the Southern Sung met the same fate in 1278. Thereupon, the new dynasty of Yuan, under the Mongol leader Kublai Khan, the grandson of Genghis Khan, was established in 1279.

Yeh-lüch'u Ts'ai passed away in the year 1243. Bansho, the author of our book, lived from the later part of the twelfth century to the middle part of the thirteenth century.

Bansho's hut, where he wrote the manuscript, was called Shoyo-an, the Hut of Equanimity, so he named the book *Shoyoroku*, "The Record of Shoyo." The book's theme, however, is not only equanimity, but also activity, as Zen has no particular character for such a term. Readers may call it the *Book of Realization*, or simply a *Book of Zen*.

I had to translate the poems into the prose form in English because of the difficulty of reproducing both rhyme and exact meaning. All names are given in their Japanese Zen pronunciation.

Chapter One
Buddha Takes His Preaching Seat

INTRODUCTION BY BANSHO

When meeting a superior student of Zen, one should shut the gate and sleep. When meeting second-rate and third-rate students, one can examine them and then plan how to teach them. It is unbearable to face an audience across the pulpit with a devil's eye. If any one of you does not agree with me, come out to the front and speak. I want to discuss the next koan with such a person.

Bansho thus gives his monks a paradox. If one lives in Zen, one's ways of living are one's teachings. We used to bow when we passed in front of our teacher's room, even though the door was shut and we were sure he was asleep. I am referring here to Soyen Shaku, who first introduced Zen to America.

A devil's eye means an artificial eye. It looks like a real eye, but it lacks true vision. A Ceylonese monk never needs a comb, as he has no hair on his head. He shaves off his hair very carefully. Just so, Zen never uses propaganda, as it has nothing to propagate.

THEME BY WANSHI

Buddha Shakyamuni took his preaching seat. Manjushri hit the table with the gavel and announced, "Such is the teaching of Buddha. All of you should observe it well, and accept it gratefully." Buddha came down from the seat in silence. The preaching was over.

Wanshi wrote themes as koans to preface his poems. He referred to a legend or tradition, to history or the sutras. You can create a theme from your own imagination, and enlarge upon or reduce the scenes to suit your own meditation.

A collection of koans is to Zen students as a docket is to lawyers. It contains mere references. No two identical cases appear in actual life.

Manjushri was the monitor in the preaching hall.

Silence is considered a virtue by many: "Smooth runs the water where the brook is deep," wrote Shakespeare. "Speech is great, but silence is greater," and "Silence is more eloquent than words," said Carlyle. "Vessels never give so great a sound as when they are empty," wrote Bishop John Jewell.

Some consider silence philosophically or aesthetically: "That silence is one of the great arts of conversation is allowed by Cicero himself, who says there is not only an art but even an eloquence in it," wrote Hannah More [a nineteenth-century British abolitionist, philanthropist, and Evangelical Christian]. And Carlyle again: "Looking around on the noisy inanity of the world—words with little meaning, actions with little worth—one loves to reflect on the great Empire of Silence, higher than all stars; deeper than the Kingdom of Death! It alone is great; all else is small."

Buddha's silence was far deeper than those expressions. In fact it was not silence at all. In the *Diamond Sutra* he said, "Subhuti, if a man should declare that the Tathagata is the one who comes, or goes, or sits, or lies, he does not understand the meaning of my teaching. Why? The Tathagata does not come from anywhere, and does not depart to anywhere; therefore, he is called the Tathagata."

Don't be cheated by Manjushri. Never mind what the monitor says, just meditate on the Buddha as your primary task.

In the *Lankavatara Sutra* there is a combined word, *Vivikta-Dharma*, which means the Dharma of Solitude. When you experience it for yourself, you will meet the Buddha in this koan. You will know, then, that Buddha preached not only coming to the seat, but also going down from it. All that we see and hear and think, all objects of consciousness, are what arise and disappear from this Dharma of Solitude.

VERSE BY WANSHI

> *Behold the Dharma of Solitude!*
> *Dame Nature sits at the loom*
> *And weaves the brocade of spring.*
> *Let her alone!*
> *Don't betray her secret,*
> *You mischievous wind!*

Wanshi seems to be blaming Manjushri, but he is really praising him, in the Zen way.

Chapter Two
Bodhidharma Walks Out from Samskrita

INTRODUCTION BY BANSHO

Penwa made a presentation twice, but he could not escape the penalty of being maimed. A brave soldier may draw his sword if he suddenly sees a diamond in the grass. An unexpected guest seldom meets an ever-ready host. People like unreal things and hesitate to face reality. Unusual things that are considered treasures usually cannot be put to any practical use. Look at the head of a dead cat—see what it is!

This is an epilogue, rather than a preface. Bansho assumes that his listeners know the dialogue between Bodhidharma and Wu Ti (a Liang dynasty emperor). The reader should first glance at the theme, and then review the Introduction and my comment.

Penwa, who lived in ancient China, found a precious jewel-in-the-rough on a mountain. He presented it to his king. To polish an uncut gem required years of work at that time, and because he was poor and ignorant of the art of polishing, he could neither hire a professional to do it nor do the work by himself. Only through the power and wealth of a king could it be accomplished. However, the king did not believe in the worth of that rough stone. He rejected the gift and, according to the law of the land, cut off the toes of Penwa's left foot, which was the penalty for a liar or a cheat. The king died, and his son could not see any value in the stone either, and had the toes of Penwa's right foot cut off. The next king, however, recognized the uncut gem for what it was, and accepted the offering of the poor maimed fellow. Afterward the polished stone was considered the best gem in China, and the king of a neighboring country offered its royal owner fifteen states for it.

Ancient soldiers fought bravely on the battlefield, but they were afraid of ghosts and monsters. One soldier drew his sword in self-defense when he saw a big diamond sparkling in the grass, believing it to be a ghost.

A Zen master was asked by a monk, "What is the most valuable thing in the world?" The master answered, "It is the head of a dead cat." "Why?" the monk asked. "Because no one can quote a price for it," the master said. The foundation of human happiness is neither the silver nor the gold standard.

THEME BY WANSHI

Wu Ti, the emperor of Liang, asked Bodhidharma, "What is the first principle of the holy Path?" Bodhidharma said, "In the world of asamskrita *there is nothing holy."* (There is neither first nor second principle.) *The emperor said, "Who are you?"* (You are a holy man, and I am a student of the holy Path—is this not correct?) *Bodhidharma said, "I know not." The emperor could not understand what the teacher meant. Bodhidharma did not see any way to enlighten the crowned student, so he left the palace and went north, crossing the Yangtzu River. He found an abandoned temple, Shaolin-szu, and stayed there nine years in meditation, gazing at the wall the whole time.*

Yangtzu-Chiang is the biggest river in China. It is also called Ch'ang-Chiang, meaning Long River. Most English writers spell the name Yangtse-Kiang.

The Han dynasty, which began in 201 B.C.E., came to an end in 220 C.E. Under the Hans the empire had grown to be as big as the United States of America is today, but the size of the empire was a source of weakness, rather than strength. Buddhism entered China during the time of Ming Ti, the second emperor of the Eastern Han dynasty, 67 C.E. From then on, the teachings of Buddha saturated the life of cultured people in spite of the dynasty changes. In the third century, China was broken into three parts: North, South, and West, the kingdoms of Wei, Wu, and Shu respectively. Toward the end of that century, North China was broken into sixteen kingdoms. The South, which no longer acknowledged any allegiance to the capital in the North, had to set up her own dynasties: Tsin, 280–419; Early Sung, 420–478; T'si, 479–501; Liang, 502–556; Ch'en, 557–588; and Sui, 589–619. The T'ang dynasty, the Golden Age of China, began in the year 620 C.E. Wu Ti, whom we meet in this koan, was the first emperor of the Liang dynasty, and his reign lasted from 502 to 549. Small kingdoms in the North had vanished by this time, except for Northern Wei, where Bodhidharma stayed for nine years and passed away.

Bodhidharma was the twenty-eighth successor of Buddha Shakyamuni, and the first patriarch of Zen in China. He came to China from Southern India in the year 520 C.E. to introduce and transmit the wisdom of Zen. Before his arrival, native scholars and monks from India had done translations of many scriptures. Bodhidharma's mission was to teach the essence of Buddhism: not theoretical doctrines, but the practical experience of enlightenment.

The first Zen book published in English, Kaiten Nukariya's *Religion of the Samurai*,[45] records the first part of the dialogue between Bodhidharma and Emperor Wu Ti as follows:

No sooner had Bodhidharma landed in Southern China than he was invited by the Emperor Wu, who was an enthusiastic Buddhist and good scholar.... His Majesty asked him, "We have built temples, copied holy scriptures, ordered monks and nuns to be converted. Is there any merit, Reverend Sir, in our conduct?" The royal host, in all probability, expected a smooth, flattering answer from the lips of his new guest, extolling his virtues and promising him heavenly rewards, but the blue-eyed Brahman bluntly answered, "No merit at all." This unexpected reply must have put the Emperor to shame and doubt in no small degree because he was informed simply of the doctrines of the orthodox Buddhist sects. He might have thought within himself, "Why not?" or asked himself, "Why is all this futile? By what authority does he declare all this meritless? What does he hold as the first principle of Buddhism?"

Wanshi abridged the dialogue to emphasize his Zen. You should repeat the words, "I know not," in silence. Whatever thought arises in you, crush it with the words, "I know not." Make your own voice the actual words of the blue-eyed monk, and let it also crush itself and vanish. The *Lankavatara Sutra* declares that those who are tied to words (*samskrita*) do not understand the truth, and that the superior state of self-realization (*asamskrita*) is beyond speech and analysis.

"As the ignorant seize upon the fingertip and not the moon, so indeed, those who are fastened to letters comprehend not my truth," the Buddha said. Wu Ti was stuck in the world of samskrita, the world of dualism— sage and fool, gain and loss, deeds and merit; Bodhidharma stepped out of it and showed him true freedom.

WANSHI'S VERSE

> *"No holy man in asamskrita."*
> *The teacher was too great.*
> *The student was too small.*
> *Winning by a close shave,*
> *Losing with no regret.*
> *Bodhidharma slipped away from the court.*
> *Alone he sits in Shaolin Temple,*
> *And holds the axle of Dharma in silence.*
> *The autumn moon hangs in the frosty sky,*
> *While the galaxy fades away*

Leaving the northern stars behind.
The teaching was thus preserved successively,
Giving both sickness and medicine
To humankind generation after generation.

A carpenter and a mason were working on the same building. A speck of plaster stuck to the nose of the mason. The carpenter shaved the speck off with his sharp ax. Bodhidharma's answer was no more, no less, like the skillful action of that carpenter.

A Chinese man was carrying some vases, tied with a rope. While he was walking, the rope broke, and the vases smashed into pieces. Bystanders saw what happened and called to the man, but he did not even look back. Instead he said, "What is the use of picking them up?" He did not "cry over spilled milk." Bodhidharma had no compromise to offer Wu Ti and no regret about his own departure.

Wanshi referred to these two stories in his verse ("Winning by a close shave, Losing with no regret").

I ask you to experience the coolness of autumn in your meditation. Wanshi is not merely describing the scenery of ancient China.

Zen is good medicine for curing delusions, but if one takes an overdose, one will get another sickness. Do not worship Bodhidharma. Do not admire his Zen. Admire your own true self.

Heart Mountain, Wyoming
May 12–June 24, 1944

PART IV
DHARMA TALKS AND ESSAYS

Editor's Note: The following talks and essays were presented and written in Los Angeles, California, unless otherwise noted.

An Ideal Buddhist

Dr. Frank Crane, a popular American writer, once said, "When we have a task we want to accomplish, we form a mind-concept of the thing desired. That is called an ideal." Now, we Buddhists have our ideal, which is none other than the accomplishment itself. Dr. Crane also said, "Have an ideal of the kind of man you want to be, and try to express that in your everyday life. Only so you can grow day by day, and achieve contentment. You may never reach your ideal; it may keep floating on and on before you. The sailor never reaches the North Star. Yet, without a North Star, he could never come to port." That was Dr. Crane's ideal. Mine is a little different from his North Star. It is all very well to put an image of your ideal in front of you, but if you cannot reach it, what is the use of deceiving and tantalizing yourself with it?

Christians never expect themselves to become God, and they think Buddhists, also, should not think to become Buddha, if Buddha is another name for God. On the contrary, we Buddhists aim to become buddhas, not in heaven or paradise, or in the lotus land of hereafter, but in this actual everyday life, in our own living world. Buddha is not a concept. It is our own mind, an achievement of our own experience. The founder of Buddhism was a man, neither God nor Son of God. Theravada Buddhists in Ceylon, Burma, or Siam call him Gotama, his family name, and Mahayana Buddhists in Tibet, China, or Japan call him Shakya, his tribal name. He was a historical personage; his given name was Siddhartha. He was called Buddha because he found ultimate truth through his enlightenment, and he was master of his thought, word, and action. He told his disciples and adherents that he was an accomplished Buddha, and that they were all future buddhas.

Buddhism shows the oneness of the whole universe. The true nature of beings is real, true, and inexhaustible sameness. From the very beginning we are all buddhas, for our minds as well as our bodies are nothing but Dharmakaya, the Buddha's true body, with infinite light and eternal life. It is our delusion to see ourselves separated from the universe, secluding ourselves in the small cells of individual egos. When you have awakened from your dream, you will know who you are, and you will realize what you have to do. Your everyday work is a part of your universal work. Your wisdom and your loving-kindness are the light and the warmth of Buddha, the vibrations of Dharmakaya itself. What need is there for any postulation of God? It would be like frost under bright sunshine. There are eighty-four thousand delusions, according to Buddhist psychology, but once you have found your inner treasure, all of them will be obliterated from your mind. If you do not sleep, you do not dream. The ideal of Buddhism is realization, and nothing else. Many other aspects of Buddhism may be considered valuable, but without this pure purpose, that is, without returning to your original source of Dharmakaya, no matter how noble and unselfish your deeds, you are still lingering in the world of delusions, and you are still far away from being a buddha.

Buddha means, "Awake, and will wake others." It means a mind with perfect wisdom and complete virtue. Those who become buddhas possess penetrating wisdom and boundless compassion. Shakyamuni Buddha manifested this during his forty-five years of activity after his attainment of buddhahood.

In Christianity, if you say you will become God, or Christ, you may be called a blasphemer, or you may be considered out of your mind, one who is thinking utterly impossible things. In Buddhism, Buddha is the name of your ideal. If you say that you cannot become a buddha, it will sound as though you are denying the possibility of ice to become water, or as if you are complaining of poverty while you have a million dollars in the bank in your own name.

Theravada Buddhists of Ceylon, Burma, and Siam believe that only one Buddha has appeared in this world during many thousands of years. They declare that the founder of Buddhism is the only Buddha in the world, and that his followers never will become buddhas in this life, and that it will take two or three rebirths or perhaps many more rebirths to be enlightened. What a delusion! Unless they open their own inner eye, they will not know even the truth of their own birth and death. How do they expect to know about a future buddha? Those theories of karma and rebirth are not the Buddha's discovery. They are previous beliefs that spread in India before the time of Shakyamuni Buddha. He adopted such theories to explain the phenomenal world, but his main purpose was to teach Dharmakaya, the source of all phenomena, the origin of the ethical and philosophical mind of the human race. Modern Buddhists need not cling to theories of rebirth. They can compare other religions, philosophies and sciences, and find new light in them.

Another feature of Buddhists is that most are vegetarians. When one dwells in brotherhood, not only the brotherhood of the human race but the brotherhood of the whole universe, one cannot enjoy food from slain animals. I am always wondering how American ladies can stand wearing the furs of wild beasts when they have such beautiful hearts and refined tastes. A professor at Clark University once said that modern women still have savage tastes, and in this regard I cannot help but agree with him. I am not asking you to cast away your furs, but if you buy some new fashion made of spotted cow skins on Market Street or around Powell Street, you yourself will be affirming the words of that professor. If you think, however, that vegetarianism is the main way to qualify as an ideal Buddhist, you are quite mistaken. If one who forbids consuming the flesh of animals is an ideal Buddhist, monkeys and rabbits would be noble adherents, since they do not eat meat. Food has something to do with our mental process, but if you cling too much to the food question, you will be caught in the net of another delusion. Just free yourself from all incoming disturbances, and first of all, get enlightened. Then a small matter like what to eat will be settled by itself.

Modern scholars say that original Sanskrit word "Buddhism" should be *Buddha-wachana*. *Wachana* means "words"; Buddha-wachana means the words of Buddha. They recognize Pali texts as scriptures written in the Buddha's spoken words. In my opinion, the original Sanskrit word for Buddhism is Buddhadharma. Dharma means the truth of ultimate reality; therefore, Buddhadharma means Buddhist truth. In Pali, it is Buddha-Dhamma. Buddha discovered this truth, and taught what he had attained through his realization for forty-five years. Dharma is the source, and wachana is the stream. If you reach the same stage of samadhi as the Buddha did, you will be a buddha yourself, but you do not have to preach the teaching with the same words, since you are living in a different world from that of the Buddha. In meditation, all of you can enter samadhi, and through samadhi you can attain enlightenment. A true Buddhist should strive to realize *Buddha-hridaya*, first of all. *Hridaya* means "heart," or "spirit." Therefore, Buddha-hridaya means the heart of enlightenment. When you acquire Buddha's spirit, that is, when you realize Dharma as clearly and as precisely as the Buddha himself, you will know for yourself every word the Buddha spoke. If you could recite all of Buddha-wachana and never see Buddhadharma as clearly as you see your own hand, you have not yet even touched Buddha-hridaya, and you will still be on the outskirts of Buddhist truth.

In the Bible you can read what Christ said: "When thou doest alms, let not thy left hand know what thy right hand doeth; that thine alms may be in secret." This is in common with the secret virtue of Buddhism. But when the words go on, "Thy Father who see-eth in secret shall recompense thee," there we see a deep cleavage between Buddhism and Christianity. As long as there is any thought of anybody, whether God or Devil, knowing of your doings, a true Buddhist would say, "You are not yet one of us." Deeds that are accompanied by such thoughts of gain are not true

Buddhist deeds, but full of tracks and shadows, and also delusions and illusions.

An ideal Buddhist should wash off all kinds of dirt and walk freely in naked truth. The perfect garment shows no seams, inside or outside; it is one complete piece, and nobody can tell where the work began and how it was woven. In true Buddhism, there ought not to be any trace of self-admiration after giving alms, much less the thought of compensation. An ideal Buddhist may keep the precepts, but will forget what has been done. Every act will unite with ethical laws harmoniously and gracefully. An ideal Buddhist will never use the term *Buddhist*. As nature's beloved child, no name is necessary. You may be a monk. You may be a layperson. It makes no difference, as long as you enjoy your emancipation, and your heart beats regularly. You will not cling to the world; therefore you will not try to escape from the world. You will be contented as a happy, peaceful dweller in this world, and will desire nothing else.

San Francisco, California
September 3, 1931

A Meeting with Sufi Master
Hazrat Inayat Khan

Senzaki and his friend Dr. Hayes, a psychologist, had gone to the San Francisco home of Mrs. Martin, the only Murshida (female Sufi teacher) in America; what follows is from a talk given later in Santa Barbara, California.

When we arrived, we were ushered into the meditation room. It was dimly lighted by a lamp covered with green silken cloth; fragrant Persian incense filled the air.

After Mrs. Martin introduced us, and after shaking hands with Murshid Inayat Khan, we were seated at a square table, Mrs. Martin facing Dr. Hayes, and the teacher facing me. My friend began talking to the teacher, asking how he liked America and its people, meanwhile selecting a cigar from his pocket, which, however, he then hesitated to light at such a meeting.

Inayat Khan smiled at me and asked, "Mr. Senzaki, will you tell me the significance of Zen?"

I remained silent for a little while, and then smiled at him. He smiled back at me. Our dialogue was over.

The psychologist, not having recognized what had happened, said, "You see, Mr. Khan, *Zen* is Japanized from the Sanskrit. Its original meaning is *dhyana*, which means meditation, and..."

At that point, Inayat Khan waved his right hand gracefully, and stopped the psychologist's speech.

Mrs. Martin then interposed, "I will get a book which describes Zen very well. It is an English translation from Japanese of *The Twelve Sects of Buddhism*. I will get it for you." Before she could rise from her seat, Inayat Khan again waved—this time with his left hand—gracefully stopping the Murshida. He looked at me.

His eyes were full of water—not the tears of the world, but water from the great ocean—calm and transparent. I recited an old Zen poem by Jakushitsu—not with my mouth, not with my mind, but with a blink of my eyes, like a flash.

> No living soul comes near that water.
> A vast sheet of water as blue as indigo!
> The abyss has a depth of ten thousand feet.
> When all is quiet and calm, at midnight,
> Only the moonlight penetrates the waves
> And reaches the bottom easily and freely.

"Murshid," I then said, "I see Zen in you."

"Mr. Senzaki, I see a Sufi in you," he replied.

Both of us then smiled, each at the other.

Mrs. Martin again interposed, "Mr. Senzaki, you should practice your English. Why don't you talk more about Zen?"

At this both the Murshid and I laughed loudly. The Murshida and the psychologist both joined in, without knowing why. The happy interview was over. I should have gone home at this time, but the psychologist seemed to wish to talk further with the Murshid, and continued with his "whys" and "wherefores," while the Murshida had to show us her collection of books and documents. So we remained there the whole evening in a discussion of "life," "death," "humanity," and "the universe."

March 3, 1935

Seven Treasures
Part One

BODHISATTVAS: This evening I will tell you about the seven treasures described in the *Saddharma-pundarika Sutra (The Lotus of the True Law Sutra,* also known as *The Lotus Sutra)*. In the time of Buddha Shakyamuni, people considered gold, silver, lapis lazuli, agate, corals, amber, and pearls to be the seven treasures. Those were costly and dear to the people of India, the same as diamonds, platinum, radium, and others are to us in this modern age. Buddha Shakyamuni compared the seven treasures of materialistic wealth to the same number of spiritual treasures. According to Chiki, the founder of the Tendai School of China, the seven spiritual treasures are as follows:

The treasure of faith
The treasure of persistence
The treasure of listening
The treasure of humility
The treasure of precepts
The treasure of self-surrender
The treasure of meditation and wisdom

Let us contemplate these seven treasures. There is a *gatha* (poem) expressing the Buddhist faith. D.T. Suzuki's translation reads:

The Buddha-body fills the world,

Universally immanent in all things;

It manifests wherever and whenever conditions are mature,

Though it never leaves the seat of Bodhi.

Please learn these four lines by heart. Buddhism is a faith that does not depend upon the existence of a being or power outside the universe. Christians believe in a God who has created this world and presides over it, directing its course and shaping its destiny. Some may think everyone should believe as they do, worshipping an external object and relying on its saving power, and they try to identify Buddhism with the same characteristics. Buddhist faith, however, does not belong to this category.

As Zen students, most of you know the koan "The Three Barriers of Tosotsu," so the gatha I just read should not be strange to you at all. The Three Barriers are these: In studying Zen, the aim is to see your own true nature. Now, where is your true nature? When you realize your own true nature, you will be free from birth and death. Now, when the light is gone from your eyes and you become a corpse, how can you free yourself? If you free yourself from birth and death you should know where you are. Now your body separates into the four elements. At this moment, where are you?

Those who have passed this koan obtained the holy treasure of faith in that instant.

There is an old saying among Zen students: "To get a glimpse of Buddha-body is not very hard, but to live on the seat of Bodhi constantly requires the spirit of a hero." When I was left alone in this country, after parting from my teacher, I knew that the Buddha-body filled America, as it is immanent universally in all things, but I had to wait seventeen years to give a lecture on Zen to the American public. Do you know why? Because the Buddha-body makes itself manifest wherever and whenever the conditions have matured. Perseverance is another name for Buddhist life. Other religions may approve of students who are eager to spread their teachings, but Buddhism always discourages such propagation by its followers. Buddhist persistence means inner cultivation, and does not aim for outer increase at all. Zen says, "Silence speaks a million words, and a million words express nothing but silence." Some of you have worked on the koans "The Four Ways of Eloquence" (Dharma; Understanding; Words; Compassion) and "The Eight Features of Buddha's Voice" (Excellent; Subtle; Harmonious; Intellectual; Powerful; Correct; Deep; Inexhaustible). Your life work is to practice them in your everyday interactions. Even though most of you will not teach Zen, or edit Buddhist magazines, you will never lose your holy treasure of persistence as long as you have your silent partner of perseverance. In my past twenty-five years in America, I had fewer regrets in my first seventeen years than I have had these past eighteen years. Do not follow my bad example. Do guard your speech. To enjoy your silence is to keep your holy treasure of persistence growing, day by day.

Nowadays good speakers are everywhere; there are almost too many. But when you stop to think, you will notice how scarce good listeners are. You all know the story of Nanin's cup of tea. Nanin, a Zen master during the Meiji era, once received a university professor who came to inquire about Zen. Nanin served the tea himself. He poured his visitor's cup full, and then kept on pouring. The professor watched the overflow until he could no longer restrain himself. He cried, "It is full now! No more can go in!" "Like this cup," Nanin said, "you are full of your own opinions and speculations. How can I show you Zen unless you first empty your cup?" The story is all right so far as it goes. But please do not use this story merely to convince others to listen to you!

This story has a copyright by the House of Egolessness, which functions throughout the study of meditation until the dawn of realization for all sentient beings. Since I respect your holy treasure of listening, I should also respect mine, and stop my speech to listen to others. We have studied three treasures now: the treasure of faith, the treasure of persistence, and the treasure of listening.

Let us leave the other four treasures—those of humility, precepts, self-surrender, and meditation and wisdom—for another time. Meanwhile, let me read my teacher's comment about the gatha I mentioned before. The treasure of faith is the source of all the other treasures. Therefore, in studying it thoroughly, both as a koan and as an object of philosophical contemplation, you will be able to hold all of the treasures firmly and permanently.

Now let us listen to my teacher's words, in a translation by D.T. Suzuki.

In the gatha recited in the beginning, the idea of sameness is rather dogmatically expressed: 'The Buddha-Body fills the world.' In this the content of sameness is called Buddha-Body or in Sanskrit, Buddhakaya. The Buddhakaya, which is also often called Dharmakaya, is the reason, life, and norm of all particular existences. When we penetrate through the diversity of all these individual phenomena, we encounter everywhere this indwelling Body and therein find the unity or sameness (samata) of things.

The principle of diversity is declared in the second line of the gatha, which makes the Buddha-Body universally immanent in all things. The Buddha-Body, the essence of existence, though absolutely one in itself, allows itself to be diversified as the lilies of the field, as the fowls of the air, as the creatures of the water, or as the inhabitants of the woods. For it is in the inherent nature of the Buddha-Body that it individualizes itself in the manifoldness of the phenomenal world. It does not stand alone outside particular existences, but it abides in them and animates them and makes them move freely. By thus abandoning its absolute transcendentality, it has subjected itself to certain conditions such as space, time, and causation. Its essence is infinite, but its manifestations are finite and limited. Therefore, the Buddha-Body has to wait to express itself in this relative world till all the necessary conditions are matured. This creation, so called, is no more than a manifestation of the self-limiting Buddha-Body.

Suppose there stands a mirror—the mirror of the Buddha-Body. Anything that comes in front of it is reflected therein, and this without any premeditation on the part of the mirror. If there comes a man, he is reflected in it; if a woman, she finds herself reflected in it; if it is a beautiful flower now which presents itself before this mirror, it is immediately and instantly reflected with all its magnificence. It is even so with things unsightly or even repugnant, for the mirror does not refuse its illuminating power to anything, high or low, rich or poor, ugly or beautiful, good or evil. Wherever and whenever conditions are ripe, all particular things will be reflected in the supranatural mirror of the Buddha-Body, without hesitation, without reasoning, without demonstration. This is the way in which the principle of karma works.

The fourth line of the gatha is more or less a continuation of the third and expresses the same sentiment from another point of view. Things are many, and are subject to constant transformation as regulated by their karma, but the Buddha-Body eternally abides in the Seat of Bodhi, which is our inmost being.

The moon is one and serenely shines in the sky, but she will cast her shadow, wherever the conditions are mature, in ever so many different places. Do we not see her image wherever there is the least trace of water? It may be filthy, or it may be clean; it may consist of only a few drops, or it may be a vast expanse, such as the ocean; but they all reflect one and the same moon as best suited to their inherent nature. The shadows are as many as different bodies of water, but we cannot say that one shadow is different from another. However small the moon may appear when there is only a drop of water, she is essentially the same as the one in the boundless sheet of water, where its heavenly serenity inspires awe and reverence. So many, and yet one in all; so diverse, and yet essentially the same; we see it reflected everywhere, and yet is not the Buddha-Body sitting, all alone, in the Seat of Bodhi?[46]

Seven Treasures
Part Two

BODHISATTVAS: So far we have studied the treasure of faith, the treasure of persistence, and the treasure of listening. Each of them is complete in and of itself when it is accomplished; the other treasures are thus incorporated in it. In comparison to these seven holy treasures, worldly treasures of any kind are worth nothing at all. A man may have lost all hope in the world, yet if he has the treasure of faith within him, he can still be happy in his Buddhist life. A terrible earthquake once destroyed the city of San Francisco, and another one destroyed Tokyo, the capital of Japan. The people of San Francisco and Tokyo lost everything but the treasure of persistence, and as you well know, they rebuilt the cities before long, and they were better than before. I am such a poor speaker in expressing my treasure of faith, but you have your treasure of listening, and this always makes this study class more interesting and more encouraging. I feel very grateful to you all.

The fourth is the treasure of humility. You may hear many impressive words attesting to humility in your social interactions, but if you know that those words are inauthentic, you will feel sickened by them. In Buddhism there is no ceremony corresponding to the Christian confession, but we say the verse of purification every full-moon night, and discipline ourselves through self-examination. I will read the purification verse for you: "All my evil actions are the endless waves of karma, caused by greed, anger, and ignorance, and performed with body, mouth, and mind. Now

I see all of them as baseless dreams. Purifying my body with the rules of the Sangha, using my mouth for the reading of sacred sutras, and pacifying my mind through deep meditation, I vow to carry myself away from the sea of delusions and reach buddhahood, so that all my actions may turn into manifestations of wisdom and grace." Thus we Buddhists keep and guard our treasure of humility.

A Zen expression says, "Heaven and earth and I have the same root. Everything in the world, therefore, is part of my true self." Just because you have obtained a little Zen understanding does not mean that you are superior to others. When you see buddha in you, you respect others more than ever, for you see that others also have buddha in them. Dogen, a Japanese monk of the Kamakura epoch, went to China and received Dharma from a Soto Zen master. When he returned to Japan, he said, "I returned home with nothing but empty hands. I learned only that the human nose is vertical and the two eyes are horizontal. The morning sun rises in the East, and in the evening it sets in the West." Here you can see the brilliance of the treasure of humility and admire it to your heart's content.

The fifth treasure is that of the precepts. Buddha Shakyamuni said on his deathbed, "After my nirvana, you ought to revere and obey the precepts as your master, as a shining lamp in the dark night, as a great jewel treasured by a poor man. Follow carefully the precepts I have prescribed. Treat them in no way different from myself." My teacher, Soyen Shaku, used to say, "What is philosophical in Buddhism is no more than a preliminary step toward what is practical in it." First of all we must keep and guard this treasure of precepts, living ethical lives as Buddhists. He also said keeping the Buddhist precepts is a threefold matter: "Buddhists must continue removing selfishness, seeking the light that is everywhere, and practicing the loving-kindness that does not contradict or discriminate."

It is simple enough, but it takes the rest of one's life, striving constantly, to practice it. Please memorize the five precepts, both in their negative and positive expressions:

First: Do not kill any living thing for your own pleasure. The positive meaning is loving-kindness toward all sentient beings.

Second: Do not take anything that does not belong to you. That is to say, live an unselfish and generous life.

Third: In married life, do not take up with another. Keep constancy strictly, and love and respect each other.

Fourth: Do not speak an untruthful word. Be honest in all your interactions.

Fifth: Do not become intoxicated. Lead a pure and sober life. This precept upholds cleanliness and righteousness.

Remember, keeping the precepts allows you to meditate well, and in meditating deeply, you can enter samadhi, the key that opens the gate of realization. The seven holy treasures are thus cooperative and mutually related.

About ten years ago a Japanese woman, whose husband was the manager of a San Francisco branch office of Yokohama Specie Bank, was taking a walk along McAllister Street. She noticed a necklace composed of some pieces of colored glass strung together in imitation of old-fashioned jewels. She asked the owner the price, and was told it cost fifty cents. She was about to buy it, when she reminded herself that she should not wear such a cheap necklace, for the sake of her husband's reputation. So she gave it up and forgot about it. The next day an American bought the necklace for fifty cents and showed it to his friend, who knew something about jewels. That friend begged the owner to sell him the necklace. So the man thought it must have a good value, and priced it at fifty dollars. The other party paid the price instantly, and displayed it in his store. One day, a customer came into the store and asked the price of the necklace. The man who had bought it for fifty dollars took a chance and named a price of five hundred dollars. Without any argument, the customer paid it and took the necklace. This customer was a clerk at Tiffany and Company in New York City, and he knew that the necklace was one of the national treasures of France. The necklace had been given to Empress Josephine by Emperor Napoleon Bonaparte. It had been stolen from the Louvre Museum in Paris, and the French government had offered a reward of one million francs for its return. The clerk at the New York jewelry store received the reward. A newspaper story and a photograph of the necklace appeared in a Japanese newspaper. The bank manager's wife read the story calmly and smiled; she was the daughter of a samurai family.

Japan is called the mecca of Buddhism nowadays, and students from all parts of the world go there to attain something precious to them. There must be some treasures still remaining in Japan, especially these seven treasures. They may be overlooked by the Japanese, but Americans are coming and discovering them. Perhaps you need not cross the Pacific Ocean. The mecca of Buddhism may come to you instead. I must warn you, however, not to be cheated by imitations.

Meister Eckhart said, "The eye with which I see God is the eye with which God sees me." Now open this very eye, and discern between the false and the genuine; see the seven holy treasures for yourself.

Seven Treasures
Part Three

BODHISATTVAS: The last two of the seven treasures are the treasure of self-surrender and the treasure of meditation and wisdom. Buddhism does not admit the existence of a self-entity, and considers all egoistic ideas to be delusions. The treasure of self-surrender teaches us how to live happily, not attaching to the self, serving others with loving-kindness. Theoretically, you can easily learn the reason why Buddhism calls "self" a phantasm. Even modern science and advanced philosophy support the statement of non-ego. Nevertheless, if we do not have the treasure of self-surrender, it is a hard task for us to make every deed unselfish. To attain this treasure, we must devote ourselves to meditation and recover our latent wisdom. Here you see again the cooperation of the treasures and their interrelationship.

My book *101 Zen Stories* includes this anecdote: A farmer requested a Tendai priest to recite sutras for his wife, who had died. After the recitation was over, the farmer asked, "Do you think my wife will gain merit from this?" "Not only your wife, but all sentient beings will benefit from the recitation of the sutras," answered the priest. "My wife will be very weak, and others will take advantage of her and get the benefit she should have, so please recite sutras just for her," the farmer said. The priest explained that it was the purpose of a Buddhist to offer blessings and merit for every living being. "That's fine," concluded the farmer, "but please make one exception: I have a neighbor who is rough and mean to me. Just exclude him from all those sentient beings." This farmer had the treasures of faith, persistence, listening, humility, and precepts, all to some extent, but the poor fellow had no treasure of self-surrender. You can see it clearly and laugh at his ignorance, but when it happens in your own case, it will not be so easily discerned.

Another story: when Yamaoka Tesshu was still a young student of Zen, he visited one master after another to have his Zen examined and thus to get instruction to deepen his understanding. He called upon Dokuon, the abbot of Shokoku-ji Monastery. To show his attainment, Tesshu said, "Mind, Buddha, and sentient beings do not exist. The true nature of phenomena is empty. There is no realization, no delusion, no sage, no mediocrity. There is nothing to give and nothing to receive." Dokuon, who was smoking quietly, said nothing, but suddenly he whacked Yamaoka with his long bamboo pipe. This made the young man quite angry. "If nothing exists," asked Dokuon, "where did this anger come from?"

Some of you express your attainment very well when you come for sanzen, and I allow you to pass your koan. You open the gate of Zen, but then where are you going? Each koan is a gateless gate. The minute you think that you have entered it, you are outside the gate. You are not allowed even to think about a koan. How can you talk to others about it? I am not trying to monopolize sanzen, as there is no such monkey business. Each of you can call yourself a Zen master and give personal guidance if you wish to do so. The pity is that when you think you have something to give to others, you have lost in that instant what you really acquired. I simply wish you not to lose your treasure of self-surrender, and keep it with your own precious Zen.

Let us go back again to the gatha expressing the treasure of faith:

The Buddha-body fills the world,
Universally immanent in all things;
It manifests wherever and whenever conditions are mature,
Though it never leaves the seat of Bodhi.

Now, which is the seat of Bodhi? Show me how you sit in it! This is your koan this evening. It is very slippery, so first of all, get a good foothold before you try to climb into the seat. Above all, be very careful while you are walking. There you will see the seventh treasure, that of meditation and wisdom. Those who cannot get rid of "self," those who express their dissatisfaction and always blame others for their suffering, are not fit to study Buddhism at all. They should remain in the world of delusions and search for gold, silver, and other materialistic treasures. They forget their own Buddha-body and refuse its manifestations. Nothing can save them; they must wake up and try to save themselves.

In the *Saddharma-pundarika Sutra*, translated from Sanskrit into English as *The Lotus of the True Law* by Herman Kern of Holland, Buddha Shakyamuni tells the Bodhisattva Mahasattva Akshayamati, "In case, young man of good family, many hundred thousand myriads of kotis of creatures, sailing in a ship on the ocean, should see their bullion, gold, gems, pearls, lapis lazuli, conch shells, stones, corals, emeralds, Musaragalvas, red pearls, and other goods lost, and the ship by a vehement, untimely gale cast on the island of Giantesses, and if in that ship a single being implores Avalokiteshvara, all will be saved from that island of Giantesses. For that reason, young man of good family, the Bodhisattva Avalokiteshvara is named Avalokiteshvara."[47] You see, there are more than seven treasures in this translation, and so there shall be more than seven virtues to be symbolized. Buddha would address his listeners as "young men of good family," just as we address our audience as "fellow students." Now I will read for you my rendition of this part, taking both the Chinese translation by Kumarajiva and the Japanese by Bunyu Nanjo as references:

"My disciples, I will tell you another cause. Suppose many hundred thousands of people sail on the great ocean searching for gold, silver, lapis lazuli, clam pearls, agate, corals, amber, and oyster pearls. In search of such seven treasures and others, should a black storm blow the drifting ship to the shore of a devil's land, if one of the passengers concentrates on the wisdom and loving-kindness of Avalokiteshvara, and calls the name of Avalokiteshvara, then everyone in the ship will escape the devil's harm. Therefore we adore Avalokiteshvara, who sees all and brings loving-kindness to all."

The world is a drifting ship, and the many people in it try to attain seven treasures: the treasures of faith, persistence, listening, humility, precepts, self-surrender, and meditation and wisdom. The misconception of "self" is the black wind that blows the ship to a devil's island, where nothing but suffering exists. A passenger who attains enlightenment will see that from the very beginning there is no delusion, and thus no suffering.

Some of you have already worked on the koan "Not the Wind, Not the Flag." Let me repeat it here. "Two monks were arguing about a flag. One said, 'The flag is moving.' The other said, 'The wind is moving.' The Sixth Patriarch happened to be passing by. He told them, 'Not the wind, not the flag; your mind is moving.'"

If you pass this koan, you can create the seven treasures by yourself whenever you need them, and then let them go back into nothingness after you finish your work.

Mumon said about this koan, "If you understand this koan intimately, you will see the two monks trying to buy iron and gaining gold." I would like to say, "Not only gold, but seven holy treasures will be in your hand."

I should add, however, another saying of Mumon's—"When the mouth opens, all are wrong"—and stop speaking.

May 28–June 11, 1935

The Ten Stages of Consciousness

BODHISATTVAS: Buddhism recognizes the equality of all beings, not only among the human ethnicities, but also among all living creatures, as well as among all things in the material world. Buddhism also acknowledges the differentiation of the phenomenal world and upholds the law of karma, through which this differentiation takes place. For instance, kings and paupers have the same buddha-nature, but their karma has manifested in different ways, and has made them as they are: kings, with highest glory and tremendous wealth, and paupers, with woeful want and forgotten names.

If both categories were made of pure gold, still their karmic processes would affect their formation accordingly. If you make a ball of pure gold, it will roll around smoothly. But if, with the same pure gold, you make a cube or a block or a pyramid, it will not move freely at all. So you see, each type of fortune, destiny, and character has been molded by itself, and no God or gods can change it. Only when we realize buddha-nature within ourselves can our karma be changed. Until the mind becomes refined enough to melt into its original buddha-nature, we are all blindfolding ourselves, and do not know what we really are. Realization of buddha-nature can be achieved by anyone who strives properly.

There are ten stages in Buddhism. Using their Sanskrit names, I will explain them one by one. *Manushya* is the human stage; above it are five stages, and below it, four. From the highest to the lowest, it goes as follows: first, *Buddha*; second, *Bodhisattva*; third, *Pratyekabuddha*; fourth,

Shravaka; fifth, *Deva*; sixth, *Manushya*; seventh, *Asura*; eighth, *Tiryag-yoni*; ninth, *Preta*; and tenth, *Naraka*.

In the Manushya realm, we think we gain comfort and happiness through knowledge. But if our so-called knowledge is not refined, we do not remain in our own realm; we become angry, and fight, and descend to the realm of asuras. The life of an asura is nothing but fighting. Even when we are living as asuras, however, we may have a good heart and the spirit of sacrifice; thus the many stories of unselfishness during the terrible First World War.

When our mind descends another step from the asura stage, we find ourselves in the tiryagyoni. "Tiryag" means a non-human animal, and yoni means "creeping (on four legs)." Therefore, tiryagyoni refers to all creatures in the animal kingdom except human beings. Animals have their own pleasures and comforts, of course, but those are short-lived—and animals do not have the human capacity for realization. If our mind goes down lower still, we feel hungry constantly; we never get any satisfaction. This is the world of the preta, ceaselessly greedy and thus continually suffering.

We should stop our subway travel by this time, but some of us do not know any limit at all. The last station is that of the narakas, the hell where there is nothing but suffering; those who descend this far down find that there is no way to climb up the steps to the next platform. Dante's *Inferno* and John Bunyan's *Pilgrim's Progress* describe skillfully the sufferings of narakas.

Now, let us climb above the human. First there is the deva realm, that of the gods. If we obtain harmony of mind and body, and conditions are perfect, both material and spiritual, we are dwelling above the stage of ordinary human beings—we are leading the life of the gods. Yet even in this happy land, unless we receive teachings about the truth of our existence, we are liable to recede a step or two, and suffer again through our own ignorance.

There is a level two floors above the human stage, that of the shravaka. *Shravaka* means "one who has heard about truth" from living buddhas.

People who lived in the Buddha's time had the opportunity to hear his noble teachings directly, and most of his disciples became shravakas. The generations that followed could not hold the teachings, because the shravaka mind was not refined enough to carry the lamp of wisdom.

The next level up is called pratyekabuddha. Although it is not the final stage of buddhahood, it includes those who work out their own way to attain some realization. Deep philosophical thinkers like Emanuel Kant, Henri Bergson, Rudolph Eucken, and William James may be called pratyekabuddhas. *Pratyeka* means "one who works by oneself" and *buddha* means "realized one."

The stage of the bodhisattva is the nearest rank to buddhahood. Bodhisattvas seek to realize the truth not only for themselves, but for the sake of all beings: the pratyekabuddhas, shravakas, devas, manushyas, asuras, tiryagyonis, pretas, and narakas. In short, a bodhisattva is a teacher of humans and gods, a leader of thinkers and sages, a true student of Buddhism, and a mentor. You and I are here to learn to be bodhisattvas, with no desire for other ranks at all.

January 14, 1936

Emancipation

BODHISATTVAS: Religion starts through seeking deliverance. When we face the impermanence and suffering of life, we yearn to attain eternity and release from suffering. Some philosophers also started from this perspective, such as Pythagoras, Plato, and Schopenhauer. Buddhism, Christianity, and other religions were born from recognition of life's dissatisfactions and imperfections. Almost every teaching from India is based on the search for deliverance. Gandhi, too, sought not only political freedom, but also true peace.

Zen aims to attain self-enlightenment without relying upon a Supreme Being or its power. As Zen students, we must save ourselves. In this respect, Zen realization should be called emancipation, rather than deliverance. Zen thought, however, was derived from Indian philosophies and religions; therefore we can trace back its source to ideas of deliverance, especially those found in the *Upanishads*.

The oldest scripture of India is the *Rig-veda*. According to Max Muller, it was composed in the era between 1200 and 1000 B.C.E., and compiled about two hundred years later. The *Rig-veda* is a collection of religious poems and ceremonial songs in which the worship of natural wonders was expressed in polytheistic forms tinged with pantheistic colors.

Several hundred years after the compilation of the *Rig-veda*, its commentaries appeared—first the *Brahmanas*, and next the *Upanishads*. In the former, we can see the idea of the hereafter, and in the latter, the idea of transmigration.

In the first part of the *Sveta-svatara Upanishad*, a late compilation, we read:

> The Brahma students say: Is Brahman the cause? Whence are we born? Whereby do we live, and whither do we go? O ye who know Brahman, tell us at whose command we abide, whether in pain or in pleasure?

Here we find the bud of the question of "I"—the self. This has much to do with the problem of transmigration.

In the *Chandogya Upanishad*, an early compilation, we see the following dialogue between father and son:

> "Fetch me from thence a fruit of the Nyagrodha tree."
>
> "Here is one, Sir."
>
> "Break it."
>
> "It is broken."
>
> "What do you see there?"
>
> "These seeds, infinitesimally small."
>
> "Break one of them."
>
> "It is broken."
>
> "What do you see there?"
>
> "Not anything, Sir."
>
> "My son, that subtle essence which you do not perceive, then, of that very essence this great Nyagrodha tree exists. Believe it, my son. That which is the subtle essence, in it all that exists has itself. It is the Self, and thou, O my son, art it."

In another part of the Upanishads, the father tells his son:

> "Place this salt in water, and then wait on me in the morning." The next morning, the father said, "Bring me the salt which you placed in the water last night."
>
> The son, having looked for it, found it not, for, of course, it was melted.

The father said, "Taste it from the surface of the water. How is it?"

The son replied, "It is salty."

"Taste it from the bottom. How is it?"

The son replied, "It is salty."

The father said, "Throw it away and then wait on me."

He did so, but salt exists forever.

Then the father said, "Here also, in the body forsooth, you do not perceive the True, my son, but there indeed it is. That which is the subtle essence, in it all that exists has its Self. It is the True. It is the Self, and thou, O my son, art it."

According to the theory of the *Upanishads*, our true self is of the same nature as Brahman, Divine Being, and we should be enjoying boundless pleasure in the world of eternity, but our delusions imprison us with individual limitations, and thus we take a long journey of transmigration from one realm of suffering to another. We must escape from this imprisonment. We must free ourselves from these delusions. This is the origin of the idea of emancipation, and both Brahmanism and Buddhism have this current of thought. The more one contemplates the ideal of the true self, the more one dislikes one's life of human desires. In that way, the *Upanishads* encouraged a pessimistic outlook.

In the *Upanishads*, there are four ways to seek emancipation:

One: Deliverance through the supreme power of a personal god. In the time of the *Rig-veda*, some people believed that one who led a moral life would be reborn in the happy world called Yama. This result could sooner be attained by paying homage to Brahman, than by following the ordinary course of cause and effect. Such an idea was common among all races at that stage of primitive development. The "Other Power" sects of Buddhism, which rely on the power of Amida or other buddhas, are the offspring of this belief.

Two: Individual emancipation. Our spirit is pure and free from the very beginning, but our attachment to the five senses conceals the brightness of the mirror of mind. Those who want to escape from the suffering of the world must drive out all sorts of desires and recover original purity and freedom. There is no necessity for a god or understanding of absolute reality to accomplish this ethical independence. Yoga aims to attain this kind of emancipation.

Three: Negation of the will to live. One who belongs to this class of emancipation sees life as nothing but delusions, and thinks that as long as there is a life, there must be suffering. Theravada Buddhism was mistakenly classified in this category, because some followers define nirvana as extinction. Schopenhauer had a similar idea.

Four: Emancipation by realizing absolute reality within oneself. This class of emancipation is monism, while the other three are either dualism or pluralism. Contrary to the other negative forms, this one is positive, and manifests in the practical world with fewer tendencies toward morbid ideas. Self is seen as small, impermanent, and impure when compared to the universe or ultimate reality, but once unified with the absolute, it becomes great, eternal, and beautiful. This oneness is called Brahma in later Vedic thought, and is called Tathata (*shinnyo* in Japanese) or Dharmakaya in Mahayana Buddhism. Shingon, Buddhist mysticism, teaches that our bodies are Buddha's body itself; and Zen sees the phenomena of birth and death as nirvana, true peacefulness itself.

What, then, is Buddhist emancipation? Buddhism sees the world in two ways. One is *sankata*, and the other, *asankata*. Sankata is the world of comparison, where everything exists in dualistic terms: high and low, good and bad, right and wrong, etc. In this world, although there is no creator or ruler, the law of cause and effect functions through material and spiritual phenomena. Everything exists only in relation to everything else. The world is simply a phenomenon of various interrelationships. When one realizes that there is nothing outside the relationship of subjective and objective elements, one begins to see the world of asankata, the creative and universal principle that flows from eternity to eternity. Before one is enlightened, one experiences the world only through the law of causation. In fact there are not two worlds at all. One's mind freely harmonizes with universal law when one practices purification and lives a life of wisdom and compassion. This is the goal of Zen.

February 18, 1936

How to Study Buddhism

BODHISATTVAS: My wish as a Buddhist monk is to have no permanent place to stay, but to be like a lone cloud floating freely in the blue sky. Even though I have been living in this shelter for Buddhist monks for six years and seven months, I have always considered myself a pilgrim on a wandering journey. It is a transient stay; therefore, I do not worry about tomorrow. It is today that I am living with gratitude. How can my regrets have anything to do with the happenings of yesterday? If I have to go away on a long trip, some other monk may make a transient stay in this shelter. As long as this principle of *annica*, the principle of impermanence, is practiced, this shelter will remain a Buddhist one. In fact, I am passing away every day. What you saw in me yesterday, you cannot see anymore. Tomorrow you will meet a man who looks like Senzaki, thinks like Senzaki, and talks like Senzaki, but he is not the Senzaki you met today. As long as you dwell in such an understanding of *anatta*, the principle of non-individuality, the friendship between you and me will be a Buddhist one.

If you desire to move our meditation hall into another location to increase our comfort and pleasure, you are clinging to delusions. Buddhists, true Buddhists, never use propaganda. I did not ask you to come to this place; your own buddha-nature led you here. A new location and a better house might draw more people, but if we have no Buddhist spirit within, what would be the use of having a crowd around us? Some may say that they are satisfied with this location and with this house, but that we must have a more attractive place for the sake of strangers. This world is, however, nothing but the realm of dissatisfaction. Wherever one goes, one must face some sort of suffering. This is the principle of *dukkha* that the Buddha repeatedly taught about. Those who come for comfort and pleasure will never be satisfied in a Buddhist house. They do not belong there from the very beginning. So why should we try to attract them?

This house is a shelter for Buddhist monks, and you are all our honorable guests. Therefore you should feel obliged to follow the principles for which this house stands. If you want to meditate, I will join you in meditation. If you want to study the scriptures, I will assist you in learning about them. If you want to keep the precepts and take monastic vows, I will ordain you as monks, nuns, *upasakas*, or *upasikas* [Buddhist laymen or laywomen] and will endeavor to live the Buddhist life with you. If you want to donate material or immaterial things, the monks will receive them in the name of *dana paramita* (the virtue of giving). You need not worry about how and where your seeds of charity are planted. Just give, and forget about your having given. This is the only way to maintain the Sangha, the community of practicing Buddhists.

No guests at a Buddhist house need concern themselves about how to spread the teaching and how to maintain the movement. Their time should be taken up in studying meditation, digesting the scriptures, and practicing what they are learning in their own lives. With this true spirit, the teachings of Buddha will continue in their proper form.

Of course, I have no objection to your starting a new movement with the understanding you have attained, but while you are coming to this meditation hall, I wish you to be the silent partner of Zen. Throw away your ideas about teaching others, and devote yourselves to study. There are 1,700 koans that you have to pass. There are 5,000 books on Buddhism written in European languages that require your reading, not to mention sutras and commentaries written in Chinese and Japanese. And as for realization, once you think you have attained something, you will have fallen ten thousand feet down, and you will have to start up from the bottom again.

I am telling you this in such a severe way because I want you to attain real Buddhist enlightenment, the true emancipation of Zen Buddhism. What some may call spiritual attainment may satisfy worldly desires, but if it is not the highest stage of nirvana, you will drop to the world of dust again like an arrow shot toward the sky. Whatever I say is the echo of my teacher's wisdom, and whatever my teacher told me is the wisdom of his teacher, and on back through seventy-nine teachers, finally reaching Buddha Shakyamuni. I could give you a longer discourse, but unless you are ready to enter samadhi, the more you hear, the more unnecessary burdens you will carry upon your shoulders. Just come, all of you, and practice true Buddhism. Follow the discipline of Zen and forget about your self-limited worldly opinions.

October 3, 1937

Zen Buddhism in the Light of Modern Thought

BODHISATTVAS: Let us consider some problems of life from the viewpoint of Zen Buddhism, which is free from the entanglement of sentiment.

The first problem is that of "miracles." The Buddha had no desire to perform miracles in order to establish any claim to a divine nature. The performing of wonders results from a complete understanding of the laws of nature; it is no secret power, no divine grace, but merely the result of wisdom.

When the King of Kosala demanded of the Buddha that he permit his monks to perform miracles, he answered, "I do not teach my disciples the law that I may say to them, 'Go, ye monks, and perform miracles before the people,' but thus I teach the law: 'Live, O monks, concealing your good deeds, and revealing your faults.' O King, this is the law I teach."

A Zen master in China once said, "Do you want to see me perform miracles? I draw the water from a well and carry it home in a pail. I chop wood and build a fire with it."

This meditation hall is sometimes quite warm in the summer, and somewhat cold even in early winter, but we always feel it is just right when we have tea together in the kitchen. This is our miracle, and we are satisfied and happy—what else could we want?

The second problem is in regard to the existence of "a secret doctrine." Is there a secret doctrine in Buddhism? One who understands esoteric Buddhism to mean that there is some hidden doctrine that is disclosed by the master to the disciple is in error. Those who have invented stories to the contrary have shown themselves to be very ignorant of the Buddhist scriptures. The Buddha expressly declared that he kept nothing hidden. He said to Ananda, his beloved disciple, when he was about to pass away, "I am not one of those teachers with a hidden teaching, who with closed fists keeps something back." A Zen master said, "I am showing my heart thoroughly, from inside out. If there is anything hidden, you are the guilty one, not I."

The third problem is "sin." What is sin? There is a dark current of thought among Christian followers regarding sin. The teachings of Jesus have been sadly prostituted by a corrupt priesthood for the purpose of power and politics; the people are kept in fearsome ignorance. Anyone acquainted with church history knows this. The Greek work *hamartia*, which is translated "sin" in the New Testament, actually means "a failure to hit the mark," or "fault," so when Jesus said to the man sick with palsy, "Son, be of good cheer, thy sins are forgiven," it should read, "Son, be of good cheer, thy failures (or thy faults) have been sent away (banished)." The original of the word "forgive" should be translated, "send away, put out, let go." This reading makes quite a difference.

The same holds true for good and evil. When we have good thoughts and perform good deeds, we have hit the mark. When we have evil thoughts and perform evil deeds, we have committed a "failure"—we have failed to hit the mark. Nowhere is there a deity involved in the matter. Our behavior is a matter of ethics. Heaven and hell are in no sense whatever to be regarded as reward and punishment, respectively. Quite simply, they result from actions, just as the sensation of burning is a result of, not a punishment for, swallowing a scalding cup of hot chocolate; or the sensation of sweetness is the result of, not the reward for, drinking a glass of honey sherbet. In all matters concerning a future life, the attitude of the Buddhist is a simple one: "Act well here and now, and whatever may happen in the future cannot but be favorable."

The fourth problem regards "Buddhism and the needs of today." If we could decide on the needs of today, then perhaps we could decide whether Buddhism could meet them or not. The greatest need of today is to realize that all life is one, which would bring about the elimination of selfishness and everything akin to it. For this, Buddhism is highly qualified to answer the needs of today, since that understanding is its basic principle. The next problem is a good example.

The fifth problem is "the question of matter." Ancient Buddhists taught that *akasa*—a substance akin to our modern ether—is formless, eternal, infinite, and uncaused, and that the material universes are constructed from that akasa, and of the four elements that emanate from it. Here it is necessary to point out that the terms commonly translated "air, fire, earth, and water," do not at all bear the meanings of the physical substances we call by those same names—it is expressly stated, for example, that the pure earth element is invisible and immaterial in the ordinary sense of the word.

In our modern phraseology we would term these elements of the ancient Buddhists as forces rather than elements, although, as far as that goes, seeing that physicists nowadays recognize no solid ultimate atom, the term forces might equally well be applied to our own chemical elements. The four elements proceeding from akasa are indeed rather nearer to our own modern conceptions of elements, for they consist of the primary forces whereby the akasa is molded into gross matter. Their best translation would be *vayu* (motility), *tejo* (radiability), *apo* (cohesion), and *pathavi* (inertia). Of these four, with akasa as their basis, the material universe is constructed; and thus in their conceptions of the ultimate constitution of matter, science and Buddhism are in agreement.

The sixth problem is "Buddhism and modern thought." The founder of Buddhism was himself a thorough-going evolutionist. He held firmly to the great law of cause and effect, to which he could find no exception anywhere; and, as he studied this law, he discovered another, namely, the law of change. To this also he could perceive no exception. These two doctrines stamp Buddhism as an original, unique, and scientific religion.

Among other things, this law of change implies a rejection of the soul theory and any permanent self. We can see forms appearing and disappearing, in an eternal state of perpetual flux. The Buddha clearly discerned this truth twenty-five centuries ago. Standing on the firm ground of facts, Buddhism welcomes all progress and has never contested the prerogative of reason to be the ultimate truth, and, accordingly, requires nothing to be accepted without inquiry. Reason, says Buddhism, not superstition, not mere tradition, not the will to believe, not pragmatic utility, must be the foundation.

Zen aims at nothing but this reason. You are, however, not allowed to speak this reason, or to think of this reason, but to live in it as the fish, without knowing it, lives in the water. When the emperor of China asked, "What merit will I get for doing so much to establish Buddhism?" Bodhidharma replied, "No merit at all."

undated

Buddhism and Women

BODHISATTVAS: Buddha's noble Eightfold Path is the road to moral and intellectual perfection. It may seem to separate into eight different directions, but since each of the eight is the right direction, it will lead you nowhere but to your own peaceful home. The eight directions are: right view, right resolution, right speech, right action, right livelihood, right effort, right awareness, and right concentration. These eight directions are provided for men and for women alike. Buddha prescribed this noble Eightfold Path for all, regardless of sex, caste, or race. It was the true road for everybody 2,500 years ago, and it is the same for us in our time.

Buddhism is a teaching for men and for women alike. There is no sex discrimination in the Dharma. This is the truth that Buddha taught. However, and I do not know how it started, there have been many words against women, even in Buddhist countries like Japan and China. Some Buddhists in those countries believe that it was women's sinful karma that caused them to have been born as women in this life. Such beliefs are certainly reason for indignant protest. The law of causation works upon men and women alike, and it works upon good karma and bad karma alike. Why condemn women exclusively, as if men can transcend the karmic process? In a true Buddhist view, no one is born as a sinner; on the contrary, we are all born to attain enlightenment, to free ourselves from worldly delusions, and to enlighten those who follow us.

In one of the Buddhist sutras, a disciple said that women have five hindrances: that they cannot become buddhas, kings, devils, angels, or gods.

Then Buddha proved to this disciple that an eight-year-old girl attained enlightenment; her understanding placed her above the gods, devils, angels, and kings, and she entered buddhahood instantly. Modern women already can become gods, devils, angels, and kings, so why should they not become buddhas? If they do not, it is their own fault.

A Chinese proverb says, "A woman should be obedient to her parents when young, to her husband when married, and to her children when she is old." Such a saying is merely a custom adhered to by traditional Asian families, and has nothing to do with the principles of Buddhism.

In the life of Buddha, nothing is said upon the subject of whether a man or a woman is better suited to access Dharma. Buddha had male disciples and female disciples, and he honored both. His male disciples were called *bhikshus*, and his female disciples, *bhikshunis*. Bhikshus were ordered to keep 250 precepts, and bhikshunis, 500 precepts. This sounds as if Buddha was quite severe with his women disciples, by requiring them to follow twice the number of rules as male disciples. However, Buddha's teachings were expressed in these precepts. For instance, the precept "speak no lie" has the positive virtue implied, "Tell the truth and enlighten others." Seeing it this way, women disciples were qualified to perform 500 virtues.

We know from the history of the life of Shakyamuni Buddha that he was a prince married to the Princess Yasodhara. Before the prince left home to seek the way of emancipation, he and his wife had a son, Rahula. After the Buddha attained enlightenment, he returned home. When Yasodhara saw him in the garb of a mendicant, she burst into tears, fell down before him, and clasped his knees. Buddha raised her up, comforted her with gentle words, and explained what he had realized. His words spoke to her heart, and she, too, became his disciple. Is this not a beautiful page in this sage's history?

Buddhism entered China in the middle part of the first century of the Christian era, and flowered in the T'ang and Sung dynasties, between the seventh century and the fourteenth century. Chinese Buddhism entered

Japan in the sixth century, and, since then, Japanese people have adopted this teaching as a keynote of their culture. Even in this modern age, they study and practice the Dharma, the Buddha's teachings, with ceaseless endeavor. The complete system of Buddha's teachings now remains in Japan. You can find some parts of Mahayana teaching in China, Korea, Tibet, Nepal, and Bhutan, and the attitude of those Buddhists toward women is positive, since they all believe that the realization of Dharma in this life is possible for men and women alike. Theravada Buddhism in Siam, Burma, and Ceylon is also quite fair to women, especially in Burma. According to Fielding Hall, women lead an ideal life there. Mr. Hall is the author of a book called *The Soul of a People*, in which the influence of Buddhism is examined. He wrote, "That man's greatest attraction is woman does not infer wickedness in woman; that woman's greatest attraction is man does not show that man is a devil. Wickedness is a thing of your own heart."

In addition to scholarship about Dharma, the penetrating wisdom of Buddha has been preserved by the Zen masters of China and Japan. They have studied not only the Dharma in written form, but also have realized and actualized the essence of Dharma. The inner treasure has been handed down from master to disciple, just as the flame of one candle might be used to light many more.

When I mention Zen, some may think that I am talking about something different from the general body of Buddhism—that Zen is some sect made in Japan and imported here. Zen is not the name of a sect. It is an expression for the realization and actualization of the Dharma. If your wish is to carry on the work of book-learning, you will not find much profit in Zen; Zen has no textbook. It considers the sutras to be wrapping paper for one's own inner treasure. Zen respects the sutras as being a means to enlightenment. Each is a golden bridge toward buddhahood. But if you do not practice meditation, you have nothing to do with Zen. When you learn meditation, you are a Zen student. The original Sanskrit word for meditation is *dhyana*, but we continue to use the Japanese word

Zen, because for many centuries now, Japan has carried the lamp of Dharma handed down from Buddha himself to the masters. In the future, you can call it by a nice English name, or one in German, French, Spanish, or Esperanto. For now, just exert yourselves in meditation, and try to find out what your real "I" looks like. Are not your book-learning and reasoning also for the same purpose? Just ignore the name, and take it for what it is. Otherwise, later on you will laugh at your own ignorance.

When Zen teaching—that is, the lamp of Dharma—entered China from India, there were at first very few students. I want to tell you that a nun was in that first group. The Chinese nun's name was Soji (Ch.: Zongchi), and she was a disciple of Bodhidharma. The fruit of meditation that she acquired was splendid. When this teaching entered Japan, the first person who attained enlightenment was a woman—Empress Danrin Kogo, who was married to Emperor Saga. So the first Japanese to receive the lamp of Dharma that had been handed down from master to disciple continuously since Shakyamuni Buddha was a woman.

Here in America, too, a woman was the first person to open her inner eye in studying Zen. Her name was Ida Russell; she was married to Alexander Russell. She went to Japan and studied under my master, Soyen Shaku.

So you see, we have had women pioneers in Buddhism—not mere scholars, but the inheritors of brilliant Buddhadharma itself. Women students: study ceaselessly, and meet your own true self face to face! When the time comes, you will see that your everyday road is none other than the noble Eightfold Path, and you yourself will be a buddha in this very life.

undated

Obaku's Transmission of Mind
Part One

BODHISATTVAS: It is such a pleasure to meet you again in this zendo. Whenever my wandering spirit gets loose, it turns North, toward this foggy city of San Francisco. Even a homeless monk must have a sort of home in the bottom of his heart. During my stay here, we will study the teachings of an ancient Zen master, Obaku Kiun (d. 850), using the translation by D.T. Suzuki in his *Manual of Zen Buddhism*.

Suzuki uses the modern Chinese pronunciation for Obaku, Huang-Po. He titles this section *Huang-Po's Sermon: From the Treatise on the Essentials of the Transmission of Mind*. He also gives the title as it is pronounced in Japanese, *Denshin Hoyo*. *Den* means "transmission," and *shin* is "Mind," with a capital M. As Zen students, you all know this Mind with a capital M. It does not mean our psychological mind, but what may be called absolute Mind, or Buddha-Mind. So *denshin* means "the transmission of Buddha-Mind." *Hoyo* means "treatise on the essentials."

The master was preaching this sermon to Pai-hsiu (Haikyu, in Japanese), the premier of the Chinese government of his time. The aim of the treatise is to show that this one Mind is the Buddha, who is not to be considered separate from sentient beings. If the listener, the premier Haikyu, can realize his own Buddha-Mind, he can lead the same life as the master, and thus the transmission of Mind will be fulfilled.

Historically speaking, this sermon was given in China in the middle of the ninth century. However, it goes beyond any specific place and time.

See it as your own case, and receive the benefit. Obaku is the name of the mountain where this master lived. His name was Kiun, but people called him Obaku, the master of Obaku Mountain, just as we call Emerson the sage of Concord. Obaku is also the name of a tree that belongs to the cork family, or cork-oak. In Japan, we call it kiwada, "yellow bark." The trees must have been growing thickly on the mountain where the master lived. A medicine that has a peculiar acrid taste like quinine is made from the bark and fruits of this tree. It always reminds me, when I think of the bitterness of this medicine, of the poignant, keen, and severe Zen of Master Obaku, although it must have been a mere coincidence that he lived on that mountain. Rinzai, who was a master renowned for his harshness, was the successor of our Obaku. His Zen tastes like a Mexican tamale. The American mind was originally spontaneous and fresh, like good coffee, but since dogmas, religious creeds, and many strange cults from strange lands have been stirred into it, it is as though too much sugar has been poured in, and it has become too sweet. It wants now the bitter, pungent taste of Zen. Let me read the first chapter:

> The Master said to Pai-hsiu: "Buddhas and sentient beings both grow out of One Mind, and there is no other reality than this Mind. It has been in existence since the beginningless past; it knows neither birth nor death; it is neither blue nor yellow; it has neither shape nor form; it is beyond the category of being and non-being; it is not to be measured by age, old or new; it is neither long nor short; it is neither large nor small; for it transcends all limits, words, traces, and opposites. It must be taken just as it is in itself; when an attempt is made on our part to grasp it in our thoughts, it eludes. It is like space whose boundaries are altogether beyond measurement; no concepts are applicable here."

For those who understand Zen, Obaku's words are not new or strange at all. It is as though they are hearing their own words; they simply nod and smile. I respect each of you as an independent and capable

Zen student, so I will not spoil your taste of Obaku's Zen with any comment or explanation. Here is Suzuki's footnote to this chapter:

> One of the first lessons in the understanding of Buddhism is to know what is meant by the Buddha and by sentient beings. This distinction goes on throughout all branches of the Buddhist teaching. The Buddha is an enlightened one who has seen into the reason of existence, while sentient beings are ignorant multitudes confused in mind and full of defilements. The object of Buddhism is to have all sentient beings attain enlightenment like the Buddha. The question is whether they are of the same nature as the latter; for if not, they can never be enlightened as he is. The spiritual cleavage between the two being seemingly too wide for passage, it is often doubted whether there is anything in sentient beings that will transform them into Buddhahood. The position of Zen Buddhism is that One Mind pervades all and therefore there is no distinction to be made between the Buddha and sentient beings and that as far as Mind is concerned the two are of one nature. What is then this Mind? Huang-po attempts to solve this question for his disciple Pai-hsiu in these sermons.

Suzuki capitalizes the first letter of both "One" and "Mind," while for "enlightened one," he uses no capitals. Other English writers of Buddhist books capitalize "Enlightened One," influenced by the sweetness of some God-idea or conception of hero-worship. In not capitalizing "enlightened one," Suzuki suggests that it is to be found in all walks of life, like a potato that can be picked up in any field. But One Mind is absolute. It has no comparison. Therefore Suzuki uses capitals for those words.

Obaku's Transmission of Mind
Part Two

The second paragraph of D.T. Suzuki's translation reads:

> This One Mind only is the Buddha, who is not to be segregated from sentient beings. But because we seek it outwardly in a world of form, the more we seek the further it moves away from us. To make Buddha seek after himself, or to make Mind take hold of itself—this is an impossibility to the end of eternity. We do not realize that as soon as our thoughts cease and all attempts at forming ideas are forgotten the Buddha reveals himself before us.

Some frequent visitors to Muso-an could not join us this evening, but all of them can be with us if they enter into samadhi at home. Samadhi is another name for Zen meditation. In this sermon, Obaku calls it One Mind, and says it "is the Buddha, who is not to be segregated from sentient beings." When you enter into samadhi, you have nothing to receive, and there is nothing to receive you. There is no place to enter, and there is nobody who enters. Obaku calls such a stage of meditation the Buddha who is not segregated from sentient beings. The minute you see Buddha as segregated from sentient beings, you are out of samadhi, and your Zen meditation becomes a failure. Why? Because you give Buddha an outer form at that moment, and hold yourself separate from Buddha. Obaku says, "Only because we seek it outwardly in a world of form, the more we seek, the further it moves away from us." Obaku's Zen does not allow even the slightest shadow of a lingering form. He uses his big stick to hit students who hanker after such a shadow. His Zen has the bitterness of strychnine and the heat of cayenne pepper. Why? Because he wants students to attain sudden and abrupt realization. He says, "To make Buddha seek after himself, or to make Mind take hold of itself—this is an impossibility to the end of eternity." Obaku's Buddha is the One Mind that is not segregated from sentient beings. One who, having committed innumerable sins, seeks to be saved by Buddha, thus segregates himself from Buddha, and deserves the blow of Obaku's big stick. Another, who tries to hold on to One Mind through dualistic speculation, merely plays a psychological game, and can never realize the essence of being. That one, too, deserves Obaku's big stick.

At the end of this paragraph, Obaku says, "We do not realize that as soon as our thoughts cease and all attempts at forming ideas are forgotten the Buddha reveals himself before us." He is thus assuring us that Zen meditation is true emancipation. Since the Buddha is another name for One Mind, he reveals himself even among religious minds of other faiths. Meister Eckhart, a Christian mystic, said, "The eye with which I see God is the very eye with which God sees me." We use these words as a koan to cut off all attempts at conceptualizing. When you work on this koan, you will see that there is no God, no "me," but just one eye, glaring eternally. You are at the gate of Zen at that moment. Don't be afraid, just keep on meditating, repeating the koan in silence: "The eye with which I see God is the very eye with which God sees me." There is no reality other than this one eye. If you repeat this again and again, you will at last find yourself at home, dwelling in One Mind without recognizing it as One Mind. You will find that your days have fewer burdens and more happiness. Your hours outside meditation will be spent in the same happy frame of mind, and you will accomplish everyday tasks easily, with calmness and contentment. You will read Zen books with new understanding, as if they were your own writings. Of course, you must continue to devote as much time to meditation as you can.

Obaku's Transmission of Mind
Part Three

BODHISATTVAS: Let us continue our study of *The Treatise on the Essentials of the Transmission of Mind* with Obaku's third paragraph: "This Mind is no other than the Buddha, and Buddha is no other than sentient beings. When Mind assumes the form of a sentient being, it has suffered no decrease; when it becomes a Buddha, it has not added anything to itself. Even when we speak of the six virtues of perfection (*paramitas*) and other ten thousand meritorious deeds equal in number to the sands of the Ganges, they are all in the being of Mind itself; they are not something that can be added to by means of discipline. When conditions (*pratyaya*) are at work, it is set up; when conditions cease to operate, it remains quiet. Those who have no definite faith in this, that Mind is Buddha, and attempt an achievement by means of discipline attached to form, are giving themselves up to wrong imagination; they deviate from the right path."

Some of you coming to this meditation class for the first time may think that we are attempting an achievement—advancing toward becoming buddhas. Christians gather at a prayer meeting and believe that their purification is more advanced than it was at their last meeting. Islamists count every bow as a stepping-stone toward Mecca. If our new friends think that we are burning incense and meditating here to accumulate meritorious deeds, the way passengers on San Francisco streetcars pay two cents for each transfer, I appreciate the compliment, but our master of this evening, the great Obaku, will deny it. He calls such an idea "wrong imagination," and warns of deviating from the right path. Perhaps his Zen is too strong this evening. Let me add some water to it, and offer you another cup.

Confucius said, "I have talked with Kwai, my best disciple, for a whole day, and he has not made any objection to anything I have said. It is as if he were stupid. I have examined his conduct now that he has gone away from me, and I have found him able to illustrate my teaching. Kwai, my disciple, is not stupid!" This is one of the Confucian analects. You see here a man of practicality who looks like a fool and his teacher, another apparent fool, admiring him. In the analects of Zen, we might say, "I have stayed with my brother monk all day long. He did not say a word. I did not hear a thing. We two stupid-heads were happy."

Confucianism is an ethical teaching with a dualistic base; therefore it attempts "an achievement by means of a discipline attached to form," as Obaku put it. Lao-Tsu said, "One excels who regards one's best achievement as inconsequential." Confucius was once a disciple of Lao-Tsu, but he did not learn the teacher's Way. Lao-Tsu never knew about Buddhism, but he attained Zen by himself. I am not degrading the teaching of Confucius, but it is not a path of perfect emancipation, as Buddhism is.

In another story, a Taoist was told by the emperor that he would be honored as a great teacher. He ran away and hid himself in the remote mountains. He washed his ears, stooping over a stream. Another Taoist happened to meet him there, and asked what he was doing. After he was told, the second Taoist said, "So, your ears became quite dusty from hearing about the world of honor. I will not allow my cow to drink this polluted water." These two "nuts" thought themselves free from attachment, but they only dreamed of a formless achievement, imagining it to be the true path. They were poor students of Taoism. Lao-Tsu said in the *Tao Te Ching*, "Heaven and earth do not act from any wish to be benevolent; they deal with all things according to their nature. Likewise, the sage does not act from any wish to be benevolent; he deals with people according to their nature."

Obaku says, "This Mind is no other than the Buddha, and Buddha is no other than sentient beings." He shows us the whole—no more, no less. Then he says, "When Mind assumes the form of a sentient being, it has suffered no decrease; when it becomes a Buddha, it has not added anything to itself." A poor potato and a good plum each grow on the same ground, but one comes from the earth, and the other drops onto it. The whole neither increases nor decreases.

"Even when we speak of the six virtues of perfection (*paramitas*) and other ten thousand meritorious deeds equal in number to the sands of the Ganges, they are all in the being of Mind itself; they are not something that can be added to it by means of discipline," Obaku says. The six paramitas are: sacrifice, moral behavior, perseverance, constancy, meditation, and wisdom. They are the natural functioning of Dharmakaya, or Mind, as Obaku calls it; therefore they are not properties to be added to Mind "by means of discipline." We Zen Buddhists devote ourselves to meditation not as a means to get enlightened, but to experience enlightenment itself. We have no God to please or bribe, no Satan of whom to be afraid, no reward or merit to expect, and no goal to set. Our task of actualization is the whole of it. Thus, we have no aim for the future, no regrets from the past, but simply apply ourselves to this task minute after minute, continuously.

Such a bunch of fools we are! When conditions are at work, that is to say, when our congenial wishes to save all sentient beings meet, the Sangha of bodhisattvahood takes shape. Some of us come from a country 6,000 miles away; some find family relationships suddenly spiritual— brothers in the world become brothers in Zen. Such a condition is called *pratyaya* in Sanskrit, *yuan* in Chinese, *en* in Japanese. Obaku further says, "When conditions cease to operate, it remains quiet." This does not mean that bodhisattvahood disappears from the world. Even in these times of fighting *asuras*, amid all the struggles of the world, at the bottom of the stormy sea of samsara the Mind remains quiet, calmly observing it all. Obaku then says, "Those who have no definite faith in this, that Mind is Buddha, and attempt an achievement by means of discipline attached to form, are giving themselves up to wrong imagination; they deviate from the right path." You see, he is not the cranky old fellow we thought he was.

Obaku's Transmission of Mind
Part Four

BODHISATTVAS: In my fourth lecture on Obaku's *The Treatise on the Essentials of the Transmission of Mind*, I will use my own translation from the original Chinese, not depending upon that of D.T. Suzuki:

Master Obaku said to Haikyo, "One Mind makes buddhas, and also makes all sentient beings. There is nothing else but this Mind. From eternity to eternity, this Mind was never born, and therefore never dies. It is not blue. It is not yellow. It has no shape. It has no form. You cannot say it exists. You cannot say it perishes. It is not new. It is not old. It is not long. It is not short. It is not great. It is not small. It transcends quantity, name, description, trace, and relation. Everything is but this Mind, and none other. The minute you think of it, you are away from it. The sky has no limit. Therefore, you cannot measure it. It is the same with Mind.

"Mind is Buddha, and none other. Sentient beings are buddhas, and none other. Those who cling to form seek Buddha without Mind and without sentient beings. The more they seek, the further they separate from Buddha. Buddha searches for Buddha, and Mind searches for Mind; even with endless repetition, it is impossible to reach. When one stops forming ideas, one can actually realize the truth. How many seekers know this bare fact?

"Mind becomes sentient beings, without decreasing itself. It also becomes buddhas and sages, without increasing itself. The six virtues (paramitas) are Mind, and none other." Again, the six virtues are sacrifice, moral behavior, perseverance, constancy, meditation, and wisdom. "They are the innate virtues of human beings. Countless deeds are nothing but the working of Mind. The virtues may be dormant powers, but they are inherent in each person equally. They are not to be cultivated outwardly. They naturally come forth when human actions are directed by Mind. It is like a calm sea. The thousands and thousands of waves do not leave the water; the water itself makes the waves. Those who, wishing to attain perfection, search for it outwardly are taking the wrong road. They are dreaming of something impossible to reach."

Some Americans are eager to attain Zen. They do not miss a single Zen book written in English. They attend Zen lectures without fail. They want to hear all about Zen monks and monasteries. Some of them collect Zen pictures and portraits of Zen masters. It is all very well to take a fancy to this strange teaching, but as for its attainment, those students are not walking in the right direction. Obaku warns them strongly: "Those who have no definite faith in this, that Mind is Buddha, and attempt an achievement by means of discipline attached to form, are giving themselves up to wrong imagination; they deviate from the right path."

The sermon of Obaku, as far as we have studied it, is to encourage students to practice meditation more than anything else. He says repeatedly, "This Mind is Buddha, and none other. All sentient beings are buddhas, and none other." Let me read again from Suzuki's translation: "This One Mind only is the Buddha, who is not to be segregated from sentient beings. Only because we seek it outwardly in a world of form, the more we seek the further it moves away from us. To make Buddha seek after himself, or to make Mind take hold of itself, this is an impossibility to the end of eternity. We do not realize that as soon as our thoughts cease and all attempts at forming ideas are forgotten, the Buddha reveals himself before us."

Mumon says in a comment in the *Gateless Gate*, "Enlightenment always comes after the road of thinking is blocked. If your thinking road is not blocked, whatever you think, whatever you do, is a dangling ghost."

Our zendo is open morning and evening for sincere students who come here to meditate. Reading or copying a Zen book is a rather heavy task. Why do you not give it up, enter into meditation, and feel yourselves becoming lighter and cooler?

Muso-an, San Francisco
March 3–July 21, 1938

Esoteric Buddhism in Japan

Shingon calls itself "esoteric Buddhism," and considers other schools of Japanese Buddhism, like Kegon, Tendai, Zen, or Jodo, to be "exoteric teachings." I am a mere student, and I am only interested in studying Buddhist thought as human experience. To do propaganda for one sect or another, or to convert others into believers, is not my business at all. There are many specialists, almost too many of them, in that line, and I am not going to butt into their field.

Religious experience is beyond the realm of cognition, and whatever is said about it expresses a mere shadow of the truth. What Shingon calls esoteric Buddhism is the very thing that Zen calls inner teaching. When you drink water, you know for yourself whether it is cold or warm. You can describe your feeling in some way, but that will never express exactly what you felt. A Zen master said, "What I have told you is no secret at all. When you realize the truth for yourself, the secret belongs to you."[48]

You see, esoteric, inner, or secret teaching is right here for anyone who is brave enough to experience it. The Theosophists are my dear friends. They read Madam H.P. Blavatsky's *The Secret Doctrine* from cover to cover, but none of them has the same brilliant wisdom as the author. Why? Because they do not know how to enter into the book. That book is not a mere matter of reading. If you actually experience what Madam Blavatsky attained, the secret belongs to nobody but you. In speaking about Shingon teachings, which come from the same source as Tibetan wisdom, it is my sincere wish to encourage all of you, including my dear friends the Theosophists, to realize the truth as it is written on their altar, "There is no higher religion than truth."

Mandalas and meditation are ways of practicing Shingon Buddhism. There is no single mandala separate from other mandalas, just as there is no mind separate from the body. To draw a Shingon mandala takes many years' work on the part of a good artist. Japanese mandalas are more than beautiful. I hope some day a wealthy Theosophist who realizes the foolishness of accumulating money will donate a Shingon mandala to this library. It will help students learn how to enter into *The Secret Doctrine*, instead of abusing printed pages like trash.

The Shingon mandalas Taizokai and Kongokai (in Sanskrit, Garbhakosadhatu and Vajradhatu) respectively represent objectivity and subjectivity. When you see the Buddha outside yourself, it is the mandala of Taizokai, and when you see it within you, it is the mandala of Kongokai. If you think you are hearing such explanations from Senzaki, you are a student of exoteric Buddhism. If you feel as though an old memory from the remote past is coming to you, before I even finish this lecture you will be stepping out of the exoteric teaching, and you will smell the fragrance of esoteric Buddhism.

In the Taizokai Mandala, 414 buddhas and bodhisattvas are depicted. Each buddha reveals the completeness of wisdom and compassion, and each bodhisattva represents helpfulness toward other beings. In the center is Vairochana, surrounded by eight buddhas. The Taizokai Mandala depicts the objective truth of the universe. It can be realized only when we actualize wisdom. Until that time, it is like a woman's pregnant condition. Taizo means "Pregnant State."

The Kongokai Mandala represents subjectivity. It is Mind. When it reveals itself as wisdom, it crushes all delusions the way a powerful weapon vanquishes enemies. Kongo means "Diamond Cutter." In this mandala, the whole universe is divided into nine blocks, each having certain numbers of buddhas and bodhisattvas, for a total of 1,461. One enters into the field of Vairochana and then moves into other blocks to save beings.

Some Christians think that they will stay in Paradise forever, hearing the music of harps played by angels. They never think of coming back from the pleasures of Heaven. Buddhists do not wish to stay long in the field of Vairochana. They come down to offer their service to humans and other sentient beings.

In Shingon depictions of esoteric truth, the Great Mandala is the Buddha-image of Vairochana, or ultimate reality. The Sammaya Mandala represents whatever is in the hand of the image, such as a flower, beads, or a sutra scroll. The Dharma Mandala refers to the Sanskrit letters in the sutra; and the Katsuma Mandala is the Buddha as represented by each individual human body. Each of these mandalas can be Kongokai or Taizokai, that is, theoretical or practical; manifesting wisdom and compassion or objectivity and resolve. Each relates to the others, so that when one mandala is activated, the others act accordingly.

If you have a statue or a picture of a buddha or a bodhisattva in your home, you can use it as a Great Mandala. Regard the whole body of that buddha or bodhisattva, from head to feet. In that moment, you are connecting with the Great Mandala. Next, you think of the reason why this buddha appeared in front of you. Some buddhas stand, and some sit, and their poses reveal their reason for being here. For instance, a meditation buddha is to calm you, and a standing buddha is to encourage your action. Some buddhas hold a flower, a rosary, or a sutra. The different poses are called Sammaya Mandala.

After looking at and connecting with the Great Mandala of the buddha, you will see the action of the buddha. How? You may ask. Your own response is the action of the buddha. An art dealer also has a response, estimating how much money he can make when he has a buddha statue for sale. He handles that buddha statue as merchandise, since he has no Shingon. When you learn calmness by contemplating a statue of a buddha, your pose is the buddha's pose, and the buddha's smiling face is yours. This is called the Katsuma Mandala or Karma Mandala in Shingon.

The sutra that Buddha Shakyamuni preached is his Dharma Mandala.

Buddha held a fruit and showed it to the audience when he preached the *Lankavatara Sutra*. If you see a statue of Buddha holding a fruit, you know it is a Dharma Mandala. Shingon students also see the Sanskrit capital letter of the name of a buddha or a sutra as Dharma Mandala. Theosophists call their founder "H.P.B." (H.P. Blavatsky) in the same way. In the world, if I call Mr. Jack London, saying "Hey, J.L.!" it is somewhat impolite, but in Shingon, if I say, "Om J.L. five-cents-a-word Svaha!" I am adoring him as a Dharma Mandala.[49] If I say, "Om F.D.R. Second-World-War, fourth-term Svaha!" it will be the same kind of adoration.

Shingon teachings emphasize the purification of body, mind, and word. When you meditate in the Shingon way, you must sit down as calmly as Buddha Shakyamuni. Americans can sit on chairs. It is not necessary to imitate the old Indian custom, sitting cross-legged. If you sit peacefully and forget that you are sitting, your whole body is purified at that moment. If the Buddha in a picture or a statue enters into you, and you enter into him, you are Buddha, and Buddha is you. In such an instance, your words are purified. Whatever words you speak, they are all Buddha's. Shingon students train themselves for this, reciting *dharani* (mystical incantations). There are hundreds of them, all of which are supposed to be the actual words of Buddha. The name Shingon means reciting the true words of Buddha. Modern philologists say that the language of most of the dharanis is a mix of broken Sanskrit and Tibetan, but since it is a symbol of faith, I rather advise Shingon students to carry it on as it is. Dharanis should be transmitted from mouth to ear, teacher to disciple, not in writing.

Shingon uses *mudras* (hand positions) in connection with purification. This is also transmitted from individual to individual. One is the lotus flower in bud. Another is the adoration of Buddha, symbolizing Buddha's head. A third is the open lotus flower. A fourth is for protection, using the Indian symbol of a weapon that crushes all delusions. A fifth is the symbol of a helmet, and represents constancy in keeping the precepts. With these mudras, you are a hero on a battlefield, vowing to crush all delusions.

As I said before, what Zen calls the inner teaching is no other than what Shingon calls esoteric Buddhism. Before Zen Buddhism went to Japan it passed through China, met Taoism there, and washed away some of the ancient ceremonies and rituals. Shingon carried with it the colorful rituals of Brahmanism, the esoteric Buddhism of China, and tinges of the indigenous religion of Tibet. Japanese Shingon was completed by Kobo Daishi.

Who was Kobo Daishi? And why do we Japanese Buddhists remember him for so long and admire him so much? Kobo Daishi was a homeless monk, just as I am now. Of course a diamond and charcoal are of the same simple element that chemistry calls carbon, but the former has its beautiful brilliance and everlasting solidity, while the latter has nothing but a shadowy black color and is liable to be reduced to ashes at any minute. Kobo Daishi means "great teacher who spread Buddhism among the people." It is a posthumous name given by Emperor Daigo, the sixtieth sovereign of Japan, eighty-six years after the monk's death. While living, the name of this monk was Kukai, which means "Ocean of Emptiness." The monk himself never thought his name would be stamped vividly on the history of Japan, but his profound knowledge and noble acts in expressing his faith and guiding the people of his time made the name the unshakable monument it is.

Kobo Daishi was born June 15, 774 C.E., in Sanuki on the island of Shikoku, in the southwestern part of Japan. He died when he was sixty-two years old, in 836. Kobo Daishi was favored by emperors and nobles, but he lived as a homeless monk. He was a good Sanskrit scholar, and studied the language systematically for the first time in the history of Japan. He mastered the spoken Chinese of his time, and went to China to study Mikkyo, esoteric Buddhism. Even though he stayed there less than three years, he brought the complete teaching to Japan, together with the cream of Chinese civilization, such as literature, fine arts, and applied science. He wrote more than one hundred books in beautiful classical Chinese on general Buddhism and esoteric teachings. He was a calligrapher, a sculptor, an architect, a poet, and an artist. Some of his works—sculptures he carved, paintings, and temples and pagodas he designed—still survive in Japan.

Kobo Daishi was certainly a Japanese Milarepa, if we can call Milarepa a Tibetan Kobo Daishi. He was a man of Saint Francis's compassion, Leonardo da Vinci's genius, Bacon's skillfulness in writing, and Martin Luther's braveness in reformation, all combined. He brought the Chinese educational system to Japan and founded a school for higher education in connection with his Kyoto temple; it was the first school in Japan to offer education to young men who were not of the noble or elite classes. He was also the inventor of the Japanese phonetic writing system.

Besides all this, he discovered hot springs and taught people their medicinal properties. He built many bath houses for public use, and encouraged people to learn cleanliness. He told the Japanese about coal and coal oil, and its usefulness as fuel. He planned roads and bridges. He suggested the building of dams and taught farmers how to conserve water for irrigation. He also introduced the manufacture of paper, brushes, and ink-blocks for writing, and even Japanese confectionery was invented by him, since it was he who brought sugar from China. He made new rulers and measures. He invented pigments and taught people how to dye their clothes. He promoted the newly introduced culture of the silkworm. Despite all these activities, the profound wisdom within him was always bright.

When old age approached, Kobo Daishi left his great temple in the city and retired to his remote mountain sanctuary on the summit of Mt. Koya, where in the year 835 C.E., on March 21, surrounded by his monks and his silent forests, he passed from this world. His grave is a mecca for throngs of devoted followers who come to pay homage to him, offering incense and candles. His loving-kindness for humanity and his contributions to Japanese civilization form his everlasting portrait, which you can see as vividly now as in the past.

I will close my lecture with a bit of Zen. Basho, the great Japanese poet, wrote:

Ume ga ka
ni notto
hi no deru
yamaji kano

The translation:

The sun rises gracefully
Beyond the long mountain road
Bringing the fragrance
Of plum blossoms

This is the Taizokai Mandala of Zen: the fragrance of plum blossoms permeates your body and mind; you are walking down the long road within the vastness of Vairochana. As for the Kongokai Mandala, I will give you a koan from the *Gateless Gate*: A monk asked Nansen, "Is there a teaching no master ever preached?" (He was asking about esoteric teaching.) Nansen answered, "Yes, there is." "What is it?" asked the monk. Nansen replied, "It is not mind, it is not Buddha, it is not things." The koan ends here. Now, what is it?

You can find the answer in any sutra. You can find it even in Patanjali[50] or the *Bhagavad Gita*. Of course you can find it in *The Secret Doctrine* of Madam Blavatsky. You may find it in the Holy Bible. When your morning coffee is neither too hot nor lukewarm, but is just the right temperature to sip, you may find the answer at the tip of a silver spoon. When your husband is in a good humor, you may find it in his handsome face. When your wife smiles at you, you may find it before she opens her mouth. It is not mind. It is not Buddha. It is not things. What is it?

Theosophical Society, San Francisco
March 13, 1938

Shingon Teachings

BODHISATTVAS: According to the Shingon teachings of Buddhism, truth should be expressed not only with words but with mind and body, for they are interdependent and cooperative; understanding the sacredness of these three, body, mind, and words, is the approach to realization.

If the mind is not unified with ultimate reality and the body consecrated to truth, beautiful words are in vain. When we look at a statue of the Buddha in the cross-legged posture, we see a figure like an unshakable mountain. What other spiritual teacher or deity is depicted in such an inspiring pose? Each word of Buddha's in the sutras is an expression of truth, for he was the Enlightened One, and knew all. These sacred words are in this world, not in some far-away paradise or world to come. When you face Buddha's image, praising his boundless wisdom and endless loving-kindness, your mind will expand into the universe, and you will enter the realm of ultimate reality. Mind, body, and words—the three are one, each for all and all for each. Unless you enter into this state, you will create karma leading to suffering and delusion. Then the behavior of your body will not harmonize with the norm of life, your mind will become dull and dark, and your words will be in vain.

Our five sense organs, the eyes, ears, nose, tongue, and sense of touch, are merely the gateways to inner wisdom. Do not, however, rely upon them and be deceived thereby; neither abuse nor neglect them. With the right mental attitude, you can enter into realization through each of these gates.

There is no noumenon outside of phenomena, and there are no phenomena apart from the noumenon. Therefore, in Shingon, if you recite one dharani, it is a symbolic intonation of truth; and if you concentrate your mind upon a mandala, there is no doubt that you will attain enlightenment. We take a mandala as a mirror of our mind.

There are too many theoretical aspects of Shingon to be disclosed in a short talk. Some day, however, you may have an opportunity to learn more about these teachings. In fact, I give the unwritten part of the teachings in every service; the unwritten is one hundred times better than the written. While some of you may not recognize it, you receive this unwritten and unspoken message during the service.

Shingon and Zen are not two different sects. A ceremony or ritual is the Shingon approach to Zen realization. To express realization, whether one uses words, actions, or meditation, one is following Shingon methods. Here is a Zen anecdote that illustrates this:

Kyogen was a disciple of Hyakujo. Isan asked Kyogen, "I am told that you have been studying under my late master, Hyakujo; moreover, that you have remarkable intelligence. The understanding of Zen through this medium, however, generally ends in intellectual and analytical comprehension, which is not of much use. Yet you may have had an insight into the truth of Zen. Tell me your understanding of birth and death. That is, what was your own being before your parents gave birth to you?" Kyogen did not know how to reply. Retiring to his room, he looked into the notes he had taken from sermons given by his late master. Having failed to find a suitable passage that he might present as his own view, he returned to Isan and implored him to teach him Zen. But Isan said, "I really have nothing to impart to you. Moreover, if I attempted to do so, you might have occasion to make me an object of ridicule later on. Besides, whatever instruction I might give you would be my own, and hence, could never be yours."

Kyogen was disappointed, and considered Isan unkind. One day, however, while he was tending the grounds, a pebble he had swept away struck a stalk of bamboo. The unexpected sound elevated his mind into a state of satori. The question proposed by Isan became transparent. His joy was boundless. He felt as if he had again met his lost parents. And he realized the kindness of his senior brother, who had refused to explain things to him before the fruit of his meditation had ripened.

Now, where is Shingon and where is Zen in this story?

The sacred oneness of body, mind, and words inspired the awakening at the moment of hearing the sound of the pebble against the bamboo. There is no difference in efficacy between the sound of a pebble striking bamboo and the sound that comes from the ringing of a bell. When you are ready for Zen, sound or no sound will become a Shingon ritual for you. But if in your struggle toward Zen attainment you have no Zen, Shingon or no Shingon, it will be but a plaything.

Think it over.

October 15, 1940

What Is Zen?
An Evening Chat

FRIENDS IN DHARMA: You and I practice Zen meditation in this humble house every once in a while, but if anyone asks us, "What is Zen?" none of us can really answer. Zen must be practiced and experienced individually; it is impossible to explain in words. You may think, then, that you can call it silence, but mere silence is not Zen. It is not a matter of "preaching" or "lecturing" about Zen, nor is it about "no words." Of course, some people preach about Zen or give lectures on Zen, but their speeches are like milk without the cream. You cannot attain full satisfaction by merely listening to another. We simply exert ourselves to be unified with Zen.

Unification with Zen is called *ts'an shan* in Chinese. "Ts'an" is to meet face to face. One visits a Buddhist temple; that is also ts'an, meaning to meet Buddha face to face. If a woman goes to the temple to show off her new dress, that is not ts'an. Even though she sees an image or statue of Buddha, her ts'an is not complete. Ts'an means that I see you in me, and you see me in you. The image or statue of Buddha symbolizes loving-kindness and wisdom. When you pay homage to the symbol, raising and putting your hands together palm to palm, you enter into Buddha and Buddha enters into you. There is complete intimacy, and nothing but loving-kindness and wisdom remain. This is real ts'an. Ts'an shan is the same; one enters into Zen and becomes nothing but Zen. *Dhyana*, a Sanskrit word, was modified in China as *shan*, and then it was Japanized as *Zen*. Now Zen is recognized universally as the actualization of Buddhist wisdom. Zen can never be confined in a form. One cannot express it with a few words or with thousands of them. If our talk this evening comes to a point where we enter into Zen and Zen enters into us, it means that our meeting is not at all in vain.

Now, what is Zen? Some think Zen is an aesthetic of simplicity and refinement; they may find articles in an old curiosity shop that are quaint and uncommon and perhaps antique, and call them Zen objects. If someone has little attachment to things worldly and acts oddly but amiably, people may call him or her a Zen person. Zen students often seem peculiar, but that just shows that they are on their way to accomplishment—they are not yet there. We wash our hands with soap, and the odor of the soap remains on our hands for a little while. That is an effect of washing, but it has nothing to do with cleanliness itself. Zen only trains us to live as we ought to live. Zen works without color, odor, or taste. One who would make a show of Zen is worse than a religious snob.

The tea ceremony of Japan was born of Zen, but it is not Zen itself. The complicated form of the tea cult bears in its odor and quietude some resemblance to Zen, but it is far from the activity of Zen, which steers life's boat across the stormy seas of this world. Zen dialogues may be mistaken as witty remarks, but they are a compressed form of philosophical discernment, and not one of them is idle talk or spicy conversation. Many use the word Zen, but very few understand what it really is. Zen sees the whole universe as one's own true self. It expresses the realization that heaven, earth, and humans grow from the same root, and everything in this world is interrelated.

Now I speak and you listen. Yet the speaker is the listener. There is only one master, but the trick of discrimination makes us think "you" and "me." This master is neither male nor female, neither rich nor poor, neither wise nor stupid. Fire cannot burn it, and flood cannot drown it. It is the effulgence of the Cross that illuminates the world. It is called "the light of love" by some. Even the sword of Mohammed ever carries its brilliance. It can never perish, but exists from eternity to eternity. Lao Tzu called it Tao, and Confucius named it *Jen*. In Buddhism we call it Tathata (as-it-is-ness), nirvana, or *satya* (reality). Any dialogue on Zen must emanate from this one master; otherwise, the dialogue is nothing but a common conversation about worldly affairs. As Zen students, first of all you must realize your true essence through practice in your everyday life. You must break out of your ivory tower of idealism and work with enthusiasm in the living world of reality.

Human investigation of the world started because people thought things existed outside themselves. They wondered what those things were: mountains, rivers, forests, clouds, stars, sun, moon, and others. Objectivity was the basis of their study. In other words, "thatness" was the subject of science and philosophy. Buddhism calls "thatness" *dhatu*, in contrast to *gitta*, which is subjectivity, or "thisness." Science helped a great deal to study "thatness," but it only explained how things are and could not give any answer as to what or why they are. Humans then started to learn about mind, and established psychology and epistemology. They learned that objectivity is merely the reflection of subjectivity, and they conceptualized and studied "mind." From the Sophists of Greece to the modern idealists, humans have studied mind objectively and failed. They studied "thisness" in the guise of "thatness," without experiencing the true "thisness" within. The true "thisness" within, or absolute reality, is called *satya*, and Buddhism teaches that satya and dhatu are not two, and that the ten thousand things of objectivity are of one suchness. Thus in Buddhism, I recognize you in me, and you recognize me in you. We call satya "reality" to indicate thusness or suchness, but there is still no such thing separate from us.

Someone asked a Chinese Zen teacher, "What is Zen?" The teacher answered, "*Ts'in*." Such a simple reply! Ts'in means "intimacy." In Japan, the most intimate relationship is that of parent and child, while in America it seems to be that of husband and wife. However, the closest one of all is one's own mind. In saying "mind," I do not mean ideas you have heard from others or have read in books. In Zen we say, "Whatever has entered through the gate of the six senses is not the true treasure." The lucidity of one's own inner being is true intimacy. The relationship of parent and child, or of husband and wife, serves to transmit this lucidity to the generations that follow. Zen is, thus, the most intimate subject one may study.

When asked, "What is Zen?" another Chinese teacher said, "*Pu,*" which means "everywhere." In other words, it is a foolish question to ask what Zen is, since Zen exists everywhere. Mountains, rivers, earth, grasses, and trees, all express Zen. There is a Zen poem:

> In spring, hundreds of flowers;
> In autumn, a harvest moon;
> In summer, a refreshing breeze;
> In winter, snowflakes accompany you.
> If useless things do not clutter your mind,
> Any season is a good season for you.

From kings to paupers, everyone has an inner shrine of Zen. On New Year's Eve, when a swooping wind scatters confetti in flying swirls, you can find the color and melody of Zen in the open, right on the street. The philosophy of Henri Bergson, who wrote *Creative Evolution*, is congenial to Zen. He said, "In this wandering planet, the whole of humanity, in space and time, is one immense army galloping beside and before and behind, each of us in an overwhelming charge able to beat down every resistance and clear the most formidable obstacles. This persistently creative life is what we mean by God: God and life are one."

The *Tripitaka*, the entire collection of Buddhist scriptures, commentaries, and historical and lexicographical records, contains 65,000 volumes. Among them, about 7,000 were translated into Chinese from the first century of the Common Era to the tenth century, the originals being in Sanskrit or Pali or other ancient languages. The most accurate translation from Sanskrit was made by Hiuen Tsiang in the seventh century. One of his translations was of the *Prajna-Paramita Sutra*, a 600-volume work.

An extract from a summary of this scripture (what we know as "The Heart Sutra") ends with a mantra, or "magic words," which read in Sanskrit as follows: *Gate gate paragate, parasamgate, Bodhi Svaha.* A literal translation of this might be: "Go, go with all sentient beings; Go, from delusion to enlightenment—Svaha."

That last word, "Svaha," is like "Amen" in Christianity. All incantations end with it. Some foolish priests merely recite the words and expect to get merit from that. Such persons are not fit to be students of Zen. Zen says even to the most earnest student, "Go away, and come back after thirty more years of meditation."

Another Chinese Zen teacher said, "*Ch'u*" when asked, "What is Zen?" "*Ch'u*" means "Go away." Sometimes American slang is quite an appropriate expression of Zen, as it is so free from the entanglement of words, and often bursts forth with the naked truth. "What is Zen?"— "Go on, beat it!" American students may admire such a dialogue of "'nough said."

"What is Zen?" "Ch'u." In this ch'u are all 600 volumes of the *Prajna-Paramita Sutra.*

Zen does not seek God or Buddha outwardly. It requires one to dig deep within one's own mind. Bodhidharma said, "I point you directly to your own mind. See your own true nature, and become Buddha by yourself." Zen is, therefore, the teaching of ts'in, intimacy. Zen uses not only the 65,000 volumes of Buddhist scriptures, but also the Bible of Christianity and the Koran of Islam as its texts. There are Zen books that are not written on paper or on palm leaves. You can read Zen books facing the great universe. A mountain creek sometimes opens its pages of Zen. Wild geese flying in the blue sky often print a sentence of Zen. Bodhidharma said, "I do not need any writing, since I transmit a teaching beyond words and ideas." Thus Zen is the teaching of *pu*, which may be found anywhere.

The best part of Zen is its action. A Zen student must be vigorous, and must strive constantly to actualize the truth. You are like the rider of a bicycle. You must pedal if you wish to keep going. If you stop, you fall. "What is Zen?"—Ch'u! What right do you have to waste precious time asking such a foolish question? Go on, beat it!

December 3, 1941

What Does a Buddhist Monk Want?
(A private letter to a friend who suggested that I get a single apartment here at the Heart Mountain internment camp)

Every morning a Buddhist monk meditates for forty minutes and recites sutras for thirty minutes, wherever he is. Like birds in the woods, some people who love silence or like to read old scriptures join him, with no invitation needed. After the service is over, some ask him questions about the sutras, and he responds for about thirty minutes more.

I lived for twelve years in Los Angeles in the same way, and now I am here in this "Relocation Center" with the other evacuees. In Los Angeles my visitors were mostly Americans, so my recitation was in Sanskrit or in English, whereas here in this place, I use texts written in the classical Chinese. My visitors are usually from the intellectual classes, and they never make a crowd. In Los Angeles I had only fifteen chairs in my meditation hall, whereas here in this apartment, twenty by twenty feet in size, I live with another family, parents and a daughter, and the visitors bring their own chairs or sit on the floor. Ten or twelve of them enjoy the tranquility of their contemplation. They are the happiest and most contented evacuees in this center.

A Buddhist monk is celibate, and leads the simplest life possible. He never charges for any kind of work he does, being only too grateful to do something for his fellow beings. He accepts and wears used clothes and old shoes. Any excess of food or money he gives away. He sleeps quietly without worries, having none in his possession.

The life here in this center is a little too luxurious for me. If I could get an apartment by myself, no matter how small, in which to have morning and evening services daily and receive visitors at hours convenient for them in order to study Buddhism with them, I would be very thankful. I wonder if America would give that privilege as alms to a monk?

I was born in Kamchatka [a far-eastern Russian peninsula that extends toward Japan's northern-most islands] sixty-seven years ago [in 1876]. Left as an orphan baby, I did not know my parents. My foster father, a Japanese scholar-monk, picked me up at the deathbed of my mother, who was, I was told later, Japanese. (I look more Chinese than Japanese.) In those days the Japanese census was not very strict, so I was booked as the first-born baby of the Senzaki family. The Senzakis lived near the temple of my foster father. I was educated in Japan in Buddhism and Christianity, and in modern science and philosophy. I became a homeless monk when I was twenty years old.

A homeless monk has no connection with any particular sect, denomination, or cathedral. He is a man without a country with regard to religion—an international Buddhist. He may be the teacher of emperors and the friend of paupers, but has no title or rank to associate him with worldly name, honor, or glory.

I came into this country as an immigrant thirty-seven years ago. For seventeen years I worked in all kinds of livelihoods to earn my living. In 1922 I started to give lectures at colleges and universities and some philosophical societies in California and neighboring states. At present I am busy every day answering questions by mail from American friends outside.

I do not cooperate with Japanese Buddhist priests, as I am in an entirely different sphere from them. They mostly preach their sectarian doctrines, with which I do not agree. They come from Japan with credentials from the Japanese government, have their own churches or temples under the presiding cathedrals in Japan, and can go back there whenever they want to. I determined from the beginning to stay in this country the rest of my life. America is my adopted country. If Buddhist priests are abused, the

Japanese government or their cathedrals will protest to American authorities on their behalf. I do not want any government or any power to protect me in that way. I am happy enough to keep my freedom of faith, and Buddhist friends in the world as my support.

I do not approve of religious propaganda. I do not want to put my name and work in the bulletin of this center. I will let students find their own way to me. Those priests can preach on Sunday if they like. I never have a day off in my work, and every day is a holiday for me. If I cannot get a separate apartment, I will stay with this present family, each member of which is my student. I do not want permission from any authority for some religious role. If anyone forces me to stop my recitations, I will simply meditate in silence. I dislike discussing politics, but I am free to talk about ethics and religion with my visitors.

Buddhism is an ethical teaching based on pure reason, independent of any tradition or the legends of any particular country or race. What is philosophical in Buddhism is no more than a preliminary step toward what is practical in it. William James's pragmatism, a well-known interpretation of true Americanism, is nearest in thought to Buddhism. Emerson and Whitman had ideas that were congenial with Buddhism, too, without realizing it.

I have twenty to thirty American friends who correspond with me these days. I am sure they all live in Buddhism. That is:

They love and respect the lives of all sentient beings;
they are against any killing for their own pleasure.
They abstain from taking anything that is not given to them.
They abstain from indulgence in sensuality.
They abstain from lying, slander, and deceit.
They abstain from intoxicating liquors and drugs.

In short, they are a group of American Puritans with Buddhist knowledge, a group of friends who practice Buddhist meditation. As I have no interest in politics, society, or commerce, our friendship stays purely in the realms of religion and philosophy. I have no church, no members, and even after I have answered those who write to me, I do not keep a file of their names and addresses.

The evacuees here are also Americans, citizens of the world. In Buddhism, guarding one's virtue is like defending a port or a fort. If I can help America to have fewer liars, cheaters, and gold-demons—if I can do my bit to improve her people's behavior and intellectual progress—that alone is something worthwhile.

Barracks 28-22-C, Heart Mountain, Wyoming
October 15, 1942

On Zen Meditation

First of all, let us meditate together. One bell signals you to prepare for meditation. Make yourselves at home and enter quietly into the palace of silence. Next, two bells ask you to meditate in your own way. A last bell ends the period of meditation. Send your kind thoughts to all friends present, and extend them to the whole world.

I have been asked to speak on Zen meditation. I could open my hand and bid you goodnight. Here in America, however, such an intuitive manner may not be understood, so I have to use an awkward way to address the subject in my awkward English. When I say something, most of you expect to get Zen from my words. But when Zen is spoken, it is already spoiled. Even if I were to speak in Japanese, as far as Zen is concerned my speech would be either too short or too long.

In your meditation, you must have nothing in front, nothing in back. Blot out your hopes for the future. Cancel out your memories of the past. In this moment, there is no time, no space. There is only one eternal present. Zen calls this the moment of great death. Don't be afraid of it. You do not have to force yourself to enter into it. If you meditate faithfully, either counting your breaths or working on your koan, you will be there, without self-consciousness, naturally and gracefully. This is the gateless gate of Zen. Without passing through this gate, you cannot enter into Zen; when you pass through this gate, you will know that there was no gate at all from the very beginning.

A monk went to a teacher for personal guidance. He was given the koan "The Sound of One Hand." The monk worked hard, but could not solve the koan. "You are not working hard enough," his teacher told him, "You are attached to food and sleep, name and fame. Cut them off all at once and become a dead man." The next time the monk appeared before his teacher, he immediately fell over as if he were dead. "You are dead, all right," observed the teacher, "but how about the sound of one hand?"

"I haven't solved that as yet," replied the monk, looking up at his teacher. "A dead man tells no story," said the teacher. "Get out, rascal!" This monk had his teacher in front of him all the time, even though he did imitate a dead man. He had the exit from his teacher's room behind him. He could jump up and run away before his teacher could hit him. He was a cunning mouse, but not a dead man.

When my teacher, Soyen Shaku, was twenty-nine years old, he went to Ceylon, and stayed there for three years. On his way home, he took a steamer from Singapore to Siam. He was very poor, and barely had enough money to be a deck passenger. He was hungry, and suffered from thirst. Nobody knew the penniless monk. The tropical heat roasted his small body. The ship had to moor at the mouth of Monam River on account of low tide. In the evening, the sky was filled with black clouds. There was no rain, no wind, just heavy, threatening atmospheric pressure. The monk was bathed in his own sweat. Then came an army of mosquitoes. They attacked him from the front, from the back, and from both sides. In vain, the poor monk tried to protect himself.

He knew how to master the situation. He took off his clothes and sat in a corner of the deck, where the ship's lamp scarcely sent its light. He meant to feed the mosquitoes to their hearts' content while he was sitting in meditation. It took him more than one hour to enter samadhi. In the beginning he heard the voices of the mosquitoes, but before long, his body was gone, all his senses were gone. Nothing in front and nothing in back. No more hunger, no more thirst. No heat, no cold. He was a truly dead man. Then a thunderstorm woke him, and a tropical shower washed him thoroughly clean. He heard the temple bell of Bangkok calling the dawn, and he smiled to himself, realizing that Buddha Shakyamuni and Bodhidharma had not cheated him at all. When he looked down he saw some wild berries scattered around him. Berries? No, they were mosquitoes, stuffed with his blood.

Fellow students, Zen never forces you to do a heroic deed, but it will come naturally to you when you find yourself in the midst of such a situation. Simply learn to have nothing in front and nothing in back while you are sitting.

Ekido, a Japanese Soto Zen master, made three vows. I will read them for you, and afterward, comment on each.

The first vow:
The cascade of life and death must be crossed over. (What is life? When is death? These problems must be solved clearly.) *Until the dawn of such a realization, I will not stop my meditation.*

The second vow:
Every hour in the day, and every hour in the night, I will try to live as Buddha and the ancestors lived. Their way is untransmissible, and can only be attained by being lived.

The third vow:
From eternity to eternity, my life is endless. Wherever I am, whenever I live, I will not have any secondary thoughts about my circumstances, whether favorable or adverse.

Ekido was born in Japan in 1805 and passed away in 1879 at the age of seventy-four. He was perhaps the last great master of the Soto sect, even though there have been good scholars and virtuous monks after him. The lamp of Dharma, however, always continues shining. Those whose eyes are not filmed over with the dust of delusions may be illuminated by its brilliant light. Let us look over the vows one by one.

"The cascade of life and death must be crossed over." Ordinary people cling to life and are afraid of death. They do not know the true meaning of life and death. Therefore I added, "What is life? When is death? These problems must be solved clearly." As a Buddhist, you do not hold your body as your own, and you do not view mind and body as two separate things. You only call it body when you recognize it through your senses, and you name it mind when you perceive it through introspection. The minute you admit a thought as your own, you cling to it and do not wish to be separated from it. This is the cause of all suffering in the world. In the *Diamond Sutra*, Buddha said, "In case good men and good women raise the desire for Supreme Enlightenment, they should thus keep their thoughts under control. A bodhisattva who retains the thought of an ego, a person, a being, or a soul is no more a bodhisattva."

I may be able to convince you intellectually, but I cannot stop the inertia of your dualistic thinking. Like a rapid cascade, your thoughts will run toward dualism, notwithstanding your comprehension about the oneness of all things. You must cross over the cascade once and for all, and actually witness for yourself true emptiness—in Buddha's words, "All that has a form is an illusive existence. When it is perceived that all form is no form, the Tathagata is recognized." The first vow of Ekido, therefore, ends with the words, "Until the dawn of such a realization, I will not stop my meditation." This vow is also for American Buddhists who wish to follow in the footsteps of Buddha and the ancestors.

The second vow: "Every hour of the day, and every hour of the night, I will try to live as Buddha and the ancestors lived." Buddhism is not greedy for adherents. There are innumerable *-ologies* and *-isms*, and each of them is frantically craving to increase its followers. Why not go to them as a welcomed customer, instead of hiding under the name of Buddhism? The vow continues: "Their way is untransmissible, and can only be attained by being lived." When hearing "Dharma was transmitted from teacher to disciple," some may think that there is something to be given, even though it may be spiritual and invisible rather than material. In the *Diamond Sutra*, Subhuti said, "I cherish no such thought that I have attained arhatship. Just because I am not at all attached to this life, I am said to be the one who enjoys the life of non-resistance." When one lives like Buddha, one is a buddha—there is no giver and no receiver. This is the way we call "untransmissible." Just live the life of Buddha and be satisfied.

The third vow: "From eternity to eternity, my life is endless. Wherever I am, whenever I live, I will not have any secondary thoughts about my circumstances, whether favorable or adverse." If you experience pleasure, just smile and let it pass. Do not try to hold on to it, for you cannot do so. If you are sad, do not stop your tears, but let that, too, pass on. Do not ask yourself why you have such sadness. It will not help you to know. All secondhand thoughts are delusions and will bring you nothing but suffering. Do you remember what Abraham Lincoln did when he met with life's difficulties? He closed his eyes and said, "This, too, shall pass." He did not get involved with secondary thoughts. He is an unclaimed Buddhist, in my viewpoint. American Buddhists should close their eyes and say, "*anicca, dukkha*, and *anatta*—this, too, shall pass," allowing both favorable and adverse circumstances to move on. You can thus live as one with Ekido and Lincoln in your American life.

A student came to Zen Master Kanzan to receive personal guidance. Kanzan asked him where he had come from, and under which master he had been practicing Zen. The student said he had been at Yogen Monastery, studying under Jakushitsu. Kanzan said, "Show me what you have learned." The student sat up cross-legged and kept silent. Kanzan said, "My monastery has too many stone buddhas. We need no more. Get out, you good-for-nothing!"

After all, Zen is not the same as *dhyana*, though the term Zen is derived from the Chinese transliteration of the original Sanskrit. Daito Kokushi said, "You may pass hours sitting in contemplation, but if you have no Zen, you are not my disciple at all."

In Zen, meditation is a gate to enter samadhi. If you experience Zen through some other ways, you are welcome to take any one of them. Zen is not a religion. Zen has no god to worship, no ceremonial rites to follow, no future abode to which the dead are destined, and no soul whose welfare need be looked after by priests or anybody else. Zen is free of all such dogmatic and religious encumbrances. When you live what you ought to live, you are a good Zen student. What else do you want?

May 27, 1947

On *The Lotus of the Wonderful Law*
Introducing Soen Nakagawa

The summer breeze from the south has brought two wandering monks to San Francisco. Before I begin my lecture on the sutra, I want to introduce to you my brother monk, Soen Nakagawa. He arrived here from Japan on April 8, on the steamship *General Gordon*, and ever since has been living a Zen life with students at our Los Angeles Zendo. We two monks had been corresponding for fifteen years without seeing each other. We met for the first time face to face on Pier 42 in San Francisco. There is a saying in Zen: "It is better to face a person than to hear his name." There is another saying: "It is better to hear the name than to face a person." I do not know which of the two applies to our case, but you will notice that both of us are happy and contented. My brother monk is a man of few words. He will make some remarks that will serve as a preface to my lecture on *The Lotus of the Wonderful Law*.

(Soen Nakagawa speaks:)
Friends in Dharma: As a monk coming from the Far East, I want to read aloud the three objectives of the Theosophical Society, and I will refer to these three objectives in my talk.

1. To form a nucleus of the Universal Brotherhood of Humanity, without distinction of race, creed, sex, caste, or color.
2. To encourage the study of comparative religion, philosophy, and science.

3. To investigate the unexplained laws of nature and the power latent in man.

Soyen Shaku, the teacher of our Senzaki-san, came to America in 1905, and at that time stayed about nine months in this city. One day he was asked to give a talk for a Japanese gathering. The audience had heard of his reputation, and expected a profound lecture to be delivered. He began as follows: "I have studied Buddhism for more than forty years and have preached the teaching here and there. But I really could not understand it until very recently. Now I understand that after all, I do not understand anything." Most of the audience was disappointed. Some people even laughed loudly.

Nangaku, a well-known Chinese Zen master and scholar, went to visit the Sixth Patriarch, Eno Daikan Zenji (Ch.: Huineng). The Sixth Patriarch asked him, "Who is it that confronts me?" In other words, "Who are you?" or "Who am I?" Nangaku was dumbfounded and could not answer. Nowadays, there is no one who can be dumbfounded like Nangaku. Everyone knows everything and can answer every question. Wolfgang Von Goethe, whose two-hundredth anniversary is this year, said in his *Faust*:

> I have, alas! Philosophy,
> Medicine, Jurisprudence, too,
> And to my cost, Theology,
> With ardent labor studied through.
> Here I stand, with all my lore,
> Poor fool, no wiser than before.
> Magister, doctor styled, indeed,
> Already these ten years, I lead,
> Up, down, across and to and fro,
> My pupils by the nose—and learn
> That we, in truth, can nothing know!

This "we, in truth, can nothing know," or "I don't understand anything" is exactly the point of Zen. We Zen monks apply ourselves day after day, year after year, to the study of this unthinkable point. But I am not talking about Zen Buddhism, religion, philosophy, or science—just NOW!

(*strike*) Can you hear this sound? *Who* is hearing this sound? *Who* is the master of hearing? You Americans can hear this sound. We Japanese also can hear this sound. So the master of hearing is "without distinction of race (American or Japanese), creed (Christian, Theosophist, or Buddhist), sex (male or female), caste, or color." Probably "the nucleus of the Universal Brotherhood of Humanity" is hearing this sound. But we can neither see nor catch "the master of hearing."

Some of you may think that there is no such a thing to be called "master of hearing." But actually we are hearing this sound (*strike*). So there must be some "master of hearing" in our body, in our mind, somewhere! But we cannot explain what it is. We wonder about this, and enter into a deep doubt.

This doubt is very good for Zen work. Doubt and doubt! Inquire and inquire! March and march! To the unthinkable point! Ask, "Who is hearing this sound?" until you reach the bottom. Then, all of a sudden, when the bottom is broken, you will realize what the "unexplained laws of nature" really are, and you will be able to realize "the powers latent in man."

This Saturday, I will perform a Noh drama about this subject, after Senzaki-san's lecture on "Noh." This Noh drama will be my answer to the question, "Who is the master who hears this sound?" (*strike*)

By that time, please give me your answer, too.

(*Nyogen Senzaki resumes:*)
Fellow Students: On August 18, 1946, we studied the *Saddharma-pundarika Sutra* together in this very room. Our subject this evening is the same scripture. The title was translated by W.E. Soothill, professor of Chinese at the University of Oxford, as *The Lotus of the Wonderful Law*. His translation from the Chinese text was published in 1930 by the

Clarendon Press, Oxford, England. The Chinese call this sutra *Miao-fa-lien hua ching*, and Japanese pronounce it as *Myoho Renge-kyo*, or *Hoke-kyo* in abbreviation.

The Chinese text of this sutra was brought from Korea into Japan in the sixth year of the reign of Emperor Bidatsu, 577 C.E. Thirty years after that date, a commentary was written by Shotoku Daishi, the Prince-Regent of Empress Suiko. He has been called the Constantine of Japan, but it would be more fitting to call him the Asoka of the Far East. He was an able administrator, a devoted servant of the country, and a gifted Buddhist scholar. He and Empress Suiko worked together to spread the teachings of Buddha through this sutra; they studied and understood deeply this profound doctrine. He ordered his people to study the *Hoke-kyo*, and showed them how to practice its doctrine in everyday life, in keeping with what the scripture says: "The land where humankind lives is paradise itself, and each person's activity shares in the work of buddhas and bodhisattvas of the past, present, and future." As a result of the royal couple's efforts, each home kept a copy of this sutra, just as American pioneer families treasured the Holy Bible. In his seventeen chapters of the Constitution, Shotoku Daishi said, "Let us not be resentful when others differ from us. All of us have hearts, and each heart has its own leanings. Their right is our wrong, and our right is their wrong. We are not unquestionably sages, nor are they unquestionably fools. All of us are simply ordinary human beings." This statement is taken directly from Chapter Twenty of the *Hoke-kyo*, "The Bodhisattva 'Never Despise'":

> For what reason was he named "Never Despise"? Because he paid respect to and commended everybody he saw, monks, nuns, men, and women disciples, speaking thus: "I deeply admire you. Wherefore? Because you are walking in the bodhisattva way and are to become buddhas." Some people took his words wrongly and beat him with clubs and sticks, or threw bricks or stones at him. But while escaping to a distance he still cried aloud: "I dare not slight you; you are all to become buddhas." And because he always spoke

thus, the haughty monks, nuns, and their disciples dubbed him "Never Despise."

Besides Buddhist teachers, Shotoku Daishi brought architects, sculptors, bronze foundry workers, tile makers, weavers, and painters from the mainland of Asia, for he wished to enlighten his people with Buddhism and its arts. He had studied under those artists, and he directed them personally in up-to-the-minute details of his creations. He founded Horyu-ji, in Nara, one of the greatest temples in Asia. He selected the site at the head of a charming valley, with massive green mountains as a background, and at last his dream stood complete before him: an arcade with tower gates, an enormous sanded court, and blue-tiled palatial structures that rose up on the mountain slopes, terrace beyond terrace. Including this architectural triumph, three of Shotoku Daishi's wooden structures still stand; they are twice as old as the oldest temple in Europe. Shotoku Daishi was responsible for the construction, in all, of forty-six temples throughout Japan. In the *Lotus Sutra*, Chapter Eleven, "The Precious Shrine," we read, "On the stage now comes perhaps the most dramatic scene in the whole pageant. Suddenly there springs up from the earth, to the midst of the sky, a stupa or shrine of stupendous size and magnificence. It is made of the seven precious things, that is, gold, silver, and various precious stones...in this stupa is the whole body of the Tathagata." Shotoku Daishi did not take these words as an account of miracles. He tried to actualize them in this very world, and was successful.

In Chapter Twenty-one, "Divine Power of a Buddha's Tongue," we read, "Therefore you should, after the extinction of the Tathagata, wholeheartedly receive and keep, read and recite, explain and copy, cultivate and practice it, as taught. In whatever land, whether in a place where a volume of the sutra is kept or in a temple, or in a grove, or under a tree, or in a monastery, or in a devotee's house, in a palace, or in a mountain, in a valley or in the wilderness, in these places you must erect a stupa and make offerings of flowers and incense. Wherefore? You should know that these spots are thrones of enlightenment. On these spots the buddhas attain to perfect enlightenment; on these spots the buddhas turn the wheel of Dharma; on these spots the buddhas enter parinirvana."

Shotoku Daishi's devotion to Buddha led him to become the first Japanese sculptor, and his genius made him one of the greatest. At Horyu-ji, you may still see what may be the tribute of his own hand to Buddhism in a sublime figure of a bodhisattva—unconventional, vital in every flowing line, the great benign face illuminated with the most beautiful smile that has ever been carved upon wood. "It is the face of a sweet, loving spirit, pathetic and tender," Ernest Fenellosa said. [51] "The impression of this figure as one views it for the first time is of intense holiness. No serious broadminded Christian could quite free himself from the impulse to bow down before its sweet, powerful smile."[52]

In Chapter Twenty-five, we read about Kannon, or Kuanyin in modern Chinese pronunciation, represented as a female Bodhisattva, and by Europeans styled the Goddess of Mercy. She is addressed as "Most Merciful, Most Pitying." In reality Kannon is beyond sex, and may be represented as male or female. This part of the sutra inspired the royal artist to produce such an immortal masterpiece. Kuanyin is said to appear in thirty-three different bodies, in all walks of life, just as did the teachers of Sudhana in the *Avatamsaka Sutra*. Shotoku Daishi himself was one of them, leaving behind so many noble and beautiful traces, not only for ancient Japan but also for our present-day world.

In Chapter Five we read the parable of the rain: "A dense cloud spreads over and everywhere covers the whole world, and pours down its rain equally at the same time. Its moisture universally fertilizes the plants, trees, thickets, forests, and medicinal herbs, with their tiny roots, tiny stalks, tiny twigs, tiny leaves; their medium roots, medium stalks, medium twigs, medium leaves; their big roots, big stalks, big twigs, and big leaves; every tree, big or little, according to its superior, middle, or lower capacity, receives its share. From the rain of one cloud, each according to its species acquires its growth and profusion of its flowers and fruits. Though produced in the same soil and moistened by the same rain, yet these plants and trees are all different."

Japan was a Buddhist land, and besides Shotoku Daishi, there were many teachers, monks and nuns, and lay men and women adherents who cultivated themselves and shared the sweet rain of Dharma with their families and friends, age after age. I have only told you about one big tree, Shotoku Daishi, as an example of how one can practice the doctrine of *Hoke-kyo, The Lotus of the Wonderful Law,* in this very world. This sutra is the most important religious text of the Far East. It is like the *Gospel of St. John* to the Christian, and the *Bhagavad Gita* to the Hindu. The key to this book is hidden in Chapter Two, "Tactful Revelation." Now, what is the key to open this treasure-house?

Before Buddha Shakyamuni preached this sutra, his disciple Shariputra asked him three times to disclose the highest teaching. The Buddha answered him, "Stop, stop. Do not speak. The ultimate truth is not even to think." The whole scripture is, therefore, merely "a finger pointing to the moon." Unless one reads clearly between the lines, what is the use of searching through page after page? Here I join my brother monk, Soen Nakagawa, and implore you to see it for yourselves.

The Theosophical Library, San Francisco, California
June 19, 1949

Bankei's Zen

FELLOW STUDENTS: In my book *101 Zen Stories* are three stories about the Japanese Zen master Bankei. I shall give a retelling of them here.

After Bankei had passed away, a blind man who lived near his temple told a friend, "Because I cannot see a person's face, I listen carefully to what is being said. With most people, beneath their words of congratulation I detect a note of envy. Beneath their words of condolence, I hear satisfaction at being better off. But Bankei's voice was always sincere. When he expressed happiness, I heard nothing but happiness; when he expressed sorrow, I heard nothing but sorrow." This story could be called a biography of Bankei. He called his Zen "the Non-born," meaning that any idea raised in the sea of the mind is untrue. Once an idea arises we name it, and in that moment we are far away from real truth.

Once a Zen student came to Bankei and asked for help, for he was plagued by a bad temper. Bankei asked him to show it to him. The student said, "Right now I can't show it to you." Bankei asked him, "Well, when can you show it to me?" The student replied, "It comes unexpectedly." Bankei said, "In that case, it must not be your true nature, for if it were, you would be able to show it to me at any time." In this story, true nature means buddha-nature, which is simultaneously the body of each of us and of the whole universe. Bankei did not use koans as themes of meditation, but his everyday talks to his students were indeed koans. In his time, Zen students read Chinese Zen books, and expressed their questions in Chinese. Teachers also used Chinese writing in reply. Japanese people read Chinese well, but did not speak the language. Therefore, these dialogues in Zen could be read but not heard. It was very unnatural, almost ridiculous. Bankei warned his students not to use Chinese classics to communicate their Zen. Americans are fortunate not to have such double trouble. They can use ordinary language, with slang expressions. If you read old Zen books written in Chinese, you will find many slang expressions of the time; Japanese readers considered them to have deep, complicated meanings. I have a book of Bankei's lectures in his plain, everyday language, and even though he lived two hundred years before us, I can actually hear his voice, instead of just reading the written words. Some day I hope to translate this book for you.

When Bankei was getting old, the cook-monk, Dairyo, decided to serve him only fresh miso. (Japanese use miso, a paste of soybeans and fermented wheat, with everything, the way we use butter in America.) When it is too old, it gets sour and tastes bad. Seeing that the miso he was being served was better than what his monks were getting, he asked the cook, "Why are you giving me fresh miso when the others receive older miso?" Dairyo explained that it was because of the master's age and position. Bankei replied, "Then you think I shouldn't eat at all!" With that he entered his room and locked the door. Dairyo sat outside the door, begging his teacher's pardon, but there was no answer. For seven days Dairyo sat outside and Bankei sat within. Finally, a layman called loudly to Bankei, "You may be all right, teacher, but this young disciple here has to eat. He cannot go without food forever." At that, Bankei opened the door, and with a smile, told Dairyo, "I insist on eating the same food as the monks. You may become a teacher some day. Don't forget this."

Bankei acted like a child in this story, but he had no intention of making anyone suffer. He considered his pupils to be his own brothers or children. One day he went to the zendo, the meditation hall. A monk had fallen asleep, and the monk on watch duty hit him hard with the big stick. Bankei asked, "Why did you hit him? Let him sleep. While he is sleeping, he is a sleeping buddha." I can imagine that at the sound of the blow, Bankei himself shrank as if he had been hit. Zendos, however, must keep rules and regulations. Here we do not whack our fellow students, but simply show the sleeper the exit. I appreciate Bankei's mild manner, but I prefer a stricter way.

Sixty years after Bankei, the teachings of Hakuin were popular among Japanese students. He is the one who created the koan "The Sound of One Hand" as an opening gate to Zen, and he prescribed many other koans to be passed one after another before entering the final stage of training. Zen teachers in Japan now follow Hakuin's way. I have no wish to attack modern Japanese teachers, but I lament their cold relationship toward their students. If Bankei were living in our day he might say, "Why don't you return to the Non-born Source, instead of imagining sicknesses and concocting remedies for them?"

I think Bankei's Zen is a good model for American students, who need not be any teacher's followers. I cannot help admiring Bankei's loving-kindness, which filled the monastery with the atmosphere of a father surrounded by his children.

April 28, 1953

PART V
CALLIGRAPHIES AND
SELECTED POEMS

Basho, the hokku poet of Japan,
Wandered alone like a ragged cloud.
He drifted aimlessly from place to place,
Like a nameless riverlet of the Autumn field.
Three centuries after his living days,
His admirers and followers commemorate him,
On this shore of the Pacific Ocean.
Even though eighty-four thousand poems
Were written in different languages,
They cannot delineate the loneliness of pattering rain
On an evening in Southern California.

Nyogen Senzaki
Commemoration of Basho
November 3, 1938
Zen Temple, 727½ E. First Street
Los Angeles

芭蕉忌

片雲逝水閑吟客
隔世天涯思慕多
八萬四千風流句
不對羅城雨一蓑

朝露路庵

Opening words *f*
Wyoming Zen-do

The evacuation cramped Japs by heads, into the units
f barracks
Fortunately, the monk could stay with a Buddhist family.
He called his share *f* space E-kyo-an, a room *f*
Wisdom-mirror.

He suffered heat with the family in Santa Anita.
He suffered cold with the family in Heart Mountain.
He and the family and a number of Buddhists in the
two places
meditated together, and recited Sutras and studied
Buddhism every morning.

America gave the monk the alms, a single room, to-day.
He now re-opens Po-Zen-Zen-kutsu, the meditation hall
f the east bound teaching

He had it twenty years in California
Inviting many Caucasian Buddhists from all parts
f world.

He has to wait exclusively the Japanese Zen students
to come,
In this snow-covered desert *f* internment,
a Wyoming plateau.
He has nothing to do with the trivialities of
the dusty world.
He rather prefers to sit alone, burning the lamp of Dhamma
Than to receive any insincere visitors and waste time.
Heart Mountain, Wyoming, Dec 20, 1942.   nyogen Senzaki

Evacuees make poinsettia,
With colored papers,
To celebrate Christmas,
In this desert of internement
They think of the scarlet cymes
In their own gardens in California.

Christmas, 1942   nyogen
                   Senzaki

紙花のポンセテアにて
祝ひけり
さらはれ人の
師走
五五の日
如幻

Autumn came naturally to the exiled life.

We commemorate again Bodhi-Dharma, our Patriarch.

Four ways of conduct, as he taught us to practise,

Were carried by us, during past twelve months.

The seeds of Zen were planted deep,

And covered well with earth.

Who knows and who cares what will happen to-morrow,
                              in this tricky plateau?
Before long, cold clouds may cover us, and snow-storm
              may visit us, with no effect to our equanimity.

                                        Nyogen Senzaki.

Oct. 3, 1943.

1 Requite hatred with lovingkindness.

2 Live within the law of causation.

3 Avoid unreasonable desires.

4 Make Dharma the standard of life.

誦居淡淡又逢秋
一歲四行不輟耰
誰識高原明日事
寒雲飛雪也風流

如幻

In this part of plateau, we have no woods, no trees around us.

If the snow-storm comes to the village of honey-comb,

One may fail to tell either east or west, south or north.

Our imagination, thus, goes back to the Gobi Desert of ancient times,

Where many Chinese monks perished on their way to India.

Thanks to America! the lamp of Dhamma burns in the exiled life.

To-day, we commemorate So-yen Shaku, the pioneer Zen teacher in the land of Liberty.

We offer incense to his portrait, with no wild flowers but the fragrance of our Faith.

Nov. 7, 1943.   Nyogen Senzaki.

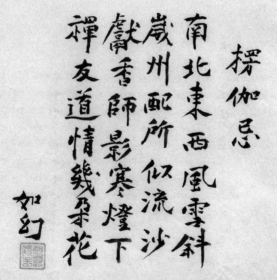

楞伽忌

南北東西風雲斜
歲州配所似流沙
獻香師影寒燈下
禪友道情幾朵花

如幻

HEART MOUNTAIN, WYOMING

This desert on the plateau
Became a village of evacuees.
The birds began to visit us from distance,
To sing their beautiful songs, these summer mornings.

Nyogen Senzaki

July 17, 1944.

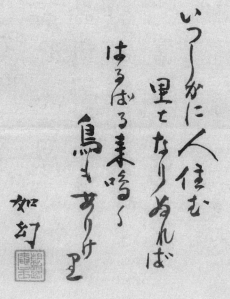

いつしかに人住む
里となりぬれば
はるばる来鳴く
鳥もありけり

如幻

My uta (Japanese ode)

とらはれて
今宵ふたゝび
　　まん丸の
月しみじみと
　　眺めける
　　　かな
加幻

Translation:

Again, I see
The full-moon in this exiled place.
The round, round moon,
In its eastern sky!

Nyogen Senzaki

"Those who live without unreasonable desires
Are walking on the road of nirvana."
So Buddha said on his death bed.
Evacuees who follow him, learning contentment
Should attain the peace of mind,
Even in this frozen desert of internment.
See a break in the clouds at east!
The winter sun rises calmly illuminating
the light of wisdom.

Nyogen Senzaki

Nirvana Day, Feb 14,
Heart Mountain, Wyoming.

涅槃會

無求無欲有涅槃
知足論仙心自安
大覺世尊當日不滅
凍雲勤處曙光寒

如幻　錦草

HEART MOUNTAIN, WYOMING

The mother was named an enemy-alien
And forced to stay within the fences.
Her son answered the call of Uncle Sam,
And gave his life in the battle field abroad.

Nyogen Senzaki

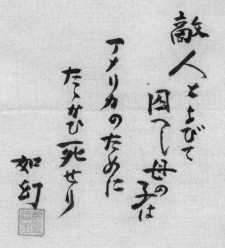

336

HEART MOUNTAIN, WYOMING

Naked mountains afar!

Colorless fields around!

Evacuees have own gardens between barracks,

They can see lively greens.

They can enjoy many flowers.

Their sons returned from the battle field,

Fought and wounded in Italy,

And called on the beloved parents,

Sisters, brothers, and friends,

Within the barb-wired fences

Nyogen Senzaki

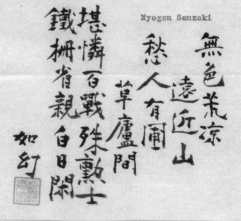

To.
Miss McAneny

HEART MOUNTAIN, WYOMING

No spring in this plateau ---

Having sleet and rain every day.

Timid hills sprinkle green by themselves

Whenever they meet the peeping sun.

All in sudden, the summer came.

Days are too hot to stay home.

The evacuees go out in the field,

Wearing their light dresses once again,

And pick up tiny flowers of the wild

While they search curious stones of ancient ages.

The third week of June,   Nyogen Senzaki
1945.

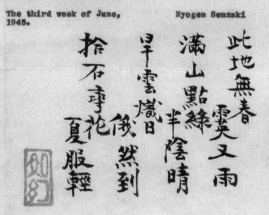

closing the meditation hall

Fellow students:
Under the Heart Mountain,
We formed Sangha three years,
And learned to practise
The wisdom of Avalokitesvara.
The gate of the barbed wire fence opens
You are now free,
To contact with the other students
Who join you to save all sentient beings
From ignorance and suffering.

Nyogen Senzaki

Aug 15, 1945

大悲山下苦修人
習得觀音三昧春
軍國秋氣開鐵柵
利生接物現應身

Bodhi-Dharma preferred the north to the south in the old days.
He left Liang and went to Wei.
One of his descendants was destined to move,
From north to south, in the present time.
He had to leave Wyoming and return to California.
Zen outwits time and space.
In this day of Commemoration, the fifth of October,
The two meet face to face.
Words are unnecessary in this family.
The monk raises his eyebrows
To warm up old relationship,
Still fearing to receive a frown for his exuberance.

Nyogen Senzaki

Pasadena,
Oct 5, 1945

達磨忌

棄南據北老胡精
遠北還南幢下兵
覿面相逢難忌避
揚眉語盡故園情

如幻

This world is the palace of enlightenment.
In his own place each person is a hero,
Striving for what he would attain.
You may have ideals ... as many as forty-eight.
Those ideals are dispersed like early stars.
Look at the new moon which rules the heaven!
If you do not realize truth at this moment,
It is nobody's fault but your own.

December 4, 1945   Nyogen Senzaki
Commemorating
Buddha's Realization

Until now the radiant moon did not
  mean so much,
And I passed many autumns in vain.

Nyogen Senzaki
October 1954

かくばかり 心を照らす
月をも
知らで すごせし いくばくの 秋

如幻

BODHIDHARMA COMMEMORATION

Without using his feet Bodhidharma came from India to China.
The flower with five petals has no form.
Autumn finds the coolness of Zen crossing the Atlantic.
Behold! This lotus mudra contains the whole affair.
October 4, 1953

CELEBRATION OF BUDDHA'S BIRTH

Who is this with the face of the unborn?
His garment is complete
With the colors of many flowers,
Blossoms of almond and peach.
The legendary Buddha declares himself at birth
The noblest in heaven and earth.
Poor child! He is too late.
The petals begin to fall;
The birds sing their old melodies.
Spring is revealed at this moment.
April 11, 1954

TRANSLATIONS OF THREE POEMS BY JAKUSHITSU

Editor's Note: Jakushitsu Genko (1289–1367) was a Japanese Zen master and poet. He traveled to China in 1319, remaining there for six years before returning to Japan where, in 1361, he established Eigen-ji. He was one of Nyogen Senzaki's favorite poets.

RYO-RYO (LONELINESS) KO-FU (OLD WAY)

Like Vimalakirti,
She shuts her mouth,
Following the old way.
All day long, she sits within the gate.
She does not tell anyone her inner treasure.
When she sees the Blue Mountain
Through the veranda, and recognizes it,
She feels she has spoken too much.

FREE HANDS
(Sasshu or San-shu in Japanese; Sa-shou in Chinese)

A flawless gem illuminates the whole mountain.
It casts pure light in every direction.
To attain this gem is not difficult.
Just keep your hands off the cliff.

THE HOUSE OF EVERGREEN: SOSUI-AN

The wind shakes the thousand-year-old evergreen.
Day and night, it raises the sound of ocean waves on
    the mountain peak.
The pines refuse to associate with the common trees.
More than a hundred feet high, they greet each other
As they try to reach the clouds.
undated

COMMEMORATION OF SOYEN SHAKU

The more he grows old, the more he becomes shameless.
This monk is still far away
From fulfilling his teacher's wishes.
Time advances without him
And he performs this commemoration
Like the prodigal son in the sutra.
His teacher trusted him forty-nine years ago
And sent him to this place to accomplish his mission.
The candle burns off year by year
Casting more shadows than light.
Tears of gratitude bathe his aged face
While the autumn wind shakes his bones.
November 21, 1950

THIRTY-THIRD COMMEMORATION
OF SOYEN SHAKU

American Zen is growing
Old enough to stand by itself.
Autumn wind colors the woods
Weaving its brocade here and there.
Who says our roshi has been buried
In the land of the Far East?
Rain patters on the window.
The lamp burns the same as ever.
Fold your hands palm to palm,
Paying homage to Soyen Shaku.
November 4, 1951

PART VI
THE AUTOBIOGRAPHY
OF SOYEN SHAKU

Translated and with Comments by Nyogen Senzaki

Preface

The writings of Dr. D.T. Suzuki are largely responsible for the fact that people familiar with the thought and culture of Asia know the meaning of the word Zen. Soyen Shaku was the first Zen master to come to the United States, sent as a representative of Japanese Buddhism to the World Parliament of Religions held in Chicago in 1893. Among the many friends he made in the United States was Dr. Paul Carus, who later invited D.T. Suzuki, a lay student of Soyen Shaku, to help him edit his monthly magazine, as well as to assist him with translations.

Soyen Shaku came again to America in 1905 and stayed in a private home, that of Alexander and Ida Russell, while teaching some of the fundamentals of Zen. His lectures of that period were translated by D.T. Suzuki into English and published in a book titled *Sermons of a Buddhist Abbot* by Open Court Publishing Company, Chicago, in 1906.

After spending twenty years in America, D.T. Suzuki returned to Japan and later, while teaching at Otani University, edited and wrote for the *Eastern Buddhist*, a magazine issued by that university. His writings, especially *Essays in Zen Buddhism*, have received scholarly recognition throughout Europe and America, and have had a far-reaching effect on Western thought.

Soyen Shaku passed from this world on November 1, 1919, leaving many disciples, followers, and more than forty books he had written in Japanese and Chinese. The teachings of this pioneer of American Zen should be widely disseminated to English-speaking people. As his admirers and devotees, my fellow student Upasika Kofu and I are venturing to translate some of his writings for our Sangha. The Chinese names are usually pronounced in the Japanese manner in this translation, instead of in Peking Mandarin or other dialects. My notes and comments are intended for beginners in Buddhism, not those specializing in Zen.

A Rip in a Buddhist Robe

[Nyogen Senzaki: We can see my teacher's private life through this fragmentary rip, or opening, even though the writing is unfinished and stops when he was a young Zen monk.]

I. FAMILY TREE

I was born in the village of Takahama, County of Oii, Province of Wakasa. The family name was Ichinose and, following the custom of the time, each householder was called "Goemon." As far as is known from our documents, the family tree started in the feudal state of Aizu, where two branches came forth from high officers under the lord of that state. From one branch, Kotaro Ichinose became the master of Castle Ao, in Wakasa. His descendents, under the name Sakuzaimon Ichinose, lived in the village called "Three Pine Trees." One of his sons, Motosuke Gorozaimon Ichinose, lived in the village of Tateishi, and was the root of the family tree of "Goemon." Gorozaimon Ichinose came to Takahama village with his second son, Tadasuke, in 1693 C.E. He passed from this world when he was eighty years old and his second son, Tadasuke, became his heir. This was the second generation. Tadasuke Ichinose passed away when he was seventy-five years old. The head of the third generation was Nagasuke Ichinose, who passed away when he was eighty-one. The head of the fourth generation was Michisuke Ichinose, who died at eighty-two. The head of the fifth generation was Hirosuke Ichinose, who lived to be only sixty-six. In the sixth generation the head of the family was Nobusuke Ichinose. He was my father, and he passed away at the age of sixty-eight. His wife, my mother, came from the Hirate family of Wada village. She was only fifty-four when she died, leaving two sons and four daughters. The first son's name was Chutaro Ichinose, and he is the seventh successor in the family line.

The first and fourth daughters died while young. The second and third daughters both married. As I write this, I am living alone in the world, my brother and sisters having passed on.

Six years ago I visited my home and wrote a poem as follows:

> Seven years I did not see my home town.
> All my family relations have gone.
> What is there to console me now?
> "Snowy Beaches and Green Leaf Mountain."

[NS: This last line is the poetical name of Wakahama and the noted mountain of Wakasa.]

II. Childhood

I was born December 18, 1859. My name was Tsunejiro Ichinose. I was quick-tempered and often sick, and this worried my mother greatly. When I was two or three years old I had a severe case of measles, barely escaping death. When I was five or six, I was very tough, and loved to wrestle with my friends, often ending in a fight. Although I was always ambitious to win, I was not strong enough, because I was so skinny. When I was seven or eight years old, I was sent to a private school at the temple of Chofuku-ji. At that time, most primary education took place at Buddhist temples, as there were no public schools. My teacher's name was Inshu, and he still lives in the same temple. He was very earnest in his endeavors to educate the children placed under his care. He used to strike me with a stick made from cherry branches. (Several years ago I visited my home town and met him and thanked him for those thrashings, and we laughed together over them.)

In that school the text was in very simple Chinese writing, focusing on morals and literature. My teacher was a monk, and he told me always to respect the Three Treasures: Buddha, Dharma, and Sangha. Also, he taught me to be filial to my parents and helpful to my brother and sisters, to be loyal to my country and faithful to my compatriots. School was open every day; our only vacation was for ten days or so in the summertime.

During the summer, we had school in the morning, and in the afternoon we had to go to a Noh teacher to learn Noh singing. Our province was well-known for Noh drama, and in our village, when we had festivals at the village Shinto shrine, we put up a stage, and many skillful Noh performers appeared there.

III. FAMILY HOME

My father was not gifted at anything in particular, but he was a serious man, and a faithful Buddhist. My mother was a very kind-hearted person who always had tears of sympathy for those in trouble. My elder brother, Chutaro, was sent in his boyhood to another temple, Joko-ji, in the village of Kohama, and was educated there by the reverends Ryuden and Kwando. This Kwando is now the abbot of Kincho Cathedral, Kamakura—near the mountain where I am staying.

My brother was a man of few words, but his good calligraphy was impressive, as were his Japanese poems and paintings, and he was, of course, a very skilled Noh singer. He took good care of our household finances.

When I started my primary education, my brother was already educated, so he was also my teacher, and I learned Confucianism from him.

Our home was not particularly wealthy, but we had ten members in the family and lived very happily. My elder brother took care of us all, winning the respect of all the elders and neighbors in our community. We had an aunt who was divorced and who had returned home to live with us, an uncle who had failed at his business, and other relations who had no other place to go. My brother took care of them all, and we lived harmoniously.

In winter we all gathered around the stove, and under the bright lights elder brother read Chinese history. Father, after drinking sake, would nod in his chair. My sister-in-law sewed, while my mother gave instructions to the maids for the next day's work.

We had a grove of bamboo outside the house which, during the heavy snows, would snap under the weight, breaking the wintry silence. In summer, we put benches outside. Each of us carried a round fan, someone would play a flute, and we would drink cool barley water; from the eaves hung pretty colored lanterns.

That was my home.

IV. Beginning Monkhood

In March 1871, at the age of twelve, I became a monk. I did not have any particular objective in mind. My elder brother had always wished to become a monk, but according to the custom of the time, as the elder son he had to accept the responsibility of managing the estate. So I put myself in the monastic life he had wanted.

Zen Master Ekkei returned to his home in our village from Myoshin-ji Monastery in Kyoto to visit his mother, who was ninety-two years old. He was a distant relative in our family line. He was ordained at a young age by Daiyu of Joko-ji and received Dharma transmission from Master Gisan of Bizen Province, who was given the Buddhist honorable name of Bukkoku Kosho by the emperor. Master Ekkei gave his position to Dokuon and opened his own zendo in Tenju-in, where he taught monks for another twenty years.

My elder brother asked our parents for permission to give me to Master Ekkei as his disciple, and they gave their consent. Master Ekkei told me, "If you want to be a hero in the monkhood, I will take you as my disciple." I said, "Yes, I will." However, I was influenced mostly by my curiosity, having been told by my parents that the emperor could have no teacher except a good Zen monk; the idea of teaching an emperor intrigued me.

Together with Master Ekkei's attendant monk Doichi-iida, I followed our master and went to Kyoto. In bidding me farewell, my relatives urged me to fulfill my mission and become the inhabitant of a great temple. My elder brother encouraged me to become a Zen master, while my parents merely admonished me to take care of my health.

Thus I left my home forever.

V. Living in the Monastery

My teacher's monastery, Tenju-in, was one of the temples in the Myoshin-ji Cathedral. Tenju-in's founder was Fujifusa, who was Prime Minister under Emperor Go-Daigo during the fourteenth century before renouncing the world and establishing the temple. I lived with my teacher and learned to recite sutras, perform ceremonies, and other things. My teacher was sixty-one years old, so other monks took care of me most of the time, as venerable teachers did not watch over such small boys. One of them, Shinjo, who himself later became the master of Seiken-ji Monastery, bore the brunt of my care. The number of monks increased month after month until there were forty of us. We had a good deal of difficulty supporting ourselves through our begging rounds, since forty men were too many for the surrounding villages to maintain. Thus, we had to divide up. Three of us went with Master Ekkei to Owari Province, to Choko-ji Monastery.

Myoshin-ji had fifty temples among its properties, and naturally there were quite a few little monks about my age there. Most of them came from wealthy families, or families of high rank, and wore pretty children's gowns. They played during their leisure time by learning ceremonies. I was living with my teacher and his disciples, who were all poor monks and were self-supporting, so I did not have many intimate friends my own age.

(NS: *At that time, Zen temples had already become important for ritual observances, and the priesthood was considered a successful position due to the need for funerals, commemorations, and other ceremonies for the citizens of Kyoto, the old capital of Japan. Monks who devoted themselves to meditation were scorned by other monks. Only one out of fifty or sixty such monks ever became Zen masters, while the others stayed in the monastery as poor mendicants the rest of their lives, or else were scattered into remote parts of the country, holding low positions as temple priests.*)

VI. A New Zendo in Owari

My first Buddhist name was Soko, but since there was another monk who had the same name, my teacher suggested that I change mine, and asked me to select a name I liked. I learned that there had been a little monklet named Soyen who had passed away during an illness, so I adopted his name.

On our trip to Owari, Master Ekkei, although he was well-known in the Rinzai School at the time, traveled like a beggar monk with a straw hat and straw sandals, and carried a bamboo staff. Doichi was very strong, and carried everyone's baggage by himself. Another monk who was small and weak carried a gourd filled with sake. Occasionally our teacher would sit down by the roadside and ask us to pour him a little cupful of sake. I was dressed not as a monk but as a traveling child, in simple clothes. My feet were tied in straw sandals. I only remember now that we passed Otsu, where I had a delicious rice pastry, and that I had my first ferry boat ride in Yabase. I remember the beautiful mountain scenery visible from the crest of Mahari, and also the station of Samegai, where I drank delicious ice-cold water! My traveling companions encouraged me onward by telling me that I would see a castle with fish made of pure gold decorating its roof-spires.

VII. From Yotsuya to Kowatari

Our zendo was at Choko-ji, Yotsuya, with sixty monks in attendance. My teacher lived in a little temple called Soken-in. As a monklet, I lived with him.

Three days after our first seclusion there, I was playing in the street, engaged in a pretend-battle with some other children. Among my playmates was a big boy of fifteen with whom I fought, hitting him so hard that I somehow drew blood. His mother was so angry that she came to my teacher and complained about me, saying, "What kind of Zen master are you? Why don't you teach your little monklet something, instead of letting him fight in the street, hurting my beloved child?"

Thus I was driven out from that temple to a nearby village, where I stayed at Taiun-ji, Kowatari. I lived separately from the monks' quarters, and studied with a priest called Tenei, who taught me reading, writing, and calligraphy. One of his pupils, Bunryo, taught me how to compose Chinese poems. I never forgot the life I had at this temple. When I visited there years later, the old priest was still alive, so I wrote a Chinese poem for him expressing my gratitude:

> Ungrateful child that I was,
> Twenty-five years passed like a dream;
> Back I came with no gift
> But to drink sake together and talk of the past.

VIII. RETURN TO KYOTO

In January 1872, the abbot of Myoshin-ji passed away, and my teacher, Ekkei, had to take his place, so he returned again to Kyoto. We monks followed him after a time. One of the elder monks taught me a poem:

> To carry the transmitted begging bowl
> Was not an easy matter.
> Our Sixth Patriarch met many difficulties.
> Thinking of that, we monks who follow him
> Generation after generation must not waste our time.
> Each afternoon we pound rice for our brother-monks,
> Tightening the pounding stone, heavy as a mountain,
> Fastened to our waists.

(NS: To pound rice a device similar to a see-saw is used. The monk steps on one end, then releases it so that the other pounding end falls on the rice. To do this, the body must have weight, so a large stone is fastened around one's waist. The procedure is very tiring.)

I was told many more Zen poems during the time by my elder brothers, and recited them loudly as I climbed the mountain roads or passed through the wide fields. I still remember vividly the anecdotes I heard then and can even now recite all those poems.

IX. JOINING MY TEACHER

In April 1872, I became one of Master Ekkei's attendant monks. An elder monk was in charge of his clothes; my duty was to carry incense for him. I followed behind him, bearing the incense bowl, and extended it to him as he performed ceremonies.

At that time, our cathedral established a school called "Prajna Forest," and we had a very good teacher, Monk Sekikan, from whom I learned Confucianism and Chinese literature. In this school, each student had to give a lecture summarizing what he had learned during the past month. Having to formulate my ideas and speak about them helped my understanding immensely. I also read Zen texts with another scholar, Toin. Although he was blind, he knew all the Zen books, particularly the *Blue Rock Collection*, by heart. If I asked him for any chapter number out of all the hundreds of chapters, he would instantly quote it, and give me a lecture in explanation as well. Thus it was that this year ended. The only difficulty I had was a rather severe skin irritation, which was cared for by one of the elder monks, who cured me unusually rapidly.

(NS: A monk told me that when Soyen was still a mere boy, he wanted to see a street dancing festival. The monk carried him on his back as one carries a baby, and sneaked out of the temple so they could follow after the street dancers. That monk loved the young monk so much that later on, when Soyen Shaku graduated from school and the elder monk had become master of a temple, he invited Soyen to lecture to his monks.)

X. My Daily Tasks and Amusements

In those days, my daily task was to recite the sutras at morning services with the other monks, and to wait on my teacher three times a day. The rest of my time was spent in school; in the evenings I would give my old teacher a massage. My teacher loved silence and spoke very little to other people; he had nothing to say to a mere boy like myself. He seemed more like an antique statue to me, inaccessible and remote, beyond any means of approach. The only times I saw him smile were when he drank a cup of sake while watching the goldfish idling in the pond. Even then, he spoke neither to me nor to the goldfish. Three times a month he allowed me to accompany him to pay homage at a Shinto shrine on Kitano Street. On our way home we paid our respects to the statue of Kobo Daishi in Toji and also paid reverence to Avalokiteshvara in Kiyomizu. I had not much faith in those temples and statues, but on the road to these places there were vaudeville houses that displayed beautiful signs, sometimes depicting a roadhouse show. Also, on our way home, some lay students would invite us to dinner; this was the most interesting part for me.

XI. Dormitory Life in Kennin Monastery

When I was fifteen years old, I went to stay at Kennin-ji, Japan's first Zen monastery, established by Myoan Eisai in the fourteenth century. There were many temples within the monastery complex. One of them, Ryosoku-in, was headed by the Rev. Shungai. He taught his students Chinese literature rather than Zen Buddhism. He asked us to write compositions on such practical subjects as "Life in the Monastery," "The History of Buddhism," or "The Biographies of Monks." There were only five monks including myself at that time. Later, when I was seventeen, there were forty of us. We had to support ourselves by begging for food around the city and surrounding villages. In our neighboring streets there were geisha houses, and we met pretty girls occasionally on the streets. Their singing and music disturbed our meditation during the long hours of the night. Among the monks there was one called "Silent Thunder," who later became a well-known Zen master. He was older than I, and it was he who encouraged me in my studies. I have recently written a poem recalling that time:

> First Zen temple in Japan.
> The ground was sacred
> And from it sprang many monk heroes.
> When I think of the time I dwelled there,
> I feel like patting those moss-covered stones
> Glowing in the light of the setting sun.

XII. Broadmindedness of My Teacher

One summer when I was the attendant monk to Shungai, my teacher, he went to visit another temple. As it was after dinner, I thought that I would have the opportunity to take a good rest, so I stretched myself out full length in the corridor of the monastery. I must have been snoring, although I did not know it, as I was in dreamland. Master Shungai came back sooner than expected, and had to pass through the very corridor where I was lying. I woke up, but pretended I was still asleep. My teacher did not step over me, but quietly walked around me to a place near my feet, saying politely, "I beg your pardon," and then went into his room. I was so ashamed! My face burned, and sweat poured down my back. I learned through that incident how to be broadminded enough to be able to teach monks.

(NS: Soyen Shaku was very severe when he gave personal guidance: he used his big stick freely, and scolded us like thunder, insulting us with scathing words. After sanzen was over, he was like sunshine after a dark storm. At first, we thought that the "Old Teacher" was acting a role; but later we found out that he really had no pretensions. When he was angry, he was really angry; and when he smiled, he really smiled. In his everyday life, he never mentioned the shortcomings of others, and used kind words on every occasion [other than in sanzen]. When he happened to see us gossiping about others' faults, he quietly stepped out, avoiding us, just as his old teacher had stepped around him, saying, "I beg your pardon.")

XIII. Commemoration for Shungai

In October 1875, our teacher Shungai passed away. He was only a little over fifty years of age. We all sank down into sadness, and then started a seclusion to commemorate him, staying within the temple for forty-nine days. Following this seclusion, we had another commemorating Buddha's realization that lasted for one week, and we carried on in the same spirit. Our Zen master for the seclusion was Dokei, who was one of the successors of my first teacher, Ekkei. All of us tried as best we could to forget everything else and just devote ourselves to meditation.

Los Angeles, California
February 15, 1951

PART VII
CORRESPONDENCE

Letters to Soyen Shaku

Translated by Professor Tsutomu Nakatsugawa and the Editor,
with the help of Mitsuo Ishida, Ph.D.

Editor's Note: This letter, perhaps the first Nyogen Senzaki ever wrote to his teacher after leaving Engaku-ji, tells of his first year of work in his village, Fukaura, in Aomori prefecture, with young people and their families. In this letter, he describes his efforts to establish the Mentorgarten amid "the flood of corruption" among the villagers, and asks for his teacher's guidance; he also deplores the Buddhist priesthood, which he sees as "utterly disinterested in saving today's society."

December 25, 189?

Greetings:

As cold weather approaches, the world rejoices with your Eminence's excellent health. Since leaving your temple last year, although worn out and ill, your disciple continues to struggle in his study as if experiencing inexhaustible karmic retributions. Time flies, and this year is already about to end. I am deeply ashamed that my progress is as slow as an ox treading the ground.

Before I met your Eminence, I thought encountering the great teachings of Buddhadharma was impossible for many lifetimes. Having met a great Zen master face to face, I pledged I would never leave the mountain, staying with you to my last moment. Little did I know that against my wishes, ill health would hinder my endeavors. Because of my karma, I spent my days in vain, able to requite little for the great benevolence I received. Sadly, I am now so far away from you.

Fortunately, the Buddha's compassion has allowed me to reach my aspiration and conviction. My aspiration is exactly what is taught in *The Book of the Inexhaustible Lamp* [compiled by Master Torei Enji]. My conviction is exactly what that book expounds. Although I lazily wasted your encouragement while I was with you, I am still committed to realizing my aspiration, even if it takes an eternity; even though I still wander aimlessly in delusion, through a deep karmic miasma.

Compared with your competent disciples, I am but a powerless speck of dirt.

I doubt if my name even remains in your mind, but my respect for your Eminence has never faltered for one day. As I sit in the hallway late in the evening, I see your caring image in the wafting incense. When the light of dawn brightens the window and the pine grove rustles in the wind, I hear your stern counsel. When the moon is high, I think of far-away Engaku-ji temple. When snow falls thick, my thoughts wander to Kosen Roshi's grave there. Your temple is always in my mind.

After receiving the bodhisattva precepts of Mahayana Buddhism from the monk who ordained me, I later again received the precepts from the Vinaya Master Unsho Risshi. While these were fortunate occurrences to savor, how could I ever have discovered my conviction for the Buddha-dharma without meeting you! Without you, how could I have nurtured my ability to follow the precepts and seek to benefit the secular world! My presence may detract from your reputation, but I do not seek your great wisdom just to gain trivial knowledge, nor do I wish to attain a noble rank that would be inappropriate for a humble being such as myself. I only pray that you will understand my unalterable conviction, and keep me under your tutelage for my future efforts.

What I am begging of you, just for the sake of myself and my small village, may appear to you as a delusory request of no significance. It is, however, a subject of intolerable anguish to me, about which I can plead to no one but you. Pray read this letter with compassion for my bad karma. I lost my mother at the age of five, and was brought up by my grandfather for the next ten years. He was the priest at a Pure Land temple, and was known for his devout conviction and benevolent deeds. I was inspired by this, and my gratitude toward Buddha's great benevolence increased. I envisioned the solemn Pure Land, and passed my days in piety, finding prayer and confession my greatest joys. When I was sixteen, my grandfather died. His last words to me were: "Corruption among Buddhist priests keeps getting worse. Although you have always wished to leave secular life and seek the great Dharma, entering monkhood may, ironically, hinder your goal. Beware of joining that pack of tigers and wolves called monks."

Later, after completing the standard academic curriculum, I returned to my parents' home and studied to be a physician. But I knew that I had been raised at the temple through the congregation's generosity, and I feared that I would face terrible karmic consequences unless I requited their kindness. I decided to relinquish my right to the family estate to my stepbrother when he came of age, and to engage myself in charitable work for the rest of my life. I relied upon the funds my grandfather left to continue my studies. While in middle school, I read Benjamin Franklin's autobiography. Following his method of character improvement, I began reviewing and recording my deeds at the end of each day, marking my negative actions with a black dot.

Observing these numerous black marks every day was disturbing. I began to feel that the Pure Land School offered little in the way of moral guidance. Due to my growing lack of confidence in myself, I looked into the Puritans' Christianity, hoping to find an alternative path, but it was in vain. It was then that I met a haiku poet who introduced me to the haiku master Basho, and it was thus that I became aware of Zen Buddhism. I began reading Zen books and chanting sutras, and gained some peace of mind. One day, while still studying medicine, I read about the Chinese monk Tokusan, who burned his commentaries on the *Diamond Sutra* and started his Buddhist study all over again. This made me resolve to become a monk. Since the only Zen temples in my home region were of the Soto School, I became a Soto Zen monk.

In the autumn of the following year, I had the good fortune to meet you and discover my aspiration and conviction. As those who toiled before us have advised, perhaps one who aspires to study Buddha's teachings and wishes to benefit the secular world should first dwell in seclusion. In this world of mounting corruption, however, I feared that the poisonous tide of hedonism was about to drown all beings, so I felt passionately that I must take time from monastic life to save others. This may ultimately reflect my lack of seriousness for Buddhist practice, but I must express my conviction honestly to you. If you think this is nothing but a worthless delusion, I will most gratefully accept your counsel.

I find that I seriously doubt that Buddhism can have the influence needed to change the secular world. Nay, I must question the ability of the Buddhist monks who have preceded me to influence that world. While the virtue of Buddhist teachings goes without saying, I believe Buddhists have been utterly disinterested in saving today's society. In my own Zen circle, for instance, Buddhist monks are increasingly contemptuous of the precepts; none abstain from alcohol. In contrast to Christians who are actively working to eliminate social ills through their Prohibition movement, no one seems to question senior monks who accept "poison water" from their congregations. While the Christians' anti-smoking campaign may have but a small effect on lessening social corruption, it is something monks who see the world through their smoke could not even attempt. Such matters may be trivial, insufficient by themselves to determine monks' worth. However, I find it outrageous that those who have renounced the secular life to save the world should engage in such behavior. Is the life of an itinerant monk not a hallowed calling that carries on Buddha's teaching to save all beings? And yet monks' conversations, revealing their total disregard for morality, make me ashamed to be in their midst.

While I do not question that a temple removed from the secular world can produce a great Zen master, I am doubtful if it is capable of producing a number of missionaries who could competently spread Buddha's teachings. Deplorably, my own conviction is not solid enough, nor is my understanding clear enough to discern an unspoiled gem hidden within the alcohol, smoke, and corruption. How could I have entered the monkhood only to be in danger of being infected by numerous new vices? I can only repent and weep! This group of so-called Buddhists being what it is, I find it unbearable to conform to such recent worthless trends and activities as the puerile Buddhist cross-sectarian movement, politically corrupt religious legislation, ceremonial displays of Buddha's relics, clumsy management on the part of sectarian headquarters, and perfunctory missionary activities.

Increasingly people despise monks as unproductive creatures. Many temples are nothing more than useless structures. Temple congregations do more harm than good in the moral sphere. All these are nothing but disappointments. While the cross-sectarian plea sent out to the world addressing the recent persecution of Christians in China has attracted attention, its validity is questionable coming from thoroughly corrupt Buddhists who have accomplished nothing.

When I was working hard back home to help out with the famine in India, Soto monks in the prefecture had no time to spare; they asked why they should help India. Instead they busied themselves in election campaigns for managerial positions. Even laypeople would be ashamed of such behavior. I regretted having joined the ranks of monks, going against my grandfather's last words.

Morality is decaying day by day. The overwhelming greed of the entire community is despicable indeed. A venomous fouling of the fundamental principle may portend a monstrous outcome. Should this not rouse those of principle to action?

Not being afraid of doing right and putting others above oneself ought to be commonplace for religious people. Then why must we search among 100,000 monks to find even one such person? Where is the influence of

Buddhism? I cannot but deplore this. Though it was my original vow to attain Buddha's Dharma for the benefit of all beings, the present flood of corruption does not permit me to focus on the eternal. I believe I must sacrifice my own practice to work in the here and now.

What I found when I returned home made it impossible to sleep at night; I could not hold back my tears. Although my village, Fukaura, is a small one of four hundred dwellings, it seemed to epitomize the evils of the modern world.

The rich were arrogant and had no sympathy for the poor. Ethics were secondary to profits. The clash of greed was seen even between parents and children. Being a small coastal village, there were many prostitution houses (in earlier times, it is said that prostitutes numbered in the three hundreds). Moral decay defied description; the only youths not corrupted were the blind and the mute. Inferior education, pathetic religious life, and loss of chastity were all regarded as routine; rape, theft, and gambling had spread to ordinary homes as if the police did not exist. Bribery of officials was taken for granted. Owing to moral laxity, the nefarious consequences of the so-called O-Bon Dance were beyond description, contributing to the fact that few innocent virgins could be found. I could only cry aloud.

Although the village had four temples, funerals and religious events were the monks' only activities. Even at Buddhist rituals, monks merely joined in drinking alcohol and singing. With the village as it was, few educators were willing to respond to a request to come to Fukaura. Even those who came lost their integrity to the decadence, and left the village in debt and shame.

I could not but feel compelled to save others before myself in spite of my own foolishness. I am making an effort to spread Buddha's Dharma using a document I have prepared, attached to this letter. I apologize for bothering you to read this lengthy material, but who else would I turn to? Is my concern a mere passion? Will it just be like spitting on a raging fire, unable to make a difference? I beg your guidance.

The youth association and the women's association attract fewer than ten attendees, but the kindergarten, the babysitter education classes, and the boys' temple congregation have gained some momentum and keep me engaged. Some thirty young children, thirty babysitters, and sixty older boys have been coming.

With the guidance of the great Buddhadharma, I have been working hard at this. I have found teaching with slides to be most effective, and our sessions always end with joyous singing. I have also begun visiting the families of children and sick children at home, as well as conducting other activities. Please refer to the attached document for more details.

While my aspiration is due to your guidance, I have yet to settle upon a means of making a living, and numerous questions are unresolved. If necessary, I would not hesitate to work at menial chores. I could be a gate-keeper or a night watchman. I earnestly await your counsel.

Ordination teachers live as lay people do, raising successors just to secure a comfortable retirement. Thus, every year or two they hold a hundred-day monastic confinement to conduct a perfunctory religious ceremony at which some senior monks receive the title of master and a permit to don a silk robe. With their Dharma transmission ceremony, they are given a colored *kesa* [Buddhist ceremonial robe] and a license. They then shout their sutras at funerals and show off their dazzling costumes at religious gatherings. I would never for the life of me descend to their level; I would rather adhere to my grandfather's advice and to my original aspiration, continuing my study while working as a cook or cleaning monk. Perhaps I can repay my debt to the world by teaching babysitters, supervising a kindergarten, and befriending boys and girls.

Present-day temple monks are indeed a useless bunch, eating meals yet doing no work. Anyone who has a heart would be loath to join their ranks. In order to adhere to Buddha's precepts, one must get out of the temple. In order to save the populace, one must part company with monks. Oh, what a strange phenomenon, and how heart-breaking! Perhaps I may have heaped too much abuse on monks, but their comportment in this prefecture makes me wish I had a sharper tongue.

Hirosaki, in my prefecture, was the site of the former domain capital, and boasts thirty-three Zen temples. Of those, only two conduct morning chanting of sutras. The monks in other temples doze in indolence. Monks in those two temples are regarded with contempt. Most monks shelter wives or mistresses at their temples, indulge themselves in the epicurean life, or engage in money-lending or other commercial activities. On religious occasions or at memorial services for their supporters, they send hired itinerant monks and split the alms for their mutual profit. Only a few temples recruit apprentice monks, while most others arrange for the succession of their own children. Stories of monks' corruption and infidelity make monthly headlines in the local newspapers.

These situations are not limited to Soto School temples, but exist in all Buddhist sects in the prefecture. The succession of temple monks seldom fails to entail secular conflicts and lawsuits. When monks fail to save the world, it is time for the world to save monks!

I bow to and revere the monkhood as the conveyor of the precepts transmitted from Buddha. The *Bonmokyo Sutra*, based on Kegon teachings, says that all beings in the universe are one with Vairochana Buddha. When one receives the precepts, one enters into the bodhisattva realm. I deeply believe this, and if I can teach this to others, then I shall no longer have to fear monastic corruption.

The vast ocean of Buddha's Dharma fills me with amazement, although I have yet to savor a single drop, and cannot help but fret at my distance from it. Today's temples, where monks squander away their time with worthless matters, are only obstacles to the pursuit of truth. Attending funerals and chanting sutras may well be an aspect of upholding the Dharma, but the ceremonies have long lost their venerable religious significance, and are now treated as social gatherings where food and drinks are served. They are not venues where Buddha's teachings are imparted or conviction for the Dharma is enhanced. They merely add to the monks' purses, and the supporters receive no benefit in return. Of course one's circumstances may not matter as long as one makes steady progress in one's study. On the other hand, one cannot rely on the power of religion when it makes no contribution to the populace. I have now firmly resolved to leave the stagnant and ruinous life of the temple and seek a situation in which to pursue my study as a social educator. Rather than offering prayers to the dead and guarding the tombs, I prefer pursuing the Dharma through educating children and babysitters.

As I am not a quick study of Buddhadharma, I do worry that this activity may further slow down my pursuit. Yet I can hardly remain a bystander looking on at this serious national affliction.

My ordination teacher here in the prefecture is a true gentleman of unmatched sincerity, but he does not agree with doing progressive missionary work, and thus merely attends ceremonies, with no family involvement. Indeed, his family members detract from his activities. His irreverent and uneducated wife interrupts him at his school numerous times each week.

In contrast to the joint missionary efforts seen among Christian couples, hardly a single monk's wife is found to have religious convictions in this prefecture (while not even the smallest temple is without a wife). As monks' families at temples serve no missionary function, expecting guidance and benevolence there is like marking the edge of a ship when searching for a sword lost overboard. I believe it is time to give up the temple.

Since ordination, I have never touched temple alms; only seasonal offerings have allowed me to keep studying. Therefore, I feel no guilt if I change course now to spread Buddha's Dharma.

I have no way of knowing if my ordination teacher feels I am an ungrateful monk who deserted him in his old age. I do owe him an enormous debt for the transmission of the precepts. Would supporting him with material things be the best way of repaying the debt? Clothing, a bed, food, drink, and medicine are offered by many people. The spiritual way of repaying him would be to promote social welfare endeavoring to practice the Four Great Vows for All. Some advise me to secure a temple position before going out to do this work. Under the oppression of the main temple and with the mistrust among the member temples, I am afraid I might not achieve my aspirations, especially since such temples, with their old habits, not only provide little for missionary work, but actually hinder it.

I wish to pursue Buddha's Dharma for life, as an itinerant monk. For some time I belonged to the Soto School, and yet I regard this school the same as other schools, and other schools as Soto. I simply must take pains to save the local religious circle that is in such an unbearable condition. If you find my aspirations for the Fukuden-e Association unlikely to achieve significant results, due to my lack of virtue and knowledge, please send another appropriate missionary.

I would then follow him and do everything to achieve his goal. I have explained my aspirations in detail, and I ask your guidance about the immediate steps I should follow. I will strictly abide by your direction.

From my experience in my first year, women are not readily counseled by men. If I could acquire a passionate female Buddhist practitioner like Christian women missionaries, one who could inculcate other women with religious conviction and inspire virtuous deeds, there would be hope for our women's morality. Regrettably such people are not readily found in today's Buddhist establishment. If you could send a woman of benevolence, she would benefit more than simply our local region.

I will be satisfied if I am allowed to practice strict adherence to the precepts and the pursuit of Buddha's Dharma. I realize that preaching and teaching are beyond my ability. It is only because I find local conditions unbearable that I dare try to reach into a deep well with a short length of twine. I would not hesitate to follow or facilitate directions from others who share my aspirations, whether they be Christians or non-religious people.

Religious persuasion aside, a pragmatic approach to encourage women's education and morality is part of *dana paramita* [the perfection of generosity]. This should be seen as superior to simple adherence to temple formalities. Realistically, I would not be satisfied with Christian teaching, much less with non-religious approaches. I deeply believe that only Buddha's teachings are capable of nurturing the whole person. Thus I appeal to your benevolence.

Lastly, I would like your guidance on another matter. When I left the secular world and became a monk, I handed my uncle all that I had saved for my educational expenses, saying to him, "I am going to enter the temple and receive the bodhisattva precepts. I feel it is dishonorable to hold wealth, and hope you will find an appropriate way to use this for the public good." My uncle, who commanded villagers' trust for his chivalry, used this fund for various public projects, but out of his familial compassion, he saved a small part in case I fell ill during my itinerant days. When I returned home, I used the remainder, some 100 yen, to establish the Fukuden-e.

At the time, I was single-mindedly engaged in my work, anticipating the compassion of the community. I had no time to do any long-term planning, nor did I gauge local responsiveness. Due perhaps to my lack of virtue, there were no contributions from the village, and temples showed no understanding. Only friends in other regions sent occasional contributions. Expenses were paid out of the initial fund, which by now is all but exhausted. I was pleased at the initial contribution, however small, that I could make. I would have invested it with merchants so I could operate on its dividends, had I known that the community would be so unsympathetic. Nothing can be done about it now.

In this prefecture, a monk's robe may cost over a hundred gold coins; each monk has a wardrobe of eight or nine such robes. They fail to realize how much more impressive it would be to contribute to social work than to flaunt an outer shell as if they are actors. They regard anyone engaged in work like mine as a lunatic or an idiot. At the same time, little girls at my kindergarten extol Buddha's virtue while shivering in the cold on wintry days like this. I barely maintain my work by selling my clothes and pawning my books. Had I the sum that a local monk would spend in an evening's indulgence, a week's expenses for the kindergarten could be covered, enabling a hundred-odd boys and girls to learn virtue and integrity in the comfort of a warm room. Sadly and helplessly I witness the decadence of this *mappo* age. I hope you will understand my frustration.

I am confident that my first year's missionary work has been a success. I have garnered such increasing friendship with the children that I have hardly any time for my own studies. Occasionally I spend the entire day with them, except for my morning and evening meditations. Though this progress promises a fruitful outcome in spite of my imperfect virtue, immediate sustenance is a very serious issue. In my judgment, I have no recourse but to visit philanthropists in Tokyo and elsewhere. To them I would express my heart, and in return I might receive contributions to establish an endowment so that I might proceed with my work.

While I am prepared to go to Tokyo next spring, I am apprehensive about a successful outcome. Since I have no contacts in the capital, I will first visit Unsho Risshi at Mejiro Soen, and then I would like to see you. I regret troubling you about my work, and yet without your benevolence years of my attempts would come to naught, leaving my home region in moral pandemonium. Please, for the sake of saving the populace, grant your consideration to facilitating the fundraising.

Christian missionaries' expenses come entirely from their congregations, members of which cut down on their own comforts and conveniences to help others. I see no reason why we Buddhists cannot emulate this. With your kind support, I believe it would not be difficult to attain my goals. I dare trouble you with this matter at the risk of being impudent, solely because the moral crisis ought not to be ignored. If I leave the temple and pursue my aspirations, my own subsistence will come from the charity of my family, so that I may concentrate on my project without worry. I am prepared to spend the rest of my life here in study and meditation.

If you kindly grant your permission, I will promptly travel to Tokyo. I fervently ask for your compassion. Although I wish to receive your guidance in numerous other matters, I will elaborate upon them when I see you in person. At this time, I request your guidance on just two items: the direction I should take, and the maintenance of the local group.

Is what I do all but a delusion? Am I contradicting my original vow when I left the secular world? I sincerely ask for your counsel to alleviate my anguish.

Here in the remote country of the deep East, snow has covered the desolate world. Old cedar trees roar in the wind as if to alarm the world. Waves pound the coast as if to scold us. In the midst of children's play and songs, I look up to Buddha's compassion. Slowly an image of winter plum blossoms emerges in the sacred garden of Buddha's Dharma at Engaku-ji. I think of your mind, pure as a snow-white blossom. I feel your benevolence, flowing with fragrance. Then a vision of bygone days returns like a dream, and fills my heart with regret as well as with fond memories of you, making me unable to write further. As the weather grows cold, I sincerely wish you the best of health, for the sake of all beings.

Your disciple, Nyogen, with nine bows.

8 P.M., March 21, 1905

Greetings.

In this far-away land, I am very pleased to hear that Your Eminence has been in excellent health. Deep snow still covers the ground here. Reading a story in the newspaper about cherry blossoms in the capital made us envious.

I gratefully received your kind letter toward the end of last year. Your warm and caring advice has pleased this novice monk immensely. I have read your letter day and night. It has been like a mirror, illuminating my mind. Even the children were thrilled at your kind gift to the group, which we dedicated to Buddha.

Your notes on the obstacles to the pursuit of Buddha's Dharma are exactly what I needed. I feel as if you wrote them particularly for me. They inspired me, incensed me, or made me feel regret and cry, but above all I was chagrined to realize how mediocre my endeavor has been. I am ashamed of having spent days in failure, due to my bad karma. How many times have I tried to write to you, and how many times have I stopped! At long last, I have thrown off my indolence and am setting brush to paper today.

Fukuden-e, which I have resolved to make my life-long endeavor, has found its spiritual direction. On the other hand, although I have made every effort to sustain it, due to my inferior virtue it has encountered obstacles; now the kindergarten stands with no support. I only pity and laugh at myself in this crisis.

I do not intend to trouble my teacher with the nonsense of a devil driven into a corner; please smile at the innocence of a wildflower. I have not been able to maintain the first kindergarten of the fishing village, although occasional letters tell me that the children are unbearably lonely, since I have not visited them lately.

In spite of my burning desire to help, I could only send cold replies to old friends; I hope you will understand my heart.

I was excited through last year at the progress made at the kindergarten at Hirosaki, thanks to some philanthropists' support. Lately, however, it has lost most of its supporters because of war-related economic pressures, and, like the other kindergarten, is struggling to sustain its activities. The greater empathy of supporters in this community makes it all the more difficult for me to disregard the situation; the emotional tangles in my mind have intensified my struggles in the darkness. I only regret my ineptitude.

My young friends know nothing of my incompetence, and cheerfully become my friends. Everywhere they surround this tattered monk, and form a family outside my family. Apart from the kindergartens, I have gained supporters of Fukuden-e in two cities, three towns, and several villages, and have been able to plant "seedlings of Buddha" there.

We have some 1,200 members, all fine friends who teach me. They offer me so much love and trust, yet my incompetence makes it difficult to respond in kind, nor can I properly encourage their education. What karmic retribution! I can only repent day and night!

Since January I have toured through southern areas. In February I wandered along the western sea, and went to northern regions in a blizzard. Now, on my way back to Hirosaki, letters fill my sack with their encouragement, making me realize that I am still seeking my way in the darkness.

As usual, I have shamefully written down my thoughts as they come.

I have made up my mind to part with the group to which I owe so much, and go to the United States. The first reason for my failure at the kindergarten is my inferior grasp of Buddha's Dharma, and my slow progress in missionary work. The second reason is the lack of funds. A blue-eyed priest said three M's are essential to missionary work: mind, muscle, and money.

I am ashamed in my nine years of monkhood I have merely wasted the alms given to me, with the only improvement being my health. Even this is nothing beyond the norm, as I was born in frail health. While achieving enlightenment is my vow, what is most necessary at this time is money.

In these pressing days of war, I cannot hope to obtain funds in this country, as I am worse off than a dog of the well-to-do; I have had to interrupt my project for lack of a mere 30 yen for a month's work. To think that a rich Japanese man spends 200 yen a month for a Western breed of dog!

Although I am deeply chagrined, I have decided that there is no way out but removing my robe and becoming a laborer to earn funds. In my judgment, although it is possible to collect small sums from my present supporters, these will fall far short of what is needed for the long-term work.

Even in rich America, one cannot expect to find everything—even dust—made of gold. Nonetheless, would I not be able to build a Buddhist school for Fukuden-e, with the second of the three Ms supporting my health? With my insufficient scholarship and knowledge, I may not be able to do anything beyond working as a laborer. Nothing should be impossible if I work with avid purpose to accumulate money; I feel I am ready.

If I live making beds, I will impart the pure fragrance of Buddha's highest wisdom. If I work as a cook, I shall pay homage to the meat to remove the sin of eating it. Whether I am a dishwasher, a shoeshine boy, or working at some other trade, Buddha's Dharma will prevail.

Having received the warmest benevolence of Your Eminence, and having studied in the footsteps of the scholars of the past, I only regret I have not been able to match them. I shall put myself into hardship by choice so I may actively accomplish my goals. As you know I have not even completed secondary school, but I am not without the ambition to find a grain of knowledge in American education, thus helping my first M, mind, out of the doldrums.

Being sentimental by nature, I tend to create hardship for myself, but I believe American people are certain to have much to offer to me. I long to see the land of America. I hope to respond with a serious poem to the astonishing discoveries of American greatness to which Dr. D.T. Suzuki has referred.

Although I resent the "Buddhism without Monks" advocated by the members of the New Buddhism group, due to my karma, I regret I must face the unfortunate circumstances of shedding my monk's robe for three years. "Buddhism without Monks" seems an inappropriate phrase indeed. Although I cannot agree with their argument that monks are unnecessary, I must accede for the moment, so that I can earn at least my subsistence through laboring in America. Not having attained the state of mind in which I might expect nothing in return, I would miss following the precepts strictly, and I would much prefer working under a Buddhist.

I tend to ask for your judgment for such trifling details, but would appreciate your frank opinion. If you would kindly offer your understanding, I would not hesitate to undertake any hardship I might encounter.

I plan to return to Hirosaki in three days, and to stay at the kindergarten until the latter part of April. I will then arrange to keep in touch with Buddhist friends after I move to America, and will plan to come for a visit with you.

Although I have made up my mind, your words have power, and I leave the final decision to your guidance. I beg your forgiveness for troubling you with this letter, as I find it difficult to keep my many thoughts to myself.

Sincerely,
Your disciple, Nyogen, with nine bows.

April 8, 1931
441 Turner Street, Los Angeles
The Purpose of Establishing Tozen Zenkutsu
(The Meditation Hall of the Eastbound Teaching)

To Your Eminence at Engaku-ji,

We members wish to allow both Americans and Japanese here in America to encounter the teachings of Buddhadharma. For this purpose we have come to a decision to construct a zazen dojo—a temple for Zen studies—in Los Angeles. In preparation, a series of lectures on Buddhism in Japanese and English was begun in San Francisco ten years ago, and is still continuing.

This year, Dharma conditions have finally ripened to allow us to invite an erudite monk of high caliber, Gyodo Furukawa Roshi, former head of Engaku-ji in Kamakura, to conduct sanzen in the morning and evening, and to give twice-weekly teisho, in addition to the various activities in which we have been engaged. While the temple will be mainly for devotion to meditation and studies, we will not neglect the kinds of activities held in Zen temples in Japan, such as chanting sutras to transfer merit and memorial services. We will chant sutras three times a day: morning, midday, and evening. On the first and fifteenth of each month we will invite Gyodo Furukawa Roshi to offer incense for more intimate services. Not only our fellow students of Buddha's Dharma, but also Zen supporters at large will equally rejoice at the benefits transmitted through generations. On occasions of remembering the deceased, everyone will be invited to come to sit, meditate, and pray just as they would if they were at a temple in Japan.

Contributions offered by Zen supporters in Japan, as well as by those sympathetic to establishing this training temple, would be used for an endowment so that true Dharma might prosper in America.

Tozen Zenkutsu Proposers (in alphabetical order)

Managers:	Shusui Anzai
	Dwight Goddard
	John Hayes
	Shingo Mogi
	Haruko Mogi
	Saladin [Paul] Reps
Accountant:	Harukichi Sato
Directors:	Nyogen Senzaki
	Nihachi Takahashi
	Shino Watanabe
	Shoko Tanaka
	Rimpei Tsuchiya

An Article Written for the Second General Conference of Pan-Pacific Young Buddhist Associations, and Related Letters

Senzaki's article, which he sent to his brother monk Ogata-san to read at the conference held in Japan in July 1934, arrived too late. As Ogata-san explains in the following letter, the article was published at his request in the Kyo-Gaku News *of Tokyo, in four consecutive daily installments beginning August 4, 1934.*

Senzaki's article is followed by a selection of Letters to the Editor in response to his piece, and then by Senzaki's responses to those, also published in the Kyo-Gaku News.

Letter from Ogata

I had not heard from you in such a long time that the receipt of your good letter made me feel the way a poor man would feel if he found an abundant treasure.

In addition to your letter to me, I received the article which you wished me to read before the Conference of Young Buddhist Associations. But the article reached me too late for the conference, so I decided to publish it in the *Kyo-Gaku News*, a popular Buddhist newspaper in Tokyo. I am sending you the clippings of your article as it appeared, together with those of the comments of a number of readers.

After the publication of your article, many people wrote both in your favor as well as against you. And not only did they write about it, but many people around here are even now making it the subject of animated discussion.

There is a saying that "true students stand for reason, while false students run after profit."

Your big spade may dig out the true student-dragons, or reveal the harmful snakes; I do not know which.

But be that as it may, no one else has written with such courage, or wielded such a strong stroke with the iron hammer of truth, as you have done.

Please write every once in a while for the benefit of those who approve of your opinion.

—*Ogata*

The Article

To the Young Buddhists of Japan:

Before writing this paper, I burnt incense and recited a sutra. Before I mail it, I will burn incense again and recite another sutra.

I have been in America for twenty-nine years. Many of you, no doubt, were not born until after I had left Japan. This, therefore, may seem to you like the voice of a Rip Van Winkle. But I must say to you that the essence of Buddhism never changes. As it was in olden times, so it is now— whether in an Eastern or a Western country.

Dr. Dwight Goddard offered me traveling expenses across the ocean in order that I might join you in this meeting of young Buddhists from all over the world, but my intimate brother monk, Ogata, will be there, so I thought it would not be necessary for me to cross the ocean and am, therefore, going to ask him to read this paper to you in my stead.

Our friend Dr. Goddard has been going to Japan yearly for seven years to study Buddhism, with a special emphasis on Zen. Last year he went to China and met my friend Tai Hau. He visited several monasteries there, and liked their atmosphere very much. Americans who go to Japan to study Buddhism are beginning to dislike the officious airs and manners of Japanese Buddhists.

Above all else, the young Japanese Buddhists should realize the reason for what I have just related. What is the cause? It is that present-day Japanese Buddhists do not understand true Buddhism, but are clinging to sectarian ideas instead.

So-called high priests come to America from Japan and endeavor to spread Buddhism among Americans. We have tried to help them as much as we can, but have had little success. With few exceptions, they are not accomplishing anything here but propaganda and the advertisement of their titles and cathedrals, like sandwich men peddling their wares. Most of them also smell of alcohol, and few of them can wait more than a few minutes before smoking. Many times have I blushed at their behavior. They may think they can do these things here in America just as they do in Japan, but they are badly mistaken. If they desire to spread the Buddhist teachings here, they should at least imitate the example of Christian ministers, or even that of the Brahman, Vedanta, and yoga missionaries from India, all of whom live pure lives just as the Chinese Zen monks do.

I see many so-called Buddhist priests in America, but none of them behave like real Buddhists. Americans who study Buddhism demand teachers who follow Buddha's precepts, as do the monks of Ceylon and Burma.

Modern priests from Japan do not speak English. Therefore they cannot have much to do with American Buddhists. Should they think, however, that they can do any good among Americans who are interested in Buddhism, and still continue their bad behavior, they are very much mistaken, for they will succeed only in making Americans disgusted with them.

Some of the Japanese high priests come to America with shaved heads and purple robes; but the Americans who study Buddhism have such a keen sense of smell that they soon find out what kinds of lives those priests have been living in Japan.

Before I left Japan, there were three kinds of monasteries: one for studying the sutras, one for keeping the precepts, and one for meditation. But all the monks in any one of these monasteries strictly kept the precepts, and not a single one of those monks aspired either to become a famous teacher or to make a commercial business of religion. The cathedrals treated the monks as though they were only novices, and they were satisfied with this, for they had no other desire than that of "living the life": spending their whole lives as humble, homeless monks. In those days such monks had free access to all monasteries, and, no matter what kind of a monastery it was, were allowed freely to come and go. But these days, I understand, each sect has its own college, and after finishing the courses in their respective institutions the monks are given "jobs"—placed in charge of sub-temples of the same sect. This is how Japan is losing its humble wandering monks: by producing workers for the business of religion. What a pity!

Therefore it is my wish to remain either in America or in Europe for the remainder of my life in my work of spreading Buddhism. These fields are broad, while those of Japan are so narrow that they offer me little hope for usefulness. I also thought, in writing this paper, that there might yet be left a few young Buddhists who would like to come to America as true Buddhist monks.

I am now fifty-nine years old. My Buddhist age [since ordination] is thirty-nine. I shall be very fortunate if I am able to continue my wanderings for even ten years longer. In this world of impermanence, who knows what will come tomorrow? My fervent wish is to find someone with true loving-kindness toward the American people to continue the cultivation of the little garden I have planted here.

I understand that modern Japanese feel that they are living in a new era, one that does not require the teaching of all the precepts. What they are actually doing, though, is contributing to the ruination of Buddhism. It is only through the keeping of the precepts that one may enter into real meditation; and it is only through meditation that one can attain enlightenment. This fact has been self-evident all the way from Buddha's time up to the present. Other-power and Self-power are not two different things. Genku, the founder of the Other-power sects, strictly kept the precepts. Shinran, his modest and humble disciple, was ashamed of himself for his failure to keep those precepts.[53]

Nowadays, those who call themselves Shinran's descendents do not even know the spirit of Shinran. How can they reach the true Buddhist ideal in any way whatever?

Nichiren was a peculiar student of Tendai, but I do not consider him one who carried the lamp of wisdom. This is proven through his followers, who are forever attacking other sects, and who never keep the precepts.

I am making this statement because I have studied the sutras ever since I was five years old, and I had finished all the Chinese translations of them by the time I was eighteen. After that, I studied Shingon and Zen. This is no idle boast! Should anyone wish to know the true teachings, let him come on over and meet me here face to face.

I have heard some Japanese priests declare that Japan should not have any monks at all; for if the monks kept the precepts, they could not even touch money, and would, therefore, be unable to exist under modern Japanese conditions. I have heard others claim that the precept requiring monks to wear the Buddha's robe is not practicable in contemporary Japanese life.

Such contentions spring from the ignorance of the true spirit of the precepts. Young Buddhists should not listen to such devil's talk. Just take a vow to Buddha, and so become a monk or nun. The first monks and nuns in Japan took self-ordination. After cathedrals had been established under close government supervision, ordination was limited to the mediation of those cathedrals. Why not deal with Buddha directly? What need is there for a middle-man, a high priest, or a cathedral?

I call that person a monk who lives a monk's life, not simply because some cathedral or some government agency has recognized him as such.

I do not know what Japanese Buddhists now believe, but I do know that those who understand Buddhism, whether in Burma, Ceylon, Siam, China, or America, do not consider anyone a monk who does not live the life of a monk, whether he may rank as a bishop, an archbishop, or a cardinal. True Buddhists consider such titles mere business labels.

From the American woman's point of view, the priest who lives a married life and still calls himself a Buddhist monk is a living insult to womanhood. I do not consider such men even lay Buddhists. They are a step below that. They need reforming.

Do not think that Buddhism is against the married life. There ought to be, however, at least one out of a thousand Buddhists who is willing to sacrifice the pleasures of the ordinary life in order to be like a soldier on a battlefield, or like a scientist who is willing to endanger his life for the benefit of humanity.

It is probable that modern Japanese have no experience other than that of secular life, but if one should wish to enter into the higher stages of Buddhism, one cannot do so within marital relations.

I am not trying to force anyone to live a single life. But I do wish that at least one true disciple would appear on this earth. And that is that.

Japanese Buddhists ought to learn from Christian friends not to smoke and not to drink. I am afraid Japanese Buddhists may have come to believe that the Mahayana teachings are against keeping the precepts just because the Theravada is very strict in its discipline. Be that as it may, it remains true that no intemperate person will ever be able to do any effective religious work in America.

One might say that smoking is not as bad as drinking; but if one is a Buddhist who has learned either Shingon or Zen, one ought not to have a leisure moment in which to enjoy smoking.

In recent years some well-known Japanese temples and towers have been burnt to ashes. Why? Because the chief abbot or high priest had the foolish habit of smoking, and the young novices learned to smoke from his example. Those high priests or abbots ought either to resign their positions or quit smoking.

Japanese Buddhist priests talk about the teaching of emptiness, but they do not practice true emptiness in thought, because they are forever attacking other sects in the belief that theirs is the only true teaching.

When writing letters to the priests of their own sects, they address them as Reverend, but address all other priests as Mister. This shows religious snobbery and narrow-mindedness. Soto Zen people believe that the Rinzai teachings are only the petty study of koans, while Rinzai Zen people declare that the Soto sect has no enlightenment at all. Soto teachers never read Rinzai books, nor do the Rinzai ever read Soto books, because the reading of other teachings is not profitable for their own business. From the very beginning they have studied Zen only to attain fame and glory as teachers, not because of loving-kindness toward all sentient beings. They are a group of foxes. That is all!

Japanese priests are beginning to mix the authority given by the teachings with that which pertains to the cathedrals, as well as to mix this authority with that of the law of the land. Once, after I had held a meeting in honor of Kobo Daishi, who contributed so much to Japanese civilization, a priest from Japan protested that I should first have gotten a permit from the cathedral and also another from the Japanese government. He thought I was selling candy in the streets without a license.

One former abbot of a Zen monastery, while here in America, blamed me for ordaining Americans as Buddhists without first having obtained a license from the Japanese government.[54] It is true that at one time I had been a fellow inmate with that abbot in a monastery, but I was not ordained there and am not, therefore, a member of his sect.

The ordination of a Buddhist is not under the control of any sect. Anyone who has been ordained a Buddhist for ten years, no matter by what sect, has the authority to ordain others also. This is one of the precepts of the Buddha himself. No cathedral has any authority over this. Cathedrals function as the main offices of their respective sects, something like those of chain stores, and therefore have no authority over the true movement carried on by homeless monks. I am not, however, inciting you young

Buddhists to do anything against the cathedrals, but recommending that you, without any desire for rank and promotion, record yourselves in them as simple novices aspiring solely to become homeless monks.

I understand that the Japanese government is now asking Buddhist priests to cooperate with it in bettering the moral life of the Japanese people. Tell the officers of the government that, first of all, they themselves should learn Buddhism, and so do their own share. Buddhism should be independent of all kinds of government work.

I believe Japanese Buddhists are now living in the hell of commerce. Some say that the cause of this is that all of them have families, but I do not think so. The main cause is that they do not know the true spirit of Buddhism. In the spirit of true Buddhism, monks who are disciples of Buddha should not keep anything—not money, not property, not food. Before the day is over, a true Buddhist should distribute all excess food in his possession to his neighbors, who may be in greater need. I understand that Franklin D. Roosevelt, the President of the United States, is considering a plan to distribute two hundred dollars per month to all people over sixty-five years of age. If he does this, he will build a Buddhist utopia.

A true Buddhist does not need gorgeous robes; nor is the shaving of his head necessary. Should anyone give him an old sack coat, let him receive it as though it were Buddha's robe. Should anyone give him an old pair of shoes, let him receive them as though they were Bodhidharma's own. If no one gives him anything, he should work for his living. If he has no work, no money, and no food, he should not eat.

To build temples or to take up collections for a propaganda fund is a great delusion. American universities have beautiful classrooms for the study of philosophy and religion. There a Buddhist monk can introduce whatever teachings he may have attained. Those who wish to study Buddhism will call for him with an automobile. He will not, therefore, need a car of his own. If he has a little cabin in which to meditate, he can live with the smile in his heart that frees him from all worldly attachments.

To illustrate how independent a monk may be here, let me tell you a little story. Years ago a priest came to me from Koya-san. He told me that one of the temples there had burned, and offered me a commission of twenty percent on all the money I could collect with which to rebuild it. I showed him the door, and told him to go and never to return.

My ideal life for a monk is not necessarily that of the old Ceylonese monks, but it is a pure, simple, and unselfish one, dedicated to the enlightenment of others.

There are many opportunities here in America for monks who live such lives. In California alone, there are now five or six places ready for good monks. In Oregon, Washington, and British Columbia, altogether there are ten or twelve more openings for monks of this sort.

There is a sect here that is now trying to make a Buddhist showing by listing and publishing the names of Americans who have been converted to Buddhism from Christianity. This is mere propaganda to boost their religious business. Any movement initiated by true Buddhist monks should take a different path.

I invite all Buddhists in Japan, especially young Buddhists, to reconsider the direction of their lives, to renounce the common life of pleasure, and to come to America as true Buddhist monks.

—*Nyogen Senzaki*

LETTERS TO THE EDITOR

From an unnamed person:
I folded my hands and paid homage to Senzaki when I read his open letter.

From Sanshiro Ishikawa:
I always profit by reading your paper. I especially appreciate the article by Senzaki that appeared recently in four consecutive installments. While I am not a Buddhist, when I read this article I could not help but pay homage to its writer, folding my hands like the Buddhists do.

I remember Nyogen Senzaki very well; but I suppose he has forgotten me. I met him more than thirty years ago. At that time, he was about twenty-two or twenty-three years old and seemed very healthy and precocious. That impression has remained in my mind. He brought to the house where a group of friends and I were gathered a gramophone record of a lecture by Soyen Shaku, to which he had us listen. This was in Tsunohazu, on the outskirts of Tokyo. After he had gone away, I predicted to my friends a bright future for that young monk.

When I read Senzaki-san's letter in your paper, I said to myself, "Of course, he is living just as I predicted."

Probably he is to America what Bodhidharma was to China—the founder of Buddhism there.

Buddhism has almost perished in Japan, but I believe it will be resurrected in America. Hereafter, the Japanese should go to America to study Buddhism. Modern Japan is not the land for a pure teaching such as Buddhism.

Nowadays, Japanese journalism has a great deal to say about the rebirth of Buddhism; but after all, the motive for this is business. It is a tragic comedy.

I have often heard that monks sometimes give each other thirty blows with a stick for instruction. Senzaki-san's words are like a big stick to Japanese Buddhists.

In closing, I wish to thank the editor for bravely publishing the article in question, even though it conflicts with the secret desires of some of his readers.

From K. Soma:

The article by Nyogen Senzaki is wonderful; it digs out the true faults of Japanese Buddhism, and exposes the roots of its weaknesses in its modern tendencies.

His article is the strongest one I have ever read. As I followed it, he seemed to be hammering at my very soul.

In the world of Buddhism, we still have this man. His being alive is proof that Buddhism has not yet perished from the earth.

Immediately after reading this article, I started to write you, but Mr. Ishikawa reached you first, making what I might have to say unnecessary. I could not, however, help expressing my appreciation to your paper for so bravely printing such a radical article.

It is not the fault of your paper that it is filled every day with poor articles, with selfish ideas, and with our imitation of the decay in the political world.

Nevertheless, I hope you may have the good fortune to publish more articles of this nature in the future, so that your readers may be more fully enlightened.

From D. Takaki:

Nowadays there is much talk about the renaissance of Buddhism. But when I think of the modern temples, of the sectarian views, I have no bright hope. At such a time the article by Senzaki is very clear and enlightening.

Those who wish to become Buddhists should read this article twice before they join any sect whatever.

When I think that in America there is the possibility of such thought as Senzaki's, I have a strange feeling. The fact is that his ideal is also the ideal of Japan, but it is impossible to put it into practice. It is true that Buddhism is already mummified in Japan; that the true movement will be reborn out of a simple idealism such as that possessed by Senzaki.

Personally, I do not subscribe to what he says. He is clinging too much to Zen and the precepts. Nor is he thinking much about his own country. Nevertheless, I admire what he says because it comes from his own experience and practice.

But I know that Senzaki-san has never read our Master Nichiren's writings. I wish he would study the Nichiren teachings thoroughly, for there he will find that true Buddhism can be practiced in this world without either precepts or meditation.

Our sect is devoting itself to the height of Japanese life, not to that of the world, and not that of America.

Senzaki-san praises Roosevelt's plan, but both he and that president are only dreaming of the impossible.

Finally, because of his courage and sincerity, I wish to pay him my respects, even though I differ with his opinions.

From K. Katsuoka:

I am not a young Buddhist, so I was not at all obliged to read Senzaki's article. But I happened to read it, and, therefore, direct this to him.

He says that he went to America twenty-nine years ago, and has never since returned to Japan. I can understand the reason. He either forgot his mother country or he does not like Japanese temples.

He wrote that he recited sutras and burnt incense both before writing and sending his article. This is a funny way to write a newspaper article. The modern Buddhist does not do such foolish things.

I understand that Senzaki refused money from Dr. Goddard with which to come to Japan. It was a good thing. If he had come, and had seen modern Japan, especially the modern Buddhist world, he would have fainted.

Twenty-nine years ago, perhaps there were some Buddhist monks, as he states in his article; but these days, even Zen monks have families and worship the "Almighty Dollar." They all are now disciples of Shinran. In fact, only the true teachings of Shinran remain as Buddhism.

Senzaki does not know that the twentieth century is an age without precepts and without discipline.

It is true that some Japanese Zen Buddhists write about the precepts and use the word in theses with which to get doctoral titles from universities, but they do not practice the precepts.

If Senzaki is a true Zen student, he should not discriminate between the good and the bad, nor say anything about them at all.

American Buddhists may dream about monks as they appeared in the old scriptures; but none of the young Japanese Buddhists have any desire to follow the examples of those petrified old Ceylonese monks.

Senzaki preaches no smoking and no drinking. Why not let such habitués alone? If one who smokes too much gets sick, the doctor will cure him. One who drinks too much will get sick and die; then he drinks no more.

Senzaki recommends the single life; but no young Japanese man ever dreams of such a life today. Buddha was once married; why shouldn't we be?

He writes of emptiness, and disapproves of sectarian ideas; but he is still clinging, not only to the precepts, but also to Zen.

Senzaki recommends the forgetting of money; but none of the modern Japanese priests refuse money; they all study about how valuable it is, and how to employ it usefully. He ought to know what good businessmen they are.

I do not wish to see the young Japanese trained according to the ideal of Senzaki. If he can find such young people in America, he is welcome to them. Buddha said, "If you wish to be enlightened, do not reject desire. There is no enlightenment outside of desire. If one understands this reasoning, he will be enlightened."

This is my last word to Senzaki. I hope he is in good health, and that he will remain in America, and never return to Japan.

From Yasura:

There is a saying, "Even a thief can find excuses." However good an article may be, if it has given the reader a distasteful feeling, it will hardly be successful with that particular reader. It is the nature of human beings that when they feel attacked, they will find some way to protect themselves, giving ample reasons for doing so.

When I read Senzaki's article in your paper, I thought it was wonderful, especially at this time. Although it will cause resentment among some readers, it will greatly edify others.

I fear, however, that some of the readers whose weak points have been touched might say, "While Senzaki may write very reasonably, the question is whether he is really practicing what he writes."

But it is a fact that in all Japan there is no one who would have written such courageous statements, attacking the whole lot of cathedrals, sects, and temples, as Senzaki has done.

Everyone knows that Japanese temples, as well as secular people, are actually preaching against their own teachings; but, economically, they cannot reform themselves, even though they know they are in the wrong. It is like a man who has a boil that is too sore to touch; he lets it alone.

The Hongwan-ji has gorgeous temples, and the so-called "Shinran generation" is living a life of luxury. No one contends that this is the practice of Buddhism. And no one even thinks that they are practicing the teaching of Shinran. Other sectarian people are doing just about the same thing. Most people just say, "What's the use?"

Now Senzaki has written a message from America that bravely digs out all weak points. It attacks high priests as well as the common monk. I am afraid that most Japanese Buddhists, instead of turning to introspection and regret for this state of affairs, may hate Senzaki and try to throw mud at him for all his pains.

A certain person has already written against Senzaki, calling him "anti-modern, inhumane, and impractical." But no matter how he may be attacked, this will not conceal the sins of Japanese Buddhists. Even if someone were able to dig up something ugly about Senzaki's own life, this would not hide the evils in Japanese Buddhism.

I myself am a priest with many faults—surely every one of those which Senzaki attacks. But I demand to know whether there be any priest or monk who has no faults in Japan today.

I know some so-called Zen masters who are living pure lives, which they, as well as others, will admit. But they are also living the lives of the wealthy, and never think of the poor who lack even food. I do not wish to study under such masters. With all my faults, I would rather remain a lowly priest and so help the poor people around me as much as my strength will permit.

NYOGEN SENZAKI'S REPLIES

From a Humble Hut in America
To the Editor:
An article which I had intended for the Second General Conference of Pan-Pacific Young Buddhists Associations was published in your paper. This is my expression of gratitude for your favor.

About four or five years ago, I wrote two articles of the same nature as the one in question; one for a popular magazine in Tokyo, and the other for a Japanese daily newspaper in Kyoto. But there was no response whatsoever from either of these. Perhaps your paper has a greater circulation than those others, or else the Young Buddhists' Conference created a demand for something of this nature.

My brother monk, Ogata, sent me the clippings from your paper of the letters you published, one of which was written by an old acquaintance, and the others by new friends. I would like to reply to them.

I shall try to write in the simplest possible language, so as not to take up too much space in your valuable paper. If you deem what I have to offer unacceptable, please throw it into the wastebasket.

The mere fact that my letter reaches your hands is evidence that my thoughts are crossing the ocean again, and I shall be satisfied with even that.

To Ishikawa-san:

I was very glad to get the clipping of your letter to the *Kyo-Gaku News*, as I remember you quite well. We met in Tsunohazu, in the home of either Uchimura or that of Fukuda.

I am a white-haired man now, and have not been able to accomplish all I wished to do. I am ashamed of this.

Two other friends have already passed away, and my teacher, the gramophone record of whose lecture you heard, also passed away some fifteen years ago.

While yet alive, my teacher once warned me, "Whenever monks hear sweet words of praise from others, they should consider them as though they were an offering of poison." So I accept your praise with self-discipline.

To Soma-san:

Zen monks are not supposed to devote themselves to writing. You praised my article. I, therefore, blame myself.

My teacher once said of himself, "My heart burns like fire, but my eyes are as cold as dead ashes." I am trying to follow his example, although still ten thousand miles behind it.

To Takaki-san:

For the last twenty-nine years not a single day has passed without my having read the *Saddharma-pundarika Sutra*. I have also read and studied all of Nichiren's writings, and see clearly that he tried to practice the Tendai theory in a Shingon way; but he was not enlightened.

You Nichiren followers should see the sutra apart from the hand of Nichiren. You respect his formula of seven letters[55] every day, but do you know that there is another formula that has only one letter? Or that there is still another formula that has no letter whatever?

When you are able to see this letterless-letter, then come to me and we shall commune with each other.

Japan has had good masters and teachers in the past, but, among them, Nichiren and Shinran were the poorest. I could write many details, and give many reasons for this statement, but I cannot occupy unduly too much of this space. I wish you could come to America and talk to me face to face.

While Nichiren bravely declared his faith, he never expected that his followers would worship him, as modern Nichirenists do, instead of digesting the sutra he so adored.

In the Tokugawa Era, Hotan wrote a book against the Nichiren teachings. In another book, two well-known Nichiren scholars had a hard time defending themselves against this attack. I wish you would go to the library and read these books.

Life is short. Don't waste your valuable time in propaganda, or any other such nonsense.

To Yasura-san:

It is very kind of you to feel so concerned about the danger with which the arrows of hatred and slander may surround me. I am not afraid of them, however. Although I am trying my best to spread true Buddhism in America, even here I may be killed by some opponent. What, though, can I do about it? If I should die, and be buried in California, there still will be poppies blooming in the spring.

To the Editor of the Kyo-Gaku News:

I do not wish to waste any more of your space, so these are my last words to Japanese Buddhists. Those who wish further discussion should either write me personally or cross the ocean to see me.

Mr. Nyogen Senzaki
2014 Second St.
Los Angeles, 33, Calif.

Dear Sir:

Some time ago I came across a publication of the First Zen Institute of America, called *The Cat's Yawn*. I was deeply interested and inquired from them whether there was a Zen Institute or Zen Master on the West Coast. They very kindly replied with the words: "...it is possible that a Zen Master might visit Mr. Nyogen Senzaki who can be reached at..." and your address.

    It would, needless to say, be a very great honor for me to meet you and/or the visiting Zen Master if such a thing could be possible. Thank you very much for your time.

Very sincerely yours,
(signed)
(Mrs.) Myra A. Stall
1874 Titus
San Diego, 1, Calif.
July 11, 1956

Los Angeles, California
July 16, 1956

Dear Mrs. Stall,

I would reply to your inquiry about a Zen Master in the following manner:

A Zen Master is like a rainbow in that you may see him at a distance, but cannot catch him in person—even with the fastest plane. Please calm your intense desire to find such a foggy, strange person.

Zen students and followers call their teacher "Master," loving and respecting him in heart; but the teacher himself never considers himself a Zen Master. If he does you may be sure that he is not a reliable teacher of Zen at all.

Those students of Zen who refer to their teacher as "the first Zen Master in America" thereby discriminate among instructors and create only a snobbish tongue group. Please do not write me any such nonsense.

If you wish to learn something of Zen, Dr. D.T. Suzuki's books are available in most libraries and in many book stores.

Here we are very busy cultivating ourselves in meditation. We consider all teachers of the world as our own teacher.

Faithfully yours,
(signed)
Nyogen Senzaki

NEWLY TRANSLATED CORRESPONDENCE

Editor's Note: In February 2008, Eido Shimano Roshi gave a talk in Japan about Nyogen Senzaki. As this book was about to go to press, a packet of Nyogen Senzaki's letters was sent to him by someone who had heard his talk. Eido Roshi translated excerpts from three of these and incorporated them into his teaching on May 7 and May 9, 2008, at the Nyogen Senzaki Fiftieth Memorial Sesshin at Dai Bosatsu Zendo. The three excerpts follow.

May 18, 1906
To my family:
To state it briefly, there are three purposes for my having come to America. The first is to raise funds for the operation of the Mentorgarten in Aomori Prefecture. But because of the problems I have been having with my eyes, I was not allowed to be on the same boat as Soyen Shaku Roshi. This eye disease also caused an unexpected problem in obtaining the trust of the Russell family.

The second purpose is for my own study. Since my main vocation is the Buddhadharma, I may not be able to pursue ordinary academic studies. However, I am now staying with a schoolteacher, and she is teaching me rhetoric, and perhaps someday I can be a journalist for an American newspaper.

But the main reason for my coming to America is to transmit Zen to this country. That's why my teacher, Soyen Shaku, used his own pocket money to pay for my travel expenses. Although my teacher has now left San Francisco, and we are apart from one another, what I am doing here now is enduring what is hard to endure; doing what is difficult to do.

I have been doing all kinds of work, including grooming horses. While working together with immigrants from Europe and Africa, I always tell myself that the land on which I now stand may someday become the land of Buddhadharma. The person who punches me today may someday become a Buddha. The person who treats me with contempt may eventually become happy. I keep repeating this to myself. It is just like the Bodhisattva [Never Despise] who is mentioned in the *Lotus Sutra*: he bowed to everyone he met, saying, "You will become a Buddha." People became angry because they thought he was making fun of them. They beat him with sticks and stones. He dodged them, but did not stop bowing, always repeating, "You will become a Buddha."

March 11, 1908
To my family:
The reason why I have not written to you often is because then you might be more worried about what I am doing here. At any rate, last summer I went to the lake between Nevada and California, and climbed about 6,000 feet high and stayed by the lake for two months. Then I went into the state of Nevada and visited Reno. However, Reno was not ready for the Buddhadharma.

After returning to Sacramento, the capital of California, I got sick, and throughout October I was in bed. In the middle of November, I came back.

Nowadays, the anti-Japanese movement is quite strong in California. We have been experiencing a lot of persecution. I have had to carry a pistol to protect myself, and a few times I was forced to face someone's pistol, and another time, a knife. I had a fight with some Caucasians.

In February I left Stockton and returned to Oakland, but we Japanese could not find any work, so for one month I could not do anything. So I stopped going to school, and with my friend, I moved to a small island, and we are engaging in agriculture. This island is about 100 miles from San Francisco Bay, near Sacramento. Every day I work ten hours a day in the fields, and in the evening my friend and I talk about the Dharma.

As the possibility of getting a job in a big city [is poor], I am now thinking I should go to the East Coast, or perhaps I should go back to Japan. I am deeply thinking now [which way to go].

1928
To Naojiro Miyamoto:
I am now sowing some inconspicuous Dharma seeds, and I will likewise end my life in this country inconspicuously. But I am convinced that fifty years from now, the seeds I have sown will sprout, and true Buddhadharma will shine in America. I have made many sacrifices, but I am following my teacher Soyen Shaku's will, and this is the main purpose for my coming to America.

I am now fifty-two years old. My hair has turned white; perhaps you would not recognize me. Essentially, what I am doing is *tsuyubarai*: cultivating the soil so that the Buddhadharma may successfully be transplanted to America.

Notes

1. Nyogen Senzaki and Ruth McCandless, *The Iron Flute* (Rutland, Vt.: Charles Tuttle & Co., 1961), pp. 161–63.
2. Ibid.
3. Friedrich Froebel (1782–1852) was a German educational reformer and founder of the kindergarten system.
4. Eido Shimano, ed. *Like a Dream, Like a Fantasy: The Zen Teachings and Translations of Nyogen Senzaki*, second edition (Boston: Wisdom Publications, 2005), p. 69.
5. Louis Nordstrom, ed. *Namu Dai Bosa: A Transmission of Zen Buddhism to America* (New York: Theater Arts Books, 1976), p. 9.
6. Shimano, pp. 9–10.
7. Nordstrom, p. xvii.
8. Shimano, p. 11.
9. The entire collection of Buddhist scriptures, commentaries, and historical and lexicographical records, in 65,000 volumes.
10. Shimano, pp. 11–12.
11. Nordstrom, p. 10.
12. Shimano, p. 70.
13. A slang word for monks.
14. Nordstrom, pp. 167–68.
15. Ibid., p. 15.
16. Ibid., p. 15.
17. Ibid., p. 16.
18. Ibid., p. 173.
19. *Mu* is the Japanese pronunciation of the Chinese *Wu*.
20. The *Shodoka*, by Yokadaishi (Ch.: Yung-chia Hsuan-ch'e), an outstanding disciple of Huineng, the Sixth Ancestor, was translated by Senzaki and Ruth Strout McCandless, published in *Buddhism and Zen* by the Philosophical Library, New York, in 1953, and reissued in paperback by North Point Press in 1987.
21. Japan had invaded China and was seeking possession of Manchuria during Senzaki's work on the *Gateless Gate*.
22. Alfonse and Gaston were names familiar to all in Senzaki's era as personifications of well-bred gentlemen whose polite behavior resulted in stalemates: each would insist that the other go first, saying, "After you, Alfonse," and "No, after you, Gaston," ad infinitem.

23. One of Senzaki's favorite sayings of the Christian mystic Johannes Eckhart, known as "Meister Eckhart."

24. Newsboys would call out as they tried to sell the latest edition of the newspaper, "Extra, extra, read all about it!"

25. After his efforts to establish what he called a Mentorgarten, based on the German kindergarten model, in Japan during the late 1890s and early 1900s, Nyogen Senzaki carried the Mentorgarten ideal with him to America, and considered his Sangha to be members of the Mentorgarten. See Introduction.

26. Also sometimes translated as Vulture Peak.

27. Senzaki was using a translation by A.L. Kitselman.

28. Kokushi means "National Teacher," or teacher of the emperor. The teacher in this case is Nan'yo Echu (Chu, abbreviated), a Dharma successor of Eno (Ch.: Huineng), the Sixth Ancestor.

29. Tangen Oshin became Nan'yo Echu's only Dharma successor.

30. This line was dropped in the extant typed manuscript.

31. A correspondence and deep friendship between Senzaki and Soen Nakagawa developed after Senzaki read the young monk's poems, shown to him by his disciple Shubin Tanahashi, in a Japanese magazine. Detailed accounts about the relationship between these two pioneers of Zen in the West can be found in *Namu Dai Bosa: A Transmission of Zen Buddhism to America* and in the Introduction by Eido Shimano Roshi to *Endless Vow: The Zen Path of Soen Nakagawa* (Boston: Shambhala Publications, 1994).

32. This translation was completed in 1930, six years before Wong Mou-lam's death, and published by the Yu Ching Press of Shanghai. Copies were imported to London by the Buddhist Society, which in 1953 brought out a new edition, edited by Christmas Humphreys, who corrected some mistakes due to the translator's imperfect knowledge of English and improved upon the awkward or clumsy phrasing of the original used by Senzaki.

33. Humphreys' polishing of Wong Mou-lam's versions read:
    Our body is the Bodhi tree,
    And our mind a mirror bright.
    Carefully we wipe them hour by hour,
    And let no dust alight
and
    There is no Bodhi tree,
    Nor stand of a mirror bright.
    Since all is void,
    Where can the dust alight?

34. Ch., Huineng.

35. This book of sacred symbols and teachings, said to have originated with the Sixth Patriarch, was used in the Igyo School of Zen, which Isan and Kyozan founded.

36. Theodor Ippolitovich Stcherbatsky (1866–1942) was a Russian scholar of Buddhist studies who was regarded as a leading authority on the emergence of Buddhist thought in India, known particularly for his detailed analysis of Vasubandu's *Abhidharmokosha*.

37. Jeanne Marie Bouvier de la Motte Guyon / Madame Guyon (1648–1717) was mar-

ried at sixteen to Jacques Guyon, a wealthy neighbor twenty-two years older than she. The marriage was not a happy one, and she found refuge in "interior prayer," which allowed her a temporary escape from the frustrations of her life. In 1681, after the death of her husband, she left France for the Duchy of Savoy, where she taught her method of interior prayer. Her writings included *Les torrents spiritual*; an account of her spiritual life called *La vie de Madame J.M.B. de la Mothe Guion*; and *Moyen court et tres facile pour l'oraison* ("A short and very easy method of prayer"). For her views she was imprisoned, first for seven months and later, after a friendship with the influential priest Francois de Salignac de la Mothe-Fenelon drew the ire of his friends, for seven years, including four years in the Bastille. In 1703, Guyon was released from prison and paroled to her elder son. She was ordered not to write or teach, although she continued to do both until her death fourteen years later. The final section of *La vie*, *Recits de captivite*, was not published until 1992.

38. Sanskrit for sandalwood (Santalum album)].

39. Sound technology conveying audible dialogue in films was a new development in Senzaki's time. The most famous film associated with the "talkies" was *The Jazz Singer*, starring Al Jolson, which was first shown in November 1927.

40. Kaiten Nukariya: "Life is not an ocean of birth, disease, old age, and death, not the vale of tears, but the holy temple of Buddha, the Pure Land, where one can enjoy the bliss of Nirvana" [*The Religion of the Samurai* (Charleston, SC, 2007)].

41. From D.T. Suzuki's footnote to Chapter Eighteen of his translation of the *Diamond Sutra*, published in his *Manual of Zen Buddhism*.

42. A *nyoi* is a short, curved rod, carved in wood or made of iron, usually about a foot and a half long. The word means "according to the mind," and thus is a symbol of a Zen master's realization and authority.

43. *Hokku* is a term for the three-line verse in a five syllable–seven syllable–five syllable pattern that began a *renga*, collaborative poetry incorporating hokku and the five-line *tanka*, in the poetic form called *haikai no renga* that originated in Japan in the middle ages, or earlier. *Haikai* means "sportive" or "playful." Basho developed the hokku form, and eventually the term *haiku* took the place of haikai and hokku, becoming an independent art form in the 1890s.

44. Translated by D.T. Suzuki as *On Believing in Mind*, a long poetic work by Sosan Ganchi (Ch.: Seng-ts'an), the Third Ancestor. Senzaki wrote an Introduction and Commentaries to stanzas ten through nineteen.

45. Kaiten Nukariya was a professor at Keiogijiku University and the Sotoshu Buddhist College of Tokyo; his book, *Religion of the Samurai*, was published in 1913.

46. Soyen Shaku, "Buddhist Faith," *Sermons of a Buddhist Abbot*, translated by D.T. Suzuki (Chicago, Ill.: Open Court, 1906).

47. Herman Kern, trans. *Saddharma-pundarika Sutra, or The Lotus of the True Law* (New York: Dover Publications, 1963).

48. Said by the Sixth Patriarch to the monk Myo; see Case Twenty-three of the *Gateless Gate*.

49. Senzaki is referring to the fact that the well-known author was paid five cents a word—a considerable sum at the time—for his fiction about the northern wilderness.

50. Patanjali was a Hindu Vedantist who lived in the second century B.C.E. and compiled *The Yoga Sutras*.

51. Ernest Fenellosa was curator of Japanese art at the Boston Museum of Fine Art and the author, with Ezra Pound, of the 1917 *"Noh" or Accomplishment: A Study of the Classical Stage of Japan.*

52. This remarkable statue, once considered a Kannon but now thought to represent Maitreya, is a National Treasure, and can be seen in the small convent Chugu-ji, alongside Horyu-ji. Chugu-ji, formerly Ikaruga Palace, was built by Prince Shotoku for his mother, Empress Anahobe no Hashibito.

53. Senzaki is referring to the founders of Shin (Pure Land) Buddhism.

54. Senzaki may mean by "ordaining as Buddhists" conducting *jukai*, the ceremony in which a student takes the precepts.

55. "Na Mu Myo Ho Ren Ge Kyo."

Bibliography

Abe, Masao. *A Zen Life: D.T. Suzuki Remembered*. New York: Weatherhill, 1986.

Carrel, Alex. *Man, the Unknown*. Garden City, NY: Halcyon House, 1935.

Chang, Garma C.C., ed. *A Treasury of Mahayana Sutras*. New York: Institute for Advanced Studies of World Religions, 1983.

Conze, Edward, trans. *The Large Sutra on Perfect Wisdom*. Berkeley, Calif.: University of California Press, 1984.

Ferguson, Andy. *Zen's Chinese Heritage*. Boston: Wisdom Publications, 2000.

Inagaki, Hisao. *A Dictionary of Japanese Buddhist Terms*, fifth edition. Berkeley, Calif.: Stone Bridge Press, 2007.

Kern, H., trans. *Saddharma-pundarika, or The Lotus of the True Law*. New York: Dover Publications, 1963.

Mou-lam, Wong, trans. *Sutra of Hui Neng* (in *The Diamond Sutra and the Sutra of Hui Neng*, translated by A.F. Price and Wong Mou-lam). Boulder: Shambhala, 1969.

Nakagawa, Soen. *Endless Vow*. Compiled and translated by Kazuaki Tanahashi and Roko Sherry Chayat, with introduction by Eido Shimano. Boston: Shambhala Publications, 1996.

Nukariya, Kaiten. *The Religion of the Samurai*. Charleston, SC: BiblioBazaar, 1913.

Sekida, Katsuki. *Two Zen Classics*. New York: John Weatherhill, 1977.

Senzaki, Nyogen. *101 Zen Stories*. Whitefish, MT: Kessinger Publishing, 2004.

Senzaki, Nyogen. *Like a Dream, Like a Fantasy: The Zen Writings and Teachings of Nyogen Senzaki*. Edited by Eido Shimano. Boston: Wisdom Publications, 2005.

Senzaki, Nyogen; Nakagawa, Soen; and Shimano, Eido. *Namu Dai Bosa: A Transmission of Zen Buddhism to America*. Edited by Louis Nordstrom. New York: Theater Arts Books, Bhaisajaguru Series, 1976.

Senzaki, Nyogen and McCandless, Ruth. *Buddhism and Zen.* New York: Philosophical Library, 1953.

Nyogen Senzaki and McCandless, Ruth. *The Iron Flute.* Rutland, Vt.: Charles Tuttle & Co., 1961.

Senzaki, Nyogen and Reps, Paul. *Zen Flesh, Zen Bones.* Rutland, Vt.: Charles E. Tuttle & Co., 1957.

Shaku, Soyen. *Sermons of a Buddhist Abbot.* Translated by D.T. Suzuki. Chicago, Ill.: Open Court, 1906.

Suzuki, Daisetz Teitaro. *Essays in Zen Buddhism* (First, Second, and Third Series). London: Rider & Co., 1970.

_____. *The Essentials of Zen Buddhism.* Edited by Bernard Phillips. New York: E.P. Dutton & Co., 1962.

_____. *An Introduction to Zen Buddhism.* New York: Grove Press, 1964.

_____. *Manual of Zen Buddhism.* London: Rider & Co., 1950.

_____. *Outlines of Mahayana Buddhism.* New York: Schocken Books, 1963.

_____. *The Training of the Zen Buddhist Monk.* New York: University Books, 1965.

_____. *Zen and Japanese Culture.* New York: Pantheon Books, 1959.

Yamada, Koun. *The Gateless Gate.* Boston: Wisdom Publications, 2004.

Index

action, 64–66, 88, 90, 303–4
Aizo Senzaki. *See* Senzaki, Nyogen
akasa, 270
alcohol, 368, 369, 370, 381, 386, 389, 396
  and Japanese teachers in Japan, 171, 177
  wine, 75, 76
Alfred, Lord Tennyson, 176
Allah, 193
alms, giving of, 240–41
Amban's Addition, 203–5
American Buddhists, 312, 313, 346, 408n25
  opportunities for, 391–92, 394
American mind, 277
Amida, 262
Amitabha, 111
Ananda, 113–14, 147–48, 269
anatta. See no-self
ancestors, vow to live like, 311, 312
Anglin, Margaret, 174
arhatship, 313
arts of Buddhism, 319, 320
asamskrita, 229, 232
asankata, 263–64
Asoka, 318
astrology, 55

asuras, 258, 284
Autobiography of Soyen Shaku, 20, 349–62
Avalokiteshvara, 162, 209, 257, 338, 360
Avatamsaka Sutra, 320

bamboo screens, 124–26
bamboo shadows, 84
bananas, 188
Bankei, 322–24
Bansho, 223–25, 226, 229–30
barbarians, 54–56
Barriers, Three, 197–99, 245
Basho, 2, 188, 294–95, 327, 367
Baso, 16
  and no mind, Buddha, or things, 131–32, 295
  sermon on the path, 154–55
  staff of, 188–90
  and this mind is Buddha, 141–43
  and this mind not Buddha, 151–53, 154
beardless foreigner, 54–56
bell, 94–96, 298, 309
Bergson, Henri, 192, 259, 302
Bhagavad Gita, 295, 321
bhikshus and *bhikshunis*, 273

Bible, 40, 189, 240, 295, 303, 321

Bidatsu, Emperor, 318

birth and death, 197–98, 245

Blavatsky, H.P., 289, 292, 295

blows, three from Tozan, 92–94

Blue Rock Collection, The, 207–19, 359

Bodhi, 100, 245, 248, 248, 254–55

Bodhi-tree, 117, 408n33

Bodhidharma, 1, 202, 275, 339, 393

  beardless, 54–56

  bringing Buddhism to China, 37, 166, 231

  called "that fellow," 54

  and Emperor Wu-Tei, 209–10, 229, 231–32

  essence of teaching of, 38

  "I know not," 16, 209–10

  life story and teaching style of, 178–79, 181

  meditation work of, 37

  pacifies mind of successor, 178–81, 197

  and Senzaki poem/calligraphy, 339, 343

  sitting in Shaolin Temple, 232–33

  why came to China?, 57, 58, 166–68, 181

bodhisattva, 90, 145, 284–85

  aspirants as, 141

  attitude of, 69, 89, 259

  and control of thought, 312

  and no thought of ego, 69, 154

  stage of, 258, 259

"Bodhisattva 'Never Despise,'" 318–19

body not one's own, 312

Bonmokyo Sutra, 372

book-learning, 274

Book of Equanimity. See *Shoyoroku*

Book of the Inexhaustible Lamp, The, 366

bowl of succession and Sixth Patriarch, 116, 118

bowls, 83–84

Brahma and Brahman, 262, 263

breath, controlling of, 68

Buddha

  before history, 70–73

  brilliance of illuminates universe, 172

  Buddhism about becoming, 237–38

  as dried dung, 110–13

  eight features of voice of, 246

  exists everywhere, 100–101

  meaning of word, 111, 191, 238

  not the mind, 151–53

  once word said must wash mouth, 111, 142

  as One Mind not segregated from beings, 279–81, 284, 285, 286–87

  and Shingon mandalas, 291

  this mind as, 141–43

  Truth not conception of, 130, 131–32

  "What is?" as question of Buddhism, 141, 216–17

Buddha-Body

  fills the world, 100, 206, 245, 247–48, 254

  as ultimate being, 110

Buddha-hridaya, 240

Buddha-Mind, 276, 277

buddha-nature, 43–45, 70

  and bad temper, 322

  and barrier of Tosotsu, 197, 245

  and birth and death, 198

  and change of karma, 257

and emptiness, 72
and Zen questions, 191–93
Buddha Shakyamuni, 110, 202
  and Avalokitesvara, 255–56
  cannot look at Zen squarely, 189
  and desire, 334, 397
  and Dharma Mandala of Shingon,
    291–92
  and elephant getting caught by tail,
    170
  going beyond belief in, 168
  image of, 296, 299
  and Lotus of the Wonderful Law,
    321
  and miracles, 268
  and not speaking or thinking, 205
  parinirvana gatha of, 123
  paying homage to image of, 146
  philosopher asks question of, 147–
    50
  poem on celebration of birth of, 343
  and precepts, 250
  reason called Buddha, 237–38
  renunciation of and return home,
    273
  and secret doctrine, 269
  servant of that one, 191–93
  and Shravakas, 259
  takes his preaching seat, 226–28
  and Tathagata does not come or
    depart, 227
  and thoughts cannot be grasped,
    180
  and transmission of enlightenment,
    37
  twirling flower before assembly, 60–
    62, 113
  vow to live as he lived, 311, 312, 313

  and woman coming out of medita-
    tion, 182–83
  and women, 272–73
Buddha-wachana, 240
Buddhadharma, 240
Buddhakaya. See Buddha-Body
Buddhism
  aim to become buddha, 237
  books written on, 266
  eightfold path of, 104, 105, 272
  and emancipation, 263–64
  entering China, 230–31
  essence is enlightenment, 37, 184
  ethical teaching based on reason,
    307
  how to study, 265–67
  and influence to change secular
    world, 368
  introduction of in North America,
    xiii
  Mumon's belief it was degenerating,
    168
  not simply in temples or propa-
    ganda, 79
  persecution of in 845 C.E., 51, 52
  as scientific religion, 270–71
  sectarian, 153
  ten stages of, 257–58
  use of term, 241
Buddhism and Zen (Senzaki and
    McCandless), 14
"Buddhism without Monks," 381,
    388
buffalo passes through enclosure,
    169–71
Bunryo, 357
Burma (Myanmar), 274

calligraphy, 12, 20, 327–41
calling name of disciple, 98, 113–14
candle blown out by Ryutan, 133–36
Carlyle, Thomas, 164–65, 227
Carrel, Alexis, 155
Carus, Paul, 349
cat
  head of dead, 229, 230
  Nansen's killing, 87–90
"catch words," 95
cathedrals, Zen, 112, 306, 388, 390–91
Cat's Yawn, The, 402
cause and effect, law of, 263–64, 270,
  272
Central Conception of Buddhism, The
  (Stcherbatsky), 149–50
Ceylon, 148, 237, 239, 310, 386, 389
Chan or Shan, 38
Chandogya Upanishad, 261
Chang-kien, 158
change, law of, 270–71
chick or egg, 139
Chiki, 244
children, 3–4, 204
  See also Mentorgarten
China
  and Bodhidharma, 57, 58, 166–68,
    181
  Buddhism's entry into, 37, 166, 231,
    273
  and war with Japan, 45, 407n21
  Zen masters in ancient, 180, 181
Chinese, translations into, 37
Cho, poem of, 172, 173, 174
Chokei, 213–15, 217, 218–19
Choko-ji Monastery, 355
Choksha Keishin, 194–95
Christianity, 4, 105, 282, 368

and God, 110, 111, 237, 238
and heaven, 291
missionaries of, 373, 376, 386
in opposition to Zen, 189–90
and persecution in China, 369
and sin, 49, 269
and soul, 44
and temptation, 64
Chu Fo Yao Chi Ching sutra, 183
"Ch'u" ("Go away"), 303, 304
Chu Kokushi, 97–99, 408n28
church-goers, 144–46
Cicero, 165, 227
clergy and religious corruption, 204
cliffs, walking over with hands free, 149
cobra of Seppo, 218–19
compassion, 5, 182, 183, 238, 264,
  290, 377
Conference of Pan-Pacific Young
  Buddhist Associations article,
  384–91
  Letters to Editor from others, 393–
    98
  Senzaki's response to letters from
    others, 398–401
confession, Christian, 249
Confucius and Confucianism, 104,
  105, 283, 301, 353, 359
consciousness
  not an entity, 149
  ten stages of, 257–59
Constantine, 318
correspondence, 20–21,
  letters to Soyen Shaku, 365–83
  newly translated, 404–6
  Stall/Senzaki, 402, 403
  and Young Buddhist Associations
    article, 384–401

Crane, Frank, 237
Creative Evolution (Bergson), 302
crying, 131, 217
cypress tree in the garden, 166–68

Dai Bosatsu group, 11–12
Dai Bosatsu Mountain, 9, 11
Daibai, 141–42
Daigo, Emperor, 293
Daito Kokushi, 313
Daiyu of Joko-ji, 354
dana paramita (virtue of giving), 266, 374
dead man, becoming, 310–11
death, 197–98, 309, 311, 312
desires, 334, 397
Devas, 258
Devil or Satan, 284
Dharani of Great Compassionate One, 11
Dharanis, 292, 297
Dharma, use of term, 21
Dharma Mandala, 291–92
Dharma of Solitude, 228
Dharmakaya, 72, 80, 110, 238, 239, 263
Dharmaraksha, 183
dharmas and *dharma-svabhava*, 149–50
dhyana, 38, 299, 313
diamond, 229, 230
Diamond Sutra, 2, 313
  and Tathagata, 227
  and thought, 69, 154, 180, 312
  and Tokusan, 134, 135
dirty job of teaching Zen, 21, 108, 205
discipline, 287
discontinuity, 128

discrimination, 212
Dogen, 198, 250
Doichi-iida, 355, 356
Dokei, 362
Dokuon, 254
doorknob, 102
doubt, 317
drum, 83, 84
dung, dried, Buddha as, 110–13
Durant, Will, 149

ear, 95–96
Eastern Buddhist magazine, 349
Eckhart, Johannes or Meister, 134, 252, 281, 408n23
economy of Zen, 64
egg or chick, 139
ego, 69, 154, 253
Eido Shimano Roshi, xiii–xiv, 1, 6–7, 32, 404
  photograph of, 34
  and Senzaki, 17, 18, 19
  and Soen Nakagawa, 10, 19
Eightfold Path of Buddhism, 104, 105, 272
Eisai, Myoan, 360
Ekido and three vows, 311–13
Ekkei, Master, 354–55, 356, 358, 362
eloquence
  four ways of, 246
  in silence, 165, 227
emancipation, 43–44, 201, 260–64, 267
  four ways in *Upanishads*, 262–64
  and Zen meditation, 281
Emerson, Ralph Waldo, 277, 307
emotion and soft Zen, 99
emptiness, 72, 154, 155, 390

empty mirror mind, 95
Engaku-ji monastery, xiii, 3, 77, 365,
    382
enlightenment
    ideal of Buddhism, 238
    and koans, 39
    and law of causation, 47–50
    purpose of Buddha's teaching, 40,
        184, 238
    requires hard work, 114
    this world is palace of, 340
    word not capitalized by Suzuki, 29
Eno. See Huineng
equality, 212, 257
esoteric Buddhism. See Shingon
    Buddhism
Essays in Zen Buddhism (Suzuki), 349
eternalism, 119–20
Eucken, Rudolph, 259
explanations, 41
eye
    devil's, 226
    One, 49
    of the true teaching, 61, 62, 113
    with which God is seen and sees, 49,
        252, 281
eyebrows, 213–15

faith
    gatha expressing, 245, 254
    treasure of, 244–45, 247, 249
family, all belong to same, 96
farmer and sutra recitation, 253–54
fatalist, 137
father, recognizing on busy street, 193
Faust (Goethe), 316
feet, 192, 219
Fenellosa, Ernest, 320, 410n51

Fifth Patriarch, 116–20
fire, 65, 109, 205
fish, 157, 174, 202
fist, raised by meditating monk, 77–
    79
five precepts, 65–66, 307
    as master, 250
    treasure of, 244, 250–51
    See also precepts
five sense organs, 296
flag, not moving of, 140, 256
flax, 100–103
flexibility, 85
"floating zendo," 8
flower, 176
Flower Festival, 48
fool, 59
four elements, 197, 198, 245, 270
four obligations, 171
fox, 47–50, 81
Franklin, Benjamin, 367
Froebel, Friedrich (1782-1852), 3,
    407n3
Fujifusa, 355
Fujin Koron journal, 9
Fukaura village, Japan, 2, 3, 365, 370–
    71
Fuketsu Ensho, 121–23, 185
Fukuden-e Association, 374, 375, 378
furs, 239

gain and loss, 126–28
Gandhi, Mahatma, 260
Ganto, 83, 84, 85
gateless gate, 309
    each koan is, 254
    must pass to actualize reality, 131
    nature of Zen, 40–42

Gateless Gate, 20, 35–206, 288
    acknowledgements regarding, 206
    collection of koans to create, 41–42
    name and dating of, 39
    translating of by Senzaki, 9, 10
Gempo Roshi. *See* Yamamoto Gempo
    Roshi
Genghis Khan, 224
Genku, 388
Gensha, 81–82, 218–19
gesture, 199
Getsuan, 67, 69
giving in, 85, 98
Gizan, Master, of Bizen Province, 354
God, 238, 284
    Buddhism crushes idea of, 191
    in Christianity vs. Buddhism, 110,
        237
    deliverance via, 262
    knowing one's doings, 240
    nameless, 105
    as "nothingness" and "Everything,"
        134
    worshipping, 193
Goddard, Dwight, 385–86, 396
Goethe, Wolfgang Von, 316–17
gold, 109, 256
good nor not-good, 116–20
Goso Hoen
    and buffalo and enclosure, 169–71
    and meeting Zen master on the
        road, 163–65
    who is it?, 191–93
    and woman with two souls, 158–62
Gosozan mountain, 191
Gospel of St. John, 321
Gotaisan mountain, 144–46
governor, 72–73

graduation in Zen, 152
Great Mandala, 291
green, Zen that is, 83–84
Gutei, 51–52
    finger of, 51–53, 58, 197
Guyon, Madame, 164, 408–9n37
Gyodo Furukawa Roshi, 382

Haikyu or Haikyo. *See* Pai-hsiu
haircuts, 22, 148, 226
Hakuin, 324
Hall, Fielding, 274
hamartia, 269
Han dynasty, 230
harmony in life, 204
Hayes, Dr., 242
head, 192
hearing, 317
Hearn, Lafcadio, 158
Heart Mountain, Wyoming, 12–14,
    20, 29
    daily routine in, 305
    poem and calligraphy from, 328–38
    Senzaki letter to friend from, 305–8
"Heart Sutra, The," 303
Heaven, 291
Hekiganroku (*Blue Rock Collection*),
    20
heroic deeds, 311
hesitation, 88, 90, 128
Hirate family of Wada village, 352
Hirosaki, 372, 379, 381
hitting or shaking students, 44
Hofuku, 213, 214
Hogen of Seiryo monastery, 127–29,
    167
Hoke-kyo (*Myoho Renge-kyo*). See
    Saddharma-pundarika Sutra

holy, nothing is, 209–10, 230, 232
honesty, 92, 251
Hongwan-ji, 397
horse runs at shadow of whip, 147–48
Horyu-ji temple, 319, 320
Hosho, 132
Hotan, 400
house, entering, 53
Huiko, 178, 179–80
Huineng (Sixth Patriarch), 1, 116–20, 358, 408n28
    and moving of mind, 137–40, 256
    and Nangaku, 316
    secret belongs to you, 289
    and stanzas expressing Essence of Mind, 117–18, 408n29
humility, treasure of, 244, 249–50
Humphreys, Christmas, 408n32
Hyakujo, 175, 297
    and his fox, 47–50, 132
    and tipping over water vessel, 175–77

"I know not," 16, 209–10, 211, 230, 232
Ichinose, Chutaro (brother of Soyen Shaku), 352, 353
Ichinose family line, 351–52
Ichinose, Nobusuke (father of Soyen Shaku), 352
Ichinose, Tsunejiro. See Shaku, Soyen
iconoclast school, 146
ideal of Buddhism, 237–41
idealism, 131, 138
Igyo School of Zen, 124
Ikegami, Bunsen, 218–19
imagination, 154–55

impermanence (annica), 265
India and Indian teachers, 107–8, 369
Inferno (Dante), 258
Ingen, 167–68
Inoue, Rev., 33
Inshu, 352–53
internment. See Heart Mountain, Wyoming
intimacy, 301–2, 303
intoxication, 251
    See also alcohol
Iron Flute, The (Senzaki and McCandless), 14
Irving, Sir Henry, 173
Isan, 124, 175–76, 297–98, 408n35
Ishikawa, Sanshiro, 393–94, 399
Islam, 282

Jakushitsu Genko, 13–14, 20, 243, 313, 344
    Senzaki's translation of poems of, 344–45
James, William, 138–39, 259, 307
Japan
    Buddhism's entry into, 273–74
    and invasion of China during WWII, 45, 407n21
    as mecca of Buddhism, 252
    protects Japanese priests, 306–7
    and story of Ts'ing, 161–62
    woman enlightened first, 275
Japanese Buddhism
    Americans visiting dislike airs of, 386
    lost true spirit of Buddhism, 391, 393
    modern degeneration of, 74, 114

and sectarianism and business of
  religion, 386, 387, 390, 391, 396
Senzaki does not cooperate with,
  306
Senzaki's criticism of, 22
Senzaki's criticism of monks of to
  Soyen Shaku, 365, 367, 368–72,
  394
and smoking and drinking, 171,
  177, 386, 389
so-called masters of, 107, 170–71,
  177
talk of renaissance of, 394–95
teachers visiting U.S. and bad prac-
  tice/habits, 386
Jesus Christ, 240, 269
jewel-in-the-rough, 229–30
Jewell, Bishop John, 227
Jodo Buddhism, 289
Jofukyo, 4
Joshu, 44, 106, 146
  and Bodhidharma and cypress tree,
    166–68
  and buddha-nature of dog, 43–46
  as church-going, 145–46
  and investigation of tea-house
    woman, 144
  and monk in meditation, 77–79
  and "Mu," 43–46, 130, 197
  and Nansen cutting cat, 87, 88, 89
  and nothingness, 76
  and path of Buddhism, 104–7
  and sandals on his head, 87, 88
  and Tesshikaku, 167
  and ultimate path, 211–12
  and washing your bowl, 63–66

Kamchatka, 306

Kangetsu Ruth McCandless. See
  McCandless, Kangetsu Ruth Strout
Kannon, 320, 410n52
Kant, Emmanuel, 259
Kanzan, 167–68, 313
karma, 47–50, 88, 257
Kashyapa. See Mahakashyapa
Kashyapa Buddha, 47
Katsuma Mandala, 291
Katsuoka, K., 395–97
Kegon Buddhism, 289, 372
Keichu's Wheel, 67–69
Kempo, 200–202
Kennin-ji Monastery, 360
Khan, Hazrat Inayat, 242–43
kill the patriarch, 45
killing, precept prohibiting, 65, 88,
  251
Kin dynasty, 223–24
Kipling, Rudyard, 163–64
Kishu, 7
knowledge, 105, 258
  can know nothing, 316–17
  threefold classification of, 201
koans
  all call out one's own master, 80
  and Bankei, 322
  each as gateless gate, 254
  in the form of statement, 57
  given as object of Zen, 195
  as key to emancipation, 43
  like brick to open, 41
  like medicine, 112
  no identical cases appear in life, 227
  and one eye only, 281
  purpose of, 39
  total number of, 266
  way to work on, 45, 46, 57

Kobo Daishi, 198, 293–94, 359, 390

Kofu, Upasika, 350

Kogo, Empress Danrin, 275

Kongokai Mandala, 290, 291, 295

Koran, 303

Kosala, King of, 268

Kosen Roshi, 366

Kowatari, 357

Kuanyin, 320, 410n52

Kublai Khan, 224

Kukai (Kobo Daishi), 198, 293–94, 359, 390

Kumarajiva, 255

kundalini, 108

Kwai, 283

Kyo-Gaku News, 384, 399, 401

Kyogen

and Isan's question, 297–98

and man in a tree, 57–59

Kyozan, 124–26, 408n35

labor, as Zen, 100

Lamb, Charles, 183

Lankavatara Sutra, 228, 232, 292

Lao-tsu, 68–69, 105, 283, 300

and changeless path and name, 105, 176

laughter and death of Nansen, 217

law-breakers, 85

law of causation, 47–50

"Leaving Santa Anita" (poem), 12

Liang dynasty, 231

life

everyday, as the path, 104–6

lived as Zen, 100–103

living long, 106

what is?, 311, 312

lightning flashes, 69, 112

lightning Zen, 79, 122

Like a Dream, Like a Fantasy (Senzaki), 6, 8, 19

Lincoln, Abraham, 313

lion, 93, 133, 134, 145, 167

listening, treasure of, 244, 246–47, 249

London, Jack, 292, 409n49

Los Angeles, xiii, xiv, 8, 15, 19, 382

Los Angeles Zendo, 315

Lotus of the True Law, The (Kern), 255

Lotus of the Wonderful Law, The (Soothill), 317–18

lotus seed, 71

Lotus Sutra, The. See *Saddharma-pundarika Sutra*

loving-kindness, 250, 256, 299, 323–24, 324, 387

Mahakashyapa, 60–61, 62, 113–15

Mahaparinirvana Sutra, 124–25

Mahayana Buddhism, 124, 125, 153, 180

keeping the precepts, 171, 389

and mind and body not two, 72

spread of and women, 274

Maitreya, 168, 410n52

as Buddha of future, 58–59, 191

Pure Land of, 124–26

as servant of that one, 191–93

Man, the Unknown (Carrel), 155–56

mandalas in Shingon Buddhism, 290–92, 295, 297

Manjushri, 144, 145

and Buddha takes preaching seat, 226–27, 228

and woman coming out of meditation, 182–83

Manual of Zen Buddhism (Suzuki), 154–55, 180, 276

Manushya stage, 257–58

Martin, Mrs., 242–43

materialists, 131, 137

matter, 270

Matthew 13:12, 189

"Maud" (Tennyson), 122

McCandless, Duncan, 14–15

McCandless, Kangetsu Ruth Strout, 9, 13–14, 14–15, 17, 32

meals in monastery, 83–84

meditation, 287, 288, 309–14, 404

experience coolness of one's own, 233

to experience enlightenment, 284

and five precepts, 251

long hours in Soto school, 108

looking without seeing, 165

and mind without thought, 95

monk in constant, 77

and one eternal present, 309

and samadhi, 314

and techniques of Indian teachers, 107–8

for ten cycles of existence, 70–71

treasure of, 244, 255

as truth of Zen, 274–75

vow to continue beyond life and death, 311–12

Mentorgarten

American Sangha as, 58, 408n25

efforts to establish, 3, 365, 371, 378–79, 404

financial troubles of, 5, 375–76

how Senzaki taught in, 3–4

raising money for in U.S., 5, 379–81, 404

and wrestling with children, 98

Mentorgarten Sangha, 8, 9, 27, 58, 408n25

merit, 231–32, 271

Milarepa, 294

mind

as Buddha, 141–43, 155

cannot be grasped, 180

as empty mirror, 95

movement of, 140

not the Buddha, 151–53, 154

pacifying of, 178–81

not, 130–31

and "What is Zen?," 301

without thought, 95

See also Buddha-Mind; One Mind

mind, essence of, 131

and Bodhidharma, 38

and determining Sixth Patriarch, 117–18, 408n33

entered into in realization, 72

silence as, 80

Ming Ti, 230–31

miracles, 268

mirror, 95, 117, 248, 408n33

Miyako Hotel, 15, 30

Mohammed, 300

Momyo Bodhisattva, 182–84

monasteries, 83–84, 127, 387

Mongols, 224

monism, 263

monks, 22, 305

always alone and poor, 74

call for Buddhism without, 381, 388

during early life of Soyen Shaku, 356

families of in Japan not missionaries, 373

and funerals and chanting sutras,
371, 372
haircuts of, 22, 148
like buffalo getting caught by tail,
169–70
may live independently in U.S.,
391–92
no monopoly on Zen, 22, 204
only those who live as, 389
and rainy season seclusion, 213
Senzaki's criticism of corrupt Japanese, 365, 367, 368–70, 370–71,
372
traveling during summer vacation,
163
moon, 84, 248–49
finger pointing at, 151, 158, 232,
321
More, Hannah, 227
mosquitoes, 310–11
mother, 203–4
Mount Grdhvakuta, 60, 408n26
mouth, 140
"Mu," 43, 44, 45, 130, 197
mudras, 292
Mueller, Max, 260
Mumon Ekai, 61, 62, 65, 256
as recorder of *Gateless Gate*, 39
unfinished verse of, 109
and Zen as gateless, 40
mushroom, Senzaki as, 1, 112, 204
Myo and robe of succession, 116,
118–19, 289
Myoshin-ji Cathedral, 355–56, 358

Nakagawa, Soen, 9, 10–12, 408n31
initial visit to U.S., 15–16, 315

lecture on not knowing, 315–17,
321
and passing of Senzaki, 18
photographs of, 30, 31, 32, 33, 34
second visit to U.S., 17
Senzaki's poem to, 114–15
as successor of Yamamoto Gempo,
16
*Namu Dai Bosa: A Transmission of
Zen Buddhism to America* (Nordstrom), 5, 8, 10, 19
"Namu Dai Bosa" Dharani, 11
Nangaku, 316
Nanin, 246
Nanjo, Bunyu, 255
Nansen
cuts cat in two, 87–90
death of, 217
and everyday life is path, 104–7
and no mind, Buddha, or things,
130–32, 154, 295
and proceeding on from top of pole,
195
Napoleon Bonaparte necklace, 251–
52
Naraka, 258
national teacher, 97, 408n28
nature, 228, 303
needs of today, 269–70
negation of will to live, 263
New Testament, 269
Nichiren, 388, 395, 400
nirvana, 263, 267, 301
no-self (*anatta*), 161, 253, 265
Noh drama, 317, 353
"non-born, the," 322
Nordstrom, Louis, 5
nothingness

clinging to, 75–76
creative source of, 68, 69
God as, 134
Nukariya, Kaiten, 178, 181, 231,
    409n40, 409n45
Nyagrodha tree, 260
nyoi, 186, 409n42

O-Bon Dance, 370
Obaku Kiun (Huang-Po), 48, 49
    description of One Mind, 277
    no attempt at achievement, 282–83
    stick, 279–81
    transmission of Mind of, 276–88
Ogata-san, 384–85, 399
Ogdai Khan, 224
old-timers in a religious group, 196
Om mani padme hum, 147
one-finger Zen, 51, 52
101 Zen Stories (Senzaki), 253–54,
    322
One Mind
    and Buddha not segregated from
        beings, 279–81, 284, 285, 286–87
    dwelling in only, 279–81
    nature of all beings, 278
    nothing can be added to, 284
    Obaku's description of, 277
"Opening Words of Wyoming
    Zendo" (poem), 13, 328
ordination
    not under control of any sect, 390
    self, 388
    by Senzaki and Japanese govern-
        ment, 390, 410n54
ordination teachers, 371, 373
original nature, 155
Oshin, 97–99

"Other Power" sects of Buddhism,
    262
outsiders, 148
Owari Province, 355

Padelford, Kokin Louise, 17
Pai-hsiu, 276, 286–87
Pancha Sila, 65–66
panentheism, 110
paramitas (six virtues of perfection),
    282, 284, 287

Parinirvana gatha, 123
Patanjali, 295, 409n50
path
    the ultimate, 211–12
    where does it begin, 200–202
peacefulness, 84
Penwa, 229–30
persistence, 244, 245–46, 249
Pestalozzi, Johann Heinrich, 100–
    101
philosopher asks Buddha question,
    147–50
philosophical knowledge, 201
pick yourself up and stand, 107–8
Pilgrim's Progress (Bunyan), 258
Plato, 260
poems, 8, 122, 343–46
    with calligraphy, 327–41
    with calligraphy from Heart Moun-
        tain, Wyoming, 328–38
"poinsettia" poem, 329
pole, proceeding from top of, 194–96
possession, 88
poverty, 76
praise, 399
Prajna Paramita, 171

Prajna-Paramita Sutra, 302–3
pratyaya, 282, 284
Pratyekabuddha, 258, 259
preaching
  Buddha takes seat of, 226–27
  simpler is better, 130
  without words, 124–26
preaching sign, 113–14
precepts, 270
  and Japanese Buddhists, 389, 396
  kept by men vs. women, 273
  monks as conveyor of, 372
  monks contemptuous of, 368
  new era when not required, 387–88
  and Shin Buddhism, 388, 395
  See also five precepts
preference, 211, 212
Preta, 258
propaganda, 22, 79, 289, 391, 392, 400
  none in Buddhism, 226, 265
  Senzaki does not approve of, 307
prophets, 40
"Pu" ("everywhere"), 302, 303
Pure Land of Maitreya, 124–26
Pure Land School, xiv, 367
"Pure White Bodhisattva," 183
purification verse, 249–50
Pythagoras, 260

questions, 133, 211, 316

Rahula, 273
rain, parable of, 320–21
reason, and stiff Zen, 99
rebirth, 239, 260
reincarnation, 55–56

religion
  corruption of, 204
  and false religion, 192
  no higher than the truth, 290
  worshiping founder of, 193
  Zen not, 314
Religion of the Samurai, The
  (Nukariya), 178–79, 181, 231–32, 409n40
Reps, Paul, 9, 20, 37
rice, pounding of, 358
Rig-veda, 260, 262
right or wrong, 102–3
Riku, Officer, 217
Rinzai, 92, 130–31, 277
Rinzai sect, 390
Risshi, Unsho, 366, 376
robes, 94, 371, 375, 391
  "A Rip in a Buddhist..." 351
  of successorship, 113, 116, 188
Roosevelt, Franklin D., 391, 395
Russell, Alexander, 6, 275, 349
Russell, Ida, 5–6, 275, 349
Russo-Japanese war of 1904-5, 5
Ryutaku-ji Monastery, 16, 17, 32
Ryutan, blows out the candle, 133–36

Saddharma-pundarika Sutra (The Lotus of the Wonderful Law), 4, 70, 204–5, 315, 317–21
  and Avalokiteshvara saving passengers, 255–56
  importance of in Far East, 321
  and seven treasures, 244
  and Shotoku Daishi, 318–21
  study of by Senzaki, 399
Saga, Emperor, 275
sage, 72–73, 283–84

Saladin Reps. *See* Reps, Paul

salt, 261–262

samadhi, 75, 81, 279, 314

Sammaya Mandala, 291

samskrita, 232

Sangha, 169–70, 250, 284

sankata, 263–64

sanzen, 128, 198, 204, 213, 254

   Soyen Shaku's mood in, 361

satya (reality), 301

Schopenhauer, Arthur, 260, 263

science, 156, 270, 301

scientific knowledge, 201

screens, 127–29

scriptures

   burning of, 2, 124, 134

   written in Pali vs. Sanskrit, 125

   See also sutras; *Tripitaka*

seasons, 106, 302

seclusion, 77

secret book of Zen, 124, 408n35

secret doctrine, 157, 268–69

Secret Doctrine, The (Blavatsky), 289, 290, 295

seeking, 105, 143, 195

   and Confucianism and Lao-Tsu, 283

   fruitlessness of, 71, 155, 279, 282, 286–87

Seijo (Chinese woman), 158–62

Seijo (Zen master), 70, 71

Seizei alone and poor, 74–76

Sekiso, 172, 173

   and proceeding from top of pole, 194–96

self-certification, 170

self-entity

   individual as small, 263

as phantasm, 161, 253, 256, 271

self-surrender, treasure of, 244, 253–54

self, true, 116–17, 261, 262

selfishness, 250

Senzaki, Nyogen

   America as adopted country of, 306

   aversion to organized religion, 4, 22

   birth and early life of, 306, 367

   as Bodhidharma of America, 393

   and desire to help others, 367, 368

   devotion to Soyen Shaku, 366, 404, 406

   dress and appearance of, 2, 22, 148

   early life study of, 388

   fifty years since passing of, xiv, 1

   and "floating zendo," 8

   given name, 3

   illnesses of, 6, 365, 404–6

   individuality of, 161

   internment of, 12–14, 223, 305–8

   last will of, 192

   leaving temple to be educator, 373–74

   and letters to Soyen Shaku, 365–81

   living as homeless monk, 4, 6, 265, 306

   in Los Angeles, 8–9, 339

   manuscripts left at death of, 19

   at McCandless' home, 14–15

   meeting Soyen Shaku, 368

   monk for sixty years, 74

   as mushroom, 1, 112, 204

   not returning to Japan, 387

   ordination of, 2–3

   passing/funeral of, 18, 19, 33, 34

   photographs of, 28, 29, 30, 31

poems commemorating Soyen
    Shaku, 345–46
"practices" Zen, xiii
resolve to be monk, 368
return to Japan in 1955, 17
with Russell family, 6
and Shaku's notes on obstacles, 378
and Soen Nakagawa, 9, 10–12
and Soyen Shaku in America, 6–7
Soyen Shaku's letter describing, 4–5
teaching way of, xiv
and visit to Hazrat Inayat Khan, 242
and "Yankee Girl," 7, 8
years in U.S. before teaching, 7–8,
    245–46, 306, 404–6
See also Conference of Pan-Pacific
    Young Buddhist Associations
    article
Seppo, 83, 84, 218–19
Sermons of a Buddhist Abbot (Soyen
    Shaku), 349
Setcho, 210, 214–15, 217, 218–19
Setsu of Cho family, 172
seven treasures, 244–57
Shakespeare, 173–74, 183, 227
Shaku, Soyen, xiii, 5–6, 250
    Autobiography of, 20, 349–62
    becoming dead man and mosqui-
        toes, 310–11
    beginning as monk, 354–57
    and Buddha-Body, 247–49
    character of, 361
    childhood of, 352–53
    death of, 7–8, 349
    does not understand anything,
        316–17
    family tree and home life, 351–54
    first Zen master to come to U.S., 349
gramophone record lecture by, 393,
    399
Kennin-ji Monastery, 360
and koan of Kashyapa, 62
letter supporting Senzaki, 4–5
lineage of, 267
and Myoshin-ji monastery, 355–56,
    358–59
photographs of, 31
poems by Senzaki commemorating,
    345–46
second visit to U.S., 349
Senzaki bowing to, 226
Senzaki letters to, 2, 365–81
service to teacher Ekkei, 359–60
and street dancing festival, 359
translation of works of, 349–50
and World Parliament of Religions,
    xiii, 5, 349
yearly memorials to, 8, 345–46
Shakyamuni Buddha. *See* Buddha
    Shakyamuni
Shao-lin-szu monastery, 179, 181,
    230, 232
Shariputra, 321
Shen-kuang. *See* Huiko
Shiba Zuda, 175–76, 177
Shiko, 209
Shingon Buddhism, 134, 263, 289–
    98, 400
    as esoteric Buddhism, 289, 293
    and Kobo Daishi, 293–94
    mandalas in, 290–92, 295, 297
    not different sect from Zen, 297–98
    and purification, 292
    and truth with word, mind, and
        body, 296, 298
Shinjinmei (Sosan Ganchi), 409n44

Shinjo, 355

Shinran, 388, 396, 397, 400

Shintoism, 353, 359

shippei staff, 185–87

Shishin, 174

Sho Butsu Yo Ji Ko sutra, 183

Shodoka ("Song of Realization")
(Yokadaishi), 43, 76, 407n20

Shogen and man of great strength,
107–9

Shokoku-ji Monastery, 254

Shotoku Daishi, 318–20

Shoyoroku (*Book of Equanimity*), 13,
20, 223–33

Shravaka, 258–59

shujosu staff, 188

Shungai, Rev., 360–61

Shuzan Shonen, 185–87

Shylock, 80

silence, 21, 60, 128, 132, 246, 299, 359
of Buddha preaching, 227
and Dharma of solitude, 228
eloquence in, 165, 227
Empire of, 164, 227
expression of truth without, 121–23
as instruction, 85
and meditating monk, 79
and meeting master on road, 163–65
quotations regarding, 227
realm of golden, 131
as safeguard, 164
three kinds of, 164
voice of, 80

sin, 268, 272, 281

Sixth Patriarch. *See* Huineng

smoking, 171, 177, 368, 369, 386,
389, 396

Sogen Asahina Roshi, xiii

Soji, 275

Soko-ji Temple, 2

Soma, K., 394, 399

Sophists, 301

Soto school, 108, 369, 374, 390

Soul of a People, The (Fielding), 274

sound, 95–96, 317

"Sound of One Hand, The," koan, 80,
310, 324

Sozan, 74, 75, 76

speakers, too many, 246

speech
does not necessarily come from
mouth, 107–8
expression of truth without, 121–23
guarding, 246, 256
and meeting master on road, 163

Spiritual Interrelationship Day, 11–
12

staff
Basho's long (*shujosu*), 188–90
short of Shuzan, 185–87

Stall, Myra A., 402

Stcherbatsky, Theodor Ippolitovich,
149–50, 408n36

stealing, 251

steals everything from you, koan of
cypress tree, 167–68

stick, 82, 109, 133, 134, 185, 190,
281, 394
and Soyen Shaku, 361
and Tozan's three blows, 91–93

stone buddhas, 108, 313

strength, man of great, 107–9

stubbornness, 199

stupa of Tathagata, 319

Subhuti, 180, 227, 313

subject to, 50

"suchness," 119–20

suffering (*dukkha*), 266

Suigan, eyebrows of, 213–15

Suiko, Empress, 318

Sung dynasty, 273

Supreme Being, 40, 119, 260

Sutra Spoken by the Sixth Patriarch on the High Seat of the Treasure of the Law (Wong Mou-lam), 117, 408n32

sutras, 296

  making temples of, 319–20

  as means to enlightenment, 274

  recitation of, 305

Suzuki, Daisetsu T. (D.T.), 154–55, 178, 180, 349

  and American greatness, 381

  at Engaku-ji, 3

  and faith, 244

  and koan of Kashyapa, 62

  and Obaku's Zen, 278

  photograph of, 30

  "preaches" Zen, xiii

  with Russells in U.S., 6

  and use of name "Zen," 38

"Svaha," 303

Sveta-svatara Upanishad, 261

Tai Hau, 385

Tai-I Botetsu, 188

Tai-san. *See* Eido Shimano Roshi

tail, 169–70, 171

Taizan temple, 144–46

Taizokai Mandala, 290, 291, 295

Takahama village, 351

Takaki, D., 394–95, 399–400

talkies, 174, 409n39

Tanahashi, Jimmy, 9, 31, 34

Tanahashi, Shubin, 9, 16, 18, 206

  photographs of, 28, 31, 33, 34

T'ang dynasty, 231, 273

Tao, 300

Tao Te Ching, 68, 283–84

Taoism, 293

taste of Zen, 135

Tathagata, 227, 312, 319

Tathata, 263, 301

Tauler, Johann, 134

tea ceremony, 300

temper, bad, 322

temptations, 64

Tendai Buddhism, 134, 244, 253, 289, 388, 400

Tenei, 357

Tenju-in monastery, 354, 355

Tenryu, 51–53, 130

Terry, Ellen, 173

Tesshikaku, 167

Tessu, Yamaoka, 254

"thatness" (*dhatu*), 301

Theosophists and Theosophical Society, 92, 289, 290, 315–16

Theravada, use of term, 21

Theravada Buddhism, 72, 171, 263

  and Buddha Shakyamuni only Buddha, 239

  and women, 274

thieves, 205, 213–15

thinking, 95, 180, 312

  blocking road to, 21, 44, 58, 288, 321

  vow of no secondary, 311, 313

third eye, 125, 196

third seat, preaching from, 124–26

thirty-third heaven, 200

"thisness," 301

three treasures, 171, 353
"Thusness," 120
Tibetan Buddhism, 147
time, not wasting, 128
Tiryagyoni stage, 258
Toin, 359
Tokusan, 2
    asking questions of master Ryutan,
        133–34
    burning of *Diamond Sutra* and
        leaving monastery, 134, 135–36,
        367
    holds his bowls, 83–86
    and lady at teashop, 135
Tosotsu, 195, 197–99, 245
Tosui, 129
Tozan mountain, 191
Tozan Ryokai, 75, 200
    three blows of, 91–93
    three pounds of flax, 100–103,
        216–17
Tozen Zenkutsu zendo, 9, 13, 382–83
transmigration, 260–61
transmission, beyond teachings, 38,
    61
    of Dharma, 113-14
    of Mind, 276
treasures
    family, 40, 41
    inner, 41
    seven, 244–57
*Treatise on the Essentials of the Trans-
    mission of Mind* (Obaku), 276–88
Tripitaka, xiv, 302–3, 407n9
truth, 85–86, 130, 290
ts'an shan, 299
"Ts'in" (intimacy), 301–2, 303
Ts'ing, 158–60

Tutzumei, 121

ultimate truth, 85–86
Ummon, 173
    and Buddha as dried dung, 110–13
    "look out," 213, 214
    and monk off the track, 172–74
    and one path, 200–202
    and Seppo's cobra, 218–19
    shujosu of, 188
    and three blows to Tozan, 91–93
    understanding, 114, 316–17
unification with Zen, 299
uniformity, 197
universal body, 161
Upanishads, 260–63
upasakas or *upasikas*, 266
uppercut, 21, 165

Vairochana, 111, 290, 295, 372
Vedanta, 92, 386
vegetarianism, 239–40
Vimalakirti, 79, 205, 344
virtue, keeping secret, 240
Vivikta-Dharma, 228

Wakuan, 54
Wang-chau, 158–60
Wanshi, 223, 224, 226–28, 230–33
water, 248
water vessel, tipping over of, 175–77
Wells, H.G., 186, 224
"What Does a Buddhist Monk
    Want?," 1–2
wheel of Keichu, 67–69
Whitman, Walt, 122, 307
"Who am I?," 316
wind, not moving of, 137–40, 256

wine, 75, 76
wisdom, 184, 299
    not the path, 154–57
    treasure of, 244, 255
wise in the ten quarters, 200
women
    and Buddhism, 272–75
    education and morality of, 374
    and five hindrances, 272–73
    Japanese, as winners of peace, 98
words, 58, 132, 173, 272–75
    answer not necessarily shown by,
      199
    being free from words and wordless,
      149
    body and mind in Shingon, 296,
      298
    Buddha-wachana, 240
    going beyond in Zen, 41, 168
    magic in, and story of man killed,
      163–64
    not being caught by, 96, 154, 211
    philosopher asking Buddha ques-
      tion, 147–49
    preaching beyond, 124–26
    and "What is Zen?," 299–300
    See also silence
world, not forsaking, 110–11
World Parliament of Religions of
    1893, xiii, 5, 349
World War, First, 258
worldly lecturers, 204
Wu Ti (Wu-tei), Emperor, 179, 209,
    229, 230, 231–32, 233
    and Liang dynasty, 231
    and merit from religious acts, 231–
      32, 271

Yama, 262
Yamamoto Gempo Roshi, 8, 9, 11,
    16, 18, 32
    photographs of, 32, 33
Yangtzu-Chiang River, 210, 230
"Yankee Girl," 7
Yasodhara, Princess, 273
Yasura, 397, 400
Yeh-lüch'u Ts'ai, 224
Yellow River, 53
yoga, 263, 409n50
Yongtsukiang, 121
Young Buddhist Association, 384,
    398
Yuan dynasty, 224

Zen
    belongs to world, 22
    crushes delusions with body, 134
    done by laymen and women and
      plants, 204
    essence of Buddhism not sect, 41
    as everyday life, 1
    exists everywhere, 302
    good medicine in right dose, 233
    holds pure teaching from Buddha,
      152–53
    inner teaching and Shingon, 293
    kept among a few students, 129
    know and understand nothing,
      316–17
    as liberation, 39
    in light of modern thought, 268–71
    meaning of word, 38, 299, 313
    meeting superior or inferior student
      of, 226
    nobility is hidden power of, 189
    not displaying in the world, 204

not sect but realization and actualization, 274
qualities of students of, 300
simpler is better, 130
"What is?," 299–304
Zen Flesh, Zen Bones (Reps), 9, 20, 23
Zen teachers or masters, 155
  in ancient China, 180, 181
  as bay connecting with ocean, 78
  conventional manner of, 77–78
  false in present age, 170–71
  as hard workers, 177
  in Japan with families, 171
  meeting on the road, 163–65
  not doubting words of, 134
  and questions, 211
  recognizing, 165
  sacrifice for students' realization, 128

and secret "home remedies," 157
Senzaki's definition of, 404
take away attachments, 21, 111–12
true beyond persons, 300–301
and use of short staff, 185
who try to imitate old masters, 81
See also Japanese Buddhism
Zen temples, 356
zendo
  and Bankei and rules within, 323–
    24
  floating, 8
  at Miyako Hotel, 15
  of Senzaki, xiv
  Tozen Zenkutsu (Wyoming), 9, 13,
    32, 328, 338, 382–83
Zuigan calls out to his own master,
  80–82, 197

About the Editor

Reverend Roko Sherry Chayat is abbot of the Zen Center of Syracuse Hoen-ji, which was founded in 1972. She began Zen practice in 1967 with Eido Shimano Roshi at New York Zendo Shobo-ji in New York City, where she also attended Dharma teachings by Hakuun Yasutani Roshi. Her training continued at Dai Bosatsu Zendo with Eido Roshi and, on his frequent visits, with Soen Nakagawa Roshi. She studied with the late Maurine Stuart at the Cambridge Buddhist Association in the 1980s. Roko Osho was ordained by Eido Roshi in 1991, and authorized by him as a Dharma Teacher the following year. He acknowledged her as his Dharma Heir in 1998.

A creative writing graduate of Vassar College, she did post-graduate work in painting at the New York Studio School, and was a reviewer for *ARTnews* in the late 1960s. Her articles have also appeared in *Sculpture* magazine, *American Ceramics, Tricycle,* and *Buddhadharma,* among other journals, and she wrote a column on art for twenty years for the Syracuse *Post-Standard* and Sunday *Stars Magazine,* for which she won several awards. She has written, compiled, and edited several books, including *Life Lessons: the Art of Jerome Witkin; Endless Vow: the Zen Path of Soen Nakagawa* (with Eido Shimano Roshi and Kazuaki Tanahashi); and *Subtle Sound: the Zen Teachings of Maurine Stuart.*

She travels widely to teach and lead retreats, and is a member of the American Zen Teachers Association and Interfaith Works of Central New York.

About Wisdom Publications

WISDOM PUBLICATIONS, a nonprofit publisher, is dedicated to making available authentic works relating to Buddhism for the benefit of all. We publish books by ancient and modern masters in all traditions of Buddhism, translations of important texts, and original scholarship. Additionally, we offer books that explore East-West themes unfolding as traditional Buddhism encounters our modern culture in all its aspects. Our titles are published with the appreciation of Buddhism as a living philosophy, and with the special commitment to preserve and transmit important works from Buddhism's many traditions.

To learn more about Wisdom, or to browse books online, visit our website at www.wisdompubs.org.

You may request a copy of our catalog online or by writing to this address:

Wisdom Publications
199 Elm Street
Somerville, Massachusetts 02144 USA
Telephone: 617-776-7416
Fax: 617-776-7841
Email: info@wisdompubs.org
www.wisdompubs.org

THE WISDOM TRUST

As a nonprofit publisher, Wisdom is dedicated to the publication of Dharma books for the benefit of all sentient beings and dependent upon the kindness and generosity of sponsors in order to do so. If you would like to make a donation to Wisdom, you may do so through our website or our Somerville office. If you would like to help sponsor the publication of a book, please write or email us at the address above.

Thank you.

Wisdom is a nonprofit, charitable 501(c)(3) organization affiliated with the Foundation for the Preservation of the Mahayana Tradition (FPMT).